George Savage

PORCELAIN

THROUGH THE AGES

PENGUIN BOOKS

BALTIMORE · MARYLAND

Penguin Books Ltd, Harmondsworth, Middlesex
U.S.A.: Penguin Books Inc., 3300 Clipper Mill Road, Baltimore 11, Md
AUSTRALIA: Penguin Books Pty Ltd, 762 Whitehorse Road,
Mitcham, Victoria

—

First published 1954
Second edition 1963

—

Second edition copyright © George Savage, 1963

–

Made and printed in Great Britain
by Hazell Watson & Viney Ltd
Aylesbury and Slough
Set in Linotype Granjon

FOR

Janice and Henry

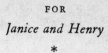

Contents

Acknowledgements

The plates illustrating this volume have been reproduced by courtesy of a number of Museums and private owners. Copyright is strictly reserved to the owners in each case, and these are enumerated in the following list:

The Boston Museum of Fine Arts: 2, 15A, 22A, 41A, 46, 50A, 50B, 52A, 52B, 53A, 56, 63C.

The British Museum: 25, 37, 42, 45, 47, 58, 59, 61.

Hastings Museum and Art Gallery: 64.

Kelvingrove Art Gallery and Museum, Glasgow: 60.

Kelvingrove Art Gallery and Museum, Glasgow, The Burrell Collection: 1, 3A, 3B, 3C, 5, 6A, 6B, 7A, 7B, 8A, 9A, 9B, 10, 12A, 12B, 12C, 14, 15B, 16A, 16B, 17A, 17B.

The Metropolitan Museum of Art, New York: 18, 19, 21A, 22B, 24A, 24B, 26, 27, 28A, 29A, 31A, 31B, 32A, 32B, 33A, 33B, 34A, 35, 36A, 36B, 38A, 38B, 39A, 39B, 40A, 40B, 41B, 43A, 43B, 44A, 44B.

The Victoria and Albert Museum, London: 54A, 54B, 55, 63A, 63B.

Dr John A. Ainslie: 57A.

Dr L. R. Janes: 8B, 11, 20B.

Mr and Mrs Sigmund J. Katz: 30A, 30B, 34B, 48A, 48B, 49A, 49B, 51, 53B, 57B, 62A.

Mr and Mrs Robert Rockliff: 62B.

Mr and Mrs Henry Stern: 20A, 28B, 29B.

Judge Irwin L. Untermyer: 21B, 23.

List of Plates

9

China. Probably 14th century. (Page 73.) A somewhat similar vase is known bearing a Yüan date.

9. (A) Vase with reticulated decoration (*ling lung*). The decoration is of sages in a landscape, the colouring turquoise, violet-blue, aubergine, and yellow. *San ts'ai*. 13½ in. China. Ming dynasty. Early 17th century. (Pages 76 and 78.)

(B) Ewer and cover of lobed form based on Near Eastern metal-work. Decorated with dragons, and floral and fruit sprays in colours. 7½ in. China. Mark and reign of Wan Li. 17th century. (Page 80.)

10. Stoneware used for architectural purposes. A roof-tile in the form of a leaping lion covered with a yellow glaze, the mane in green. 17 in. China. Ming dynasty. 16th–17th century.

11. Large bowl decorated with the Eight Immortals, of which four are shown. *Wu ts'ai* colouring. China. Reign of Wan Li. 17th century. (Page 76.)

12. (A) Furniture for the writer's table. A brush-rest with the decoration outlined in clay threads – the so-called *cloisonné* type. *San ts'ai* colouring – aubergine and yellow against a turquoise ground. 5¾ in. China. Ming dynasty. 17th century. (Page 76.)

(B) Vase and cover of baluster shape decorated in characteristic under-glaze blue. On the cover, boys playing a game. On the body, mandarins with attendants. 15¾ in. China. Reign of K'ang Hsi. 17th century. (Page 83.)

(C) Bottle-shaped vase with borders of *ju-i* heads. On the body, a Dog – or Lion – of Fo (Buddha). Slight gilding. 11 in. China. Ch'ing dynasty. Reign of K'ang Hsi.

13. A figure in *blanc de chine* from Tê Hua. The subject, a European, is an obvious caricature. The European costume of the period is well rendered. China. Tê Hua. Fukien Province. 18th century. (Page 80.)

14. A very rare set of twelve supper trays decorated with prunus blossom in aubergine and white outlined in black, the borders in green and yellow. Enamel on biscuit. Width of each tray 5⅛ in. China. Ch'ing dynasty. Reign of K'ang Hsi. (Page 77.)

15. (A) Furniture for the writer's table. A brush holder in the shape of a pine-trunk with cones and a squirrel. In brown clays of differing colours. Yi Hsing ware. Ch'ing dynasty. 18th century. (Page 82.)

(B) Club-shaped vase with seeded green ground and floral motifs, the rectangular reserves with peony sprays and emblematic devices. 18 in. China. Ch'ing dynasty. Reign of K'ang Hsi.

16. (A) *Rouleau* vase with powder-blue ground covered with gilt floral motifs, the reserves with floral sprays in enamel colours. 17¼ in. China. Ch'ing dynasty. Reign of K'ang Hsi. (Page 84.)

(B) Pierced basket with twig handles, made for export to a European silver-pattern. Chinese. Ch'ing dynasty. Reign of Ch'ien Lung. (Page 88.)

17. (A) Bowl with a grey-green celadon glaze, and an inlaid decoration

of cloud scrolls and flying phoenix. 7⅞ in. Korea. Koryu dynasty. 13th–14th century. (Page 117.)

(B) Vase of depressed globular form with two loop handles, a shoulder ridge with vertical flutings below. Pale grey-green celadon glaze with a well-defined brownish crackle. 6¼ in. Siam. Sawankhalok. About 14th century. (Page 119.)

18. A pilgrim bottle of Böttger's red stoneware with a black surface. Two handles in the form of female masks. Decoration, a landscape derived from Chinese porcelain, painted in colours and gold. 6¾ in. Meissen. c. 1715. (Page 119.)

19. A very rare tea-jar and cover from a service made for the Archbishop-Elector, Clement Augustus o Cologne, and bearing his arms. *Chinoiseries* somewhat in the manner of J. G. Höroldt, and attributed to C. F. Herold. 5⅜ in. Meissen. c. 1735. (Page 132.)

20. (A) Head of a Child. Böttger's white porcelain. 6 in. Meissen. c. 1720. (Page 132.)

(B) Teapot and cover, the cover with a twig handle. Floral decoration in high relief. Meissen. c. 1720. (Page 132.)

21. (A) Plate with a continuous landscape border, the centre painted with a fantastic animal in a style generally attributed to A. F. von Löwenfinck. 9¼ in. Meissen. c. 1730. (Page 133.)

(B) An unusually spirited Harlequin from the *Commedia dell'Arte*. He holds a flagon on his knee. By J. J. Kändler. 6½ in. Meissen. c. 1738. (Page 135.)

22. (A) A Triton blowing a horn in the form of a shell. Attributed to J. J. Kändler. A somewhat similar model of a Nereid was done by J. F. Eberlein. Meissen. c. 1740. (Page 136.)

(B) Large dish from the Swan Service made for Count Heinrich von Brühl. The border bears his coat of arms as well as scattered Oriental flowers. The surface is modelled in low relief with swans and herons amidst waves. 13¼ in. Meissen. c. 1740. (Page 136.)

23. An exceptionally fine Magpie (one of a pair). An early model by J. J. Kändler. 21 in. Meissen. c. 1733. (Page 134.)

24. (A) Tureen, cover, and stand. *Schwarzlot* painting with borders of strap-work and foliage. From a hunting service, perhaps by Jakob Helchis (or Helkis). Tureen 7¼ in. Stand 14 in. Vienna. c. 1735. (Page 147.)

(B) Dish with scalloped edge, painted with panels of diapers and flowers with supporting caryatids. In colours with gilding. 9⅛ in. Vienna. c. 1730. (Page 147.)

25. *The Medicine Seller*, brilliantly and amusingly modelled by Simon Feilner. 6¼ in. Höchst. c. 1753. (Page 152.) In German – *Theriakverkäufer*, a seller of medicines flavoured with sugar.

26. An important group of a Chinese Emperor under a draped and scrolled baldachin receiving an artist and a scholar. Originally a table centre. 15⅞ in. Höchst. c. 1765. Perhaps derived from a group – *der türkische Kaiser* – made at the same factory about 1753. The group illustrated

has been attributed (doubtfully) to J. P. Melchior. (Page 152.)

27. *Lalage* – a character from the *Commedia dell' Arte*. She hold a dish in one hand, and a spoon upraised in the other. 7½ in. Nymphenburg. *c.* 1760. By F. A. Bustelli. (Page 155.)

28. (A) Mug of barrel shape with a female mask in relief on the handle. Painted in colours with a *chinoiserie*. 4 in. Vienna. *c.* 1725. (Page 147.)
    (B) A rare partridge. This bears the incised mark, ¼. Berlin. Wegely's factory. *c.* 1755. (Page 153.)

29. (A) *A Tartar Horseman attacked by a Lion*. Probably part of a table decoration. By F. A. Bustelli. 9½ in. Nymphenburg. *c.* 1760. (Page 155.)
    (B) A pastoral figure in a more sentimental vein. 10¾ in. Höchst. *c.* 1765. (Page 152.)

30. (A) and (B) A Chinese man and woman taking tea. An important pair of figures showing the characteristic style of Franz Anton Bustelli. Nymphenburg. *c.* 1760. (Page 155.)

31. (A) A group of miners hammering a spike into rock. Modelled by Simon Feilner at Fürstenberg. 7½ in. Cf. Plate 25. Fürstenberg. 1758. (Page 158.)
    (B) An unusual group representing a booth at a Fair, inscribed *Marchand de Mode*. The back of the booth is painted with merchandise – hats, wigs, parasols, and so forth. Probably by Jean Louis. 6⅛ in. by 5¾ in. Ludwigsburg. *c.* 1770. (Page 162.)

32. (A) A group of the Three Fates with the infant son of the Elector, Karl Theodor. Modelled by Konrad Linck to commemorate the boy's death. 9 in. Frankenthal. *c.* 1773. (Page 160.)
    (B) Group of two soldiers agreeing on a truce. The base is ornamented with cannon and other trophies. Attributed to Karl Vogelmann. 7 in. Kelsterbach. 1761–4. (Page 165.)

33. (A) Coffee pot of Vienna porcelain painted with scenes depicting Apollo and the Chariot of the sun, Apollo slaying the python, and Apollo and Diana, in enamel colours, with various scrolls, *putti*, birds, and animals in addition. By Ignaz Bottengruber of Breslau, *c.* 1725. 8¾ in. (Page 168.)
    (B) Cream-pot and cover on three paw feet painted with the subject of Christ and the Woman of Samaria. Baroque scroll-work. Ignaz Preissler (Preussler). Vienna porcelain. 5¾ in. 1725–30. (Page 168.)

34. (A) Teapot of early Meissen porcelain decorated with a man and a woman playing musical instruments. The reverse depicting a shepherd and shepherdess. 4¾ in. *c.* 1730. Bartholomäus Seuter of Augsburg. (Page 168.)
    (B) Sucrier and cover of Meissen porcelain decorated with diamond-point engraving, the incisions filled with black pigment. *c.* 1750. 4⅜ in. (Page 170.) By Canon A. O. E. von dem Busch of Hildesheim.

35. An extremely rare example of the earliest successful European soft porcelain. Ewer with two handles above grotesque winged busts. Painted in underglaze blue with flowers and Renaissance ornament.

11⅝ in. Italy. Medici porcelain. Florence. *c.* 1580. (Page 175.)

36. (A) *Cachepot* decorated with figures from the *Commedia dell' Arte*. 6⅜ in. Italy. Capo-di-Monte (Naples). *c.* 1750. (Page 177.)

(B) Large dish with scalloped edge painted in enamel colours with a woman in a tall head-dress. 12¼ in. Italy. Doccia. *c.* 1746. (Page 177.) This dish is attributed to the hand of Anton Anreiter.

37. Superb figure of Dr Baloardo, one of the principal characters of the Italian Comedy. Spain. Buen Retiro. *c.* 1765. (Page 177.)

38. (A) Ewer decorated in underglaze blue with birds, *lambrequins*, and flower festoons. 7⅞ in. France. Rouen. 1680–95. (Page 180.)

(B) *Cachepot* with gadrooned borders and grotesque mask handles, painted with *chinoiseries* and some gilding. 4¼ in. France. Saint-Cloud. 1715–30. (Page 183.)

39. (A) Cane handle, the upper part painted with an Oriental vase and flowers in colour. 2½ in. France. Saint-Cloud. *c.* 1740. (Page 183.)

(B) Fountain in the form of a covered urn with flowering vines. The dolphin, coloured in turquoise green, is in low relief, and the mouth forms the aperture for a bronze-gilt spout. 12½ in. France. Mennecy. *c.* 1750. (Page 186.)

40. (A) Figure of an actor in a comic rôle. France. Mennecy. *c.* 1755. (Page 186.)

(B) Vase of baluster shape with vertical flutings, decorated in colour with Chinese figures, floral sprays, and diaper patterns in colour. 11 in. France. Chantilly. *c.* 1735. (Page 185.)

41. (A) Covered bowl decorated in gold silhouette with birds of Oriental derivation. France, Vincennes. *c.* 1750. (Page 188.)

(B) Powder horn. Turquoise ground. On one side, a stag hunt. On the other, hunting trophies and flowers. Metal mounts. 6½ in. France. Vincennes. *c.* 1753. (Page 195.) Made for Marie Josephe, Dauphine of France, daughter of Frederick Augustus, Elector of Saxony, and mother of Louis XVI.

42. *Jardinière* painted with a scene representing Perseus and Andromeda after Lemoyne. 8¾ in. France. Vincennes. *c.* 1753. (Page 195.)

43. (A) *Hercules and Omphale* attended by Cupid kneeling, the base decorated with applied flowers. Derived from an engraving after a painting by Lemoyne. 8¾ in. France. Vincennes. *c.* 1750. (Page 198.) A somewhat similar group is found in English porcelain from Chelsea.

(B) *The Bather*, copied from a statue in marble by Falconet which was exhibited at the Paris Salon in 1757. The figure in *biscuit* porcelain, the base in *ormolu* set with glazed plaques which have a turquoise ground, and flower sprays in panels. 22 in. France. Sèvres. 1758. Page 198.) The success of this model was such that it was copied with slight variations at Ludwigsburg, Meissen, Berlin, Zürich, and Copenhagen.

43. (A) Portrait bust in *biscuit* porcelain of Marie Jeanne Gomart de Vaubernier, Comtesse du Barry, after Augustin Pajou. Mounted on a

fluted column of glazed porcelain decorated in colours and gilding, and bearing the monogram, DB. 15 in. France. Sèvres. 1772. (Page 198.)

(B) *Jardinière*. Turquoise ground with diaper pattern in gold. Painted with a scene representing the signing of a marriage contract, after a painting by Teniers. Decorated by Dodin. 5¾ in. France. Sèvres. 1760. (Page 195.)

45. Tray painted with *L'Education de L'Amour* after Carle van Loo. Gilding by Noël. 15 in. France. Sèvres. 1760. (Page 195.)

46. One of a pair of vases in biscuit porcelain showing the characteristic Louis Seize style. France. Sèvres. 1776. (Page 196.)

47. Biscuit group. *Le Baiser Donné*. 7 in. France. Sèvres. 1765. (Page 198.)

48. (A) The first English porcelain. A small cream jug decorated with the flowering tea-plant in relief. Chelsea. Triangle period. *c.* 1745. (Page 223.)

(B) Superb figure of a Beggar. Chelsea. Raised anchor period. *c.* 1752. (Page 223.)

49. (A) Group: Pastoral figures of Lovers with a Lamb. Perhaps painted in the studio of William Duesbury. Chelsea. 'Girl in a Swing' type. *c.* 1751. (Page 227.)

(B) Group: Pastoral figures of Lovers with a Dove. Perhaps painted in the studio of William Duesbury. Chelsea. 'Girl in a Swing' type. *c.* 1751. (Page 227.)

This, and (A) above, are recorded for the first time.

50. (A) *The Girl in a Swing*. A finely modelled figure from which this class of porcelain takes its name. Chelsea. *c.* 1751. (Page 227.) This model is also represented in London at the Victoria and Albert Museum.

(B) An amusing group depicting the Fable of the Fox, the Stork, and the Water-jar. Chelsea. 'Girl in a Swing' type. *c.* 1751. (Page 227.)

51. A very rare group of a Chinese woman with a small boy who is playing a game similar to diabolo. A cat watches the game with interest. Chelsea. Raised anchor period. *c.* 1750. This game has an extremely ancient history, and was played by the early Greeks. (Page 226.)

52. (A) *Isabella d'Andreini* – an important Italian Comedy figure which probably pairs with Dr Baloardo from the same factory. Chelsea. Raised anchor period. *c.* 1750. (Page 226.) Isabella married Andreini, director of the Gelosi troupe of players, in 1580.

(B) Peacock on a high base derived from a Meissen model. Chelsea. Raised anchor period. *c.* 1750. (Page 226.)

53. (A) *The Dancers*, or the Masqueraders. The group is based on the Tyrolese Dancers modelled at Meissen by J. F. Eberlein. A contemporary Chinese version decorated in enamels of the *famille rose* is also known. The Chelsea model is mentioned in a factory auction sale catalogue of the period. Chelsea. Red anchor period. *c.* 1754. (Page 224.)

(B) Octagonal dish decorated with the subject of 'Hob in the Well.'

This dish is decorated in the style of Sakaida Kakiemon, and may be accepted as characteristic of Japanese work of this kind. Chelsea. Raised/red anchor period – transitional. *c.* 1752. (Page 223.)

54. (A) Tureen and cover in the form of a life-size rabbit. 9 in. by 14½ in. Based on a fashion popular at the Meissen factory shortly before. Chelsea. Red anchor period. *c.* 1755. (Page 224.)

(B) *The Reaper,* probably symbolic of Summer from a set of the Seasons. 12½ in. *Rococo* scroll base. Chelsea. Gold anchor period. *c.* 1763. (Page 225.)

55. Vase and cover in the style of Sèvres, the subject, Venus and Adonis, being derived from François Boucher. Claret ground with gilding. 13¾ in. Chelsea. Gold anchor mark. *c.* 1763. (Page 225.)

56. Richly decorated pair of figures representing a Gardener and his Companion, adapted with some differences from a Chelsea group of the gold anchor period. Bow. *c.* 1760. (Page 232.)

57. (A) A rare and interesting chamber candlestick of leaf-form painted with flowers in underglaze blue. Bow *c.* 1755. (Page 229.)

(B) Sauceboat decorated in colour, and modelled in the form of overlapping leaves. Longton Hall. *c.* 1752. (Page 252.)

58. *The Duke of Brunswick* – Prince Ferdinand von Braunschweig – derived from an equestrian figure by J. J. Kändler at Meissen. One of the finest existing figures to come from this small Staffordshire factory. Longton Hall. *c.* 1756. (Page 253.)

59. An early group of a Chinese man and woman. See Plate 51 for another group in this style. Derby. 1755 or earlier. (Page 236.)

60. (A) and (B) *Map-seller and Companion.* Derby. *c.* 1765. (Page 237.) These figures are also known in a later version from Derby, and were derived from a Chelsea model of the red anchor period.

61. *The Dead Bird.* Two biscuit figures modelled by Jean-Jacques Spängler of Zürich. Derby. *c.* 1795. (Page 238.)

62. (A) *La Nourrice.* A group made originally at the Avon pottery, near Paris, at the beginning of the 17th century, and later in porcelain at Mennecy. A Chelsea version is rare, but comparatively well known, and was made shortly after 1750. The one shown is an extremely rare type of which only two or three examples are known to exist. Attributed to Worcester. Perhaps about 1755. (Page 249.)

(B) Stand for a dessert basket moulded with vine leaves, the basketwork with a primrose yellow ground. Derived originally from Meissen, somewhat similar dishes were made at Chelsea and Derby. Worcester. *c.* 1760. (Page 246.)

63. Highly-modelled vase and cover painted in colours. This type appears from several factories, with some minor modifications, and is usually the work of Mr Tebo, his mark sometimes being stamped into the base. Another version from Worcester is surmounted by an eagle-like bird similar in modelling to some early Bow examples. 16½ in. Worcester. *c.* 1770. (Page 249.)

List of Text Figures

PORCELAIN THROUGH THE AGES

Judge the art of a country, judge the fineness of its sensibility, by its pottery; it is a sure touchstone. Pottery is pure art; it is art freed from any imitative intention.

SIR HERBERT READ

Enthusiasm is not a method of judgement.

GIOVANNI MORELLI

A detective policeman discovers a burglar from the marks made by his shoe by a mental process identical with that by which Cuvier restored the extinct mammals of Montmartre from fragments of their bones.

THOMAS HENRY HUXLEY

For in the Market-Place, one Dusk of Day.
I watch'd the Potter thumping his wet clay :
   And with its all obliterated Tongue
It murmur'd – Gently, Brother, gently, pray!

RUBÁ'IYÁT OF OMAR KHAYYÁM
OF NISHAPUR

Preface

THIS study of the art and history of porcelain is the first of a reasonably comprehensive nature to be published in a widely accessible form. I have, therefore, endeavoured to make it useful to the general reader to whom the subject is new, as well as of interest to the student who would like a view of the whole field uncluttered by too much detail.

I have appended an extensive Bibliography for the benefit of those who would like to pursue the subject in more detail. It is, however, a branch of the arts on which very few popular expositions have been written, apart from Museum handbooks. This is, I think, undeserved because, in addition to its intrinsic interest, both pottery and porcelain can throw much light on the manners, customs, and the arts and crafts of other peoples and other times. I hope, too, that the information provided may be of some service in bringing to light, and restoring to their rightful place, treasures of the past which are at present resting neglected and forgotten because of the lack of generally available information.

The larger museums in Britain and America have important collections which will repay study. Many of the provincial museums have collections of considerable value to the student, and these often have local interest. Many of these museums have, from time to time, published inexpensive monographs on various aspects of the subject, which are naturally worth acquiring. These apart, however, it will be found that most information of value is enshrined in sumptuous and expensive volumes, many of which were originally issued in strictly limited editions. The more important art journals frequently publish articles on new research and other matters of interest to the student and collector.

It is customary to acknowledge the assistance one has received in the preparation of a book of this nature. In the present case these expressions of gratitude are not merely perfunctory, but acknowledge much assistance of the greatest value generously and willingly given.

I am primarily indebted to the publishers for giving me an opportunity to contribute a work of this nature to the widely-read Pelican series. Interest in the subject has been increasing steadily during the last few years, and an inexpensive source of information will, I feel sure, fill a need which has become the more obvious within recent times, particularly as so many museum handbooks are out of print and virtually unobtainable.

My thanks are due to Mr William King of the British Museum; Mr R. J. Charleston of the Victoria and Albert Museum; to Sir William Burrell and Mr Andrew Hannah, Keeper of Glasgow's Burrell collection; to Mr Wm J. Macaulay, Glasgow's Curator of the Department of Arts; and to Mr J. Manwaring Baines of the Hastings Museum, for assistance in the provision of illustrative material. Dr L. R. Janes and Mr and Mrs Robert Rockliff have also provided photographs of examples in their collections.

In America, Miss C. Louise Avery of the Metropolitan Museum of Art has given me valuable assistance with the provision of illustrations, and in other ways. Mrs Yves Henry Buhler of the Boston Museum of Fine Arts has very generously sent me photographs of some of the porcelain in the Museum's Collection, and Judge Irwin L. Untermyer has allowed me to use two examples from his important collection.

I am especially grateful to my good friends, Mr and Mrs Sigmund J. Katz, not only for some important photographs from their superb collection of early English porcelain, but for much salutary criticism of work in progress. Mr and Mrs Henry Stern have lent me specimens for illustration, and have assisted in other ways. The Coalport Porcelain Company were good enough to provide me with information on the latter history of this factory, and very willingly answered my inquiries. I am indebted to Mrs Diana Imber for invaluable assistance with the *minutiae* of proof-reading.

Finally, I am grateful to Dr John Ainslie, not only for allowing me to use an illustration from his scholarly collection of Bow porcelain, but for calling my attention to a number of new possibilities in the history and development of early English porcelain manufacture. In a book of this nature it has not been possible to include all the points which have arisen from time to time since they are, to some extent, speculative, and discussion must be reserved for a more appropriate place.

I have taken particular pains to avoid the use of illustrations which have appeared elsewhere, although I have included a few which have previously been recorded in publications not generally available. The field covered, however, is vast, and the illustrations ought to be multiplied by many times. In a volume so inexpensive as the present that is impossible, and herein lies the principal reason why many books are both highly-priced and difficult to obtain.

It remains to say that some of the information contained herein is based on incomplete evidence. In a few instances I do not entirely agree with what I, myself, have written, but unless there have been strong reasons for diverging from the generally accepted view, I have thought it right not to confuse the reader with controversies and arguments. It is as well to bear in mind in reading books of this nature that opinion often has to be accepted in place of fact, and that research is still going on into many of the points discussed.

G. S.

Guestling, Sussex

Introduction

THE twentieth century has seen an enormous advance in the acquisition of technical knowledge. Objects which were once the luxuries of kings, princes, and the nobility have now become the commonplace essentials of daily life. People today are surrounded by possessions of a kind undreamed of even a century ago, and this has been achieved principally by the development of mass-production techniques. Despite the immense value of these techniques in raising living standards to heights unparalleled in the relatively short history of man, they have, at the same time, divested his belongings of that quality of individuality which formerly they enjoyed.

When anyone can buy a porcelain cup and saucer at a nearby china store, it is difficult to convey some sense of the esteem with which a cup and saucer of this material was regarded barely two centuries ago. And, in a day and age when the term 'art' suggests that what follows will be something about painting, sculpture, or architecture, it is only to be expected that a true appreciation of the aesthetic value of some kinds of Chinese porcelain, for instance, may be acquired only with difficulty. Nevertheless, porcelain made prior to 1800 bears about as much resemblance to most present-day porcelain as an original painting does to a half-tone block.

It is not my primary purpose to evaluate porcelain as an art, although it would not be desirable to ignore this aspect of the subject. This, however, is examined in a later section, and I am at present concerned to discuss the methods formerly used in its manufacture, the materials from which it was made, and a few other aspects of the subject which provide background material for the more detailed review of the productions of the various factories and kiln sites.

In the absence of direct evidence of a historical nature, the attribution of a specimen of porcelain to its place and time of origin depends, partly, on the recognition of the material used in its fabrication, and partly on the style displayed in its form and decoration. Despite the fact that a number of authorities are inclined to rely principally on artistic considerations, experience leads me to consider material and methods of manufacture to be the safest determining factors, more particularly because many of the earlier and more valuable things have been copied with a certain amount of exactness. These copies are not sufficiently close to defy detection, but much knowledge and experience is frequently necessary to differentiate between true and false.

The subject of porcelain is vast, and a volume of this size could not, in any sense, be exhaustive. Nearly all of the present chapters – and, in many cases, even the subsections – have, in the past, provided material for a book. It is, however, only during the last few decades that the subject has been seriously studied. The addition of new material to our store of knowledge has, within recent years, been so considerable that many of the older works are out of date, and need a great deal of experience to read them with profit. Specialized works, however important they may be in their own circumscribed field, suffer from serious drawbacks, inasmuch as they are compelled to assume in the reader a knowledge of the wider field to which the subject is related. This book, therefore, seeks to provide an introduction to more detailed study, since it supplies a somewhat cursory view of the whole which is, I think, sufficient to put the various parts into perspective.

Except in the case of English porcelain, I have allotted space to each part more or less in keeping with its importance to the subject as a whole. English porcelain is much more accessible as a subject for study, and is likely to be of more general interest in England and the United States.

Mention should be made of the somewhat peculiar position of nineteenth-century porcelain. Although I have said little, I have still treated it in greater detail than its importance warrants, since many of my readers may wish to identify specimens in their possession. During this period porcelain was made in such immense quantities that specimens have not uncommonly survived, but these things were made at a time when factories were rapidly becoming vast commercial undertakings and individuality was in process of being submerged by an increasing technical facility which placed too great a value on the merely elaborate and over-decorated.

Lest my reader think my comments are prejudiced, I quote below the words of W. B. Honey, one of the great authorities of our time on this subject –

It may be remarked that the charge of artistic insignificance in the nineteenth-century wares is by no means due to the familiar contempt for the insufficiently antique. The period of the Napoleonic wars marks a definite break with the old traditions of craftsmanship. The financial and cultural impoverishment they caused left the industrializing process, already well begun by Wedgwood, irrevocably complete.[1]

Beyond this, little need be said. The fact has been recorded, and the causes succinctly stated. Curiously enough, however, we see the same thing happening in China as in Europe, and world-wide degeneration on this scale has no parallel in earlier times.

There is, at present, a considerable demand for the better-quality industrial porcelain of the nineteenth century, principally among interior decorators, more particularly those of America.

Today there exists a radical division between the factories on the one hand, and artist-potters on the other. The latter work in their own studios. Their pots are made by hand, and are usually glazed and decorated in traditional ways. These methods now have no commercial application, and such work is often prized for its decorative value. Except in a few instances, however, it is too derivative to have any permanent aesthetic value.

*

As I shall later record, porcelain was first made in China more than twelve hundred years ago. Pottery, or earthenware, is a much older material, and pots of this kind made by prehistoric man are comparatively common.

Most Chinese porcelain is made from two principal ingredients, *kaolin* (white china clay) which is an extremely pure

1. *Old English Porcelain.*

aluminium silicate, and *pai-tun-tzŭ*, a rock which is, chemically, a silicate of potassium and aluminium. The latter is generally written in the French form of *petuntse*, the two being synonymous terms.

Kaolin is used in pottery for its property of taking and retaining almost any desired shape. It is plastic. *Pai-tun-tzŭ* can be fused into a kind of natural glass by exposing it to intense heat of the order of 1,450 degrees Centigrade. Obsidian is another natural glass which is formed by high volcanic temperatures.

Pai-tun-tzŭ is often called a feldspathic rock, *feldspar* being the generic name for the group to which it belongs. A feldspathic glaze is made from the same material, whereas non-feldspathic glazes are invariably a kind of glass, usually containing a percentage of lead.

The feldspathic rock in porcelain manufacture is ground to powder and mixed with *kaolin*. This yields a more or less plastic substance which is shaped in one of the ways presently to be described. If the mixture is fired in a kiln at the appropriate temperature, it becomes porcelain. The clay is refractory, that is to say, it needs a higher temperature to fuse it than is needed to fuse the rock. It is for this reason that the object holds its shape whilst the vitrifying heat is applied, but if the normal firing temperature be grossly exceeded, the embryo pot may be reduced either to a shapeless lump, or may be deformed. In such cases it is termed a 'waster'. Every kiln firing produced some 'wasters', but the value of a particular porcelain body was, to some extent, determined by the *quantity* of 'wasters' in each firing. Even the best designed kilns tended to be hotter in some places than others, and porcelain bodies varied in their behaviour according to the source from which they were drawn. The most useful allowed a fairly considerable temperature latitude, which meant that they would take a certain amount of over-firing with collapsing, but the worst had a very critical temperature range between the desired point of vitrification and collapse, and this demanded close control of temperature or the acceptance of a high kiln-wastage factor. This aspect, however, assumes much greater importance with early European soft-paste porcelains later to be discussed.

The question of the *source* of materials is one which demands elaboration. In these days of refined and reasonably pure substances, whose behaviour under normal conditions can be predicted with a fair measure of certainty, the point is one which is apt to be overlooked. Early potters devoted considerable time and trouble to the location of beds of suitable raw materials, and, having found them, tended to use nothing else, experiment being fraught with dangerous possibilities.

Naturally, since the methods of refinement then in use only removed the coarsest impurities, the effect of those remaining often governed results to some extent. Thus it is that porcelain made from *kaolin* and feldspathic rock drawn from one particular source will differ noticeably from porcelain made with what are, fundamentally, the same materials taken from another, the differences being caused by the variable factor of the impurities present. Since these impurities are unknown, in the sense that they cannot be added to pure materials in the same manner as that in which they originally appeared, it will usually prove impossible to reproduce much old porcelain without access to the beds from which the clay and rock were originally taken. This is basic to the detection of forgeries, and, no matter how close they may be superficially, they must always fail to stand up to comparative examination with modern scientific techniques. Indeed, the principle is capable of much wider application than to ceramic[1] substances alone.

Porcelain made from *kaolin* and *petuntse* is termed hard-paste (or true) porcelain, and came, in the first place, from China. Because Chinese porcelain was much prized in Europe, research was continually directed towards the discovery of the secret of manufacture from the end of the fifteenth century onwards.

The nature of the Chinese materials was first recognized at Meissen, in Saxony, shortly after 1700, but not before another substance superficially resembling this kind of porcelain had been elaborated, first in Italy at the end of the sixteenth century, and again, about seventy years later, in France. This substance is termed soft-paste (or artificial) porcelain.

1. From the Greek, *keramos*: potter's earth. Pron. keramik.

Whilst the terms 'hard' and 'soft' refer to the firing (Chinese porcelain, for instance, being given a 'hard' or high-temperature firing), they are usually taken to refer to the degree of hardness exhibited by the porcelain. To some extent this is borne out in practice, but it is not always a reliable guide.

The arcanists responsible for the development of soft-pastes were faced with the task of discovering the nature of a material which was white, hard, resonant when struck, and translucent. There were no exact methods of chemical analysis available, and the experimentalists had to proceed from surface appearances and analogy. They had to find substances which would give all these qualities, and, at the same time, possess the property of plasticity to a degree which would make it possible to shape vessels by ordinary ceramic methods.

They could hardly be expected to appreciate the part played by the feldspathic rock, and it is unlikely that, in these early days, kilns could have been built to attain the exceedingly high temperatures necessary to fuse the rock. This aspect of the problem caused considerable trouble at Meissen, where the part played by *petuntse* was first appreciated.

The recognition of glass as a possible material for investigation must have occurred at a very early date. Glass is transparent, and if tin oxide be added to the ingredients, it becomes milky-white and translucent. Nevertheless, it could not be shaped by methods ordinarily used in pottery. The component substances have no cohesion before they are melted, and the transition from a solid to a syrupy liquid is extremely rapid. Therefore, glass must either be cast in moulds or blown.

Clay, on the other hand, is plastic, and retains its shape during heating, whilst glass provides the translucent and resonant properties. A mixture of clay and ground glass, therefore, would have been tried by experimentalists at an early date, even though it was, no doubt, a long time before a suitable clay, the best kind of glass, and the correct kiln design, could all be brought together to make a workable soft porcelain.

This glassy porcelain was used with varying success for many years, but the temperature gap between vitrification and collapse was critical, and kiln-wastage often high, which caused further experiments to be directed towards stabilizing the body, thus making firing operations less hazardous. The first major variation on the basic formula came from the English factory at Bow, near London, about 1750. This called for the addition of up to fifty per cent of bone-ash (calcined animal bones) to the ingredients. About 1800 the hard-paste body was itself modified by the addition of bone-ash to form the standard English bone-china body.

In England, from about 1748, a porcelain was made of which the principal ingredient was soap-rock. This substance, common in Cornwall, is a natural mixture of china clay and steatite, and the wares made from it are correctly classified as a 'soft' porcelain, although, basically, the principle is much the same as that involved in the manufacture of the 'hard' variety.

*

The ability to discriminate between hard and soft porcelain bodies is essential to the student. The recognition of the nature of the material is frequently the first step towards putting a specimen in its correct classification as to place and date of manufacture, and, this apart, much valuable soft porcelain has been copied at a later date in a hard porcelain body.

Porcelain is composed of the body, to which is added a thin outer skin of glaze. The mixture of clay and other ingredients before subjection to the firing process is often referred to as the 'paste'.

Glaze is glass-like in appearance, and its purpose, originally, was to seal a porous body against penetration by liquid. It is strictly unnecessary with hard porcelain, since the degree of vitrification is such that the body is not porous. It is essential with some soft porcelains, particularly the bone-ash types, since these retain a measure of porosity.

Attention should first be directed to the glaze. Usually the hard porcelain glaze was fired in one operation with the body at the same high temperature. It is made from powdered feldspathic rock, is thin, hard, and brilliant in appearance, and is fused intimately with the body in a way which will be fairly obvious. Occasionally, a feldspathic glaze was put on in a second firing. In this case, the temperature was slightly less, and a flux added to lower the melting point of the rock. Such glazes are apt to be somewhat thicker, and can be seen to contain minute bubbles in suspension. The surface is often slightly pitted, and the Chinese refer to this type of glaze as 'chicken skin' which it somewhat resembles.

The glaze of soft porcelain was invariably added after the first firing at a considerably lower temperature. It is usually a kind of lead glass, and is thick, lying on the surface as a perceptible coating. With some varieties it exhibits a network of tiny cracks over the surface, known as 'crazing'. The Chinese occasionally induced this deliberately as decoration, but, in European porcelain, it is invariably a manufacturing defect. Leadless glazes were introduced after 1820.

Often soft porcelain glazes were difficult to control. They gathered in pools in hollows and crannies, and sometimes formed drops at the base. The bases of European porcelain have frequently been ground on an abrasive wheel to remove surplus glaze. Since the glaze was soft it will often show multiple scratches on the surface as the result of wear and handling.

Damage can often be extremely revealing. If a piece of hard porcelain is chipped, the fracture has the same appearance as will be shown by a similar accident to (say) a thick glass bottle. A soft-paste chip, on the other hand, usually exhibits a granular surface appearance not unlike that of a very fine sand, more particularly with the varieties containing bone-ash.

Most old porcelain collects dirt on the base if this is unglazed. In such cases a scrub with a nail-brush can help in diagnosis. Dirt is immediately removable from hard porcelain, but adheres much more strongly to the soft variety, and it may prove completely impossible to clean it off.

A somewhat crude test is to use a file on the base. A small file of triangular section should be employed, and the base gently filed with one of the edges. Ordinarily, hard porcelain cannot be cut in this way, or only with the greatest difficulty, whereas soft porcelain can be cut with relative ease. Once it is ascertained that the file is removing the material the test is complete, and it is useless to proceed further. One occasionally sees porcelain with unnecessarily deep file-cuts, sometimes repeated two or three times, which only help to spoil a specimen and provide no additional information.

Bone-china falls somewhere about midway between these two groups, but since it was not made until at least 1800, the necessity for differentiation no longer exists in the same degree, as will presently become apparent.

If porcelain is held up to a source of light it will be seen to be translucent. This quality varies from the slightest transmission to a quite brilliant illumination. During the nineteenth century plaques were made (called *lithophanies*) especially intended to be viewed in this way.

Certain kinds of early porcelain exhibit 'moons' when viewed by transmitted light. These are circular bright patches, and are commonest in early English and French soft porcelains, but are occasionally to be seen in early hard porcelain from Meissen and Vienna.

The student is often urged to examine the *colour* of specimens which is revealed by transmitted light, being informed, for instance, that Worcester always shows a greenish tinge by this method. For the most part I consider this test of doubtful value, except in those cases where it is able to reveal manufacturing idiosyncrasies which help in identification, of which the 'moons' referred to are a typical example. The actual colour to be seen in this way depends on a number of factors which are by no means invariably present. Certain bodies, for example, have a natural orange translucency that was, at one time, regarded as a defect. It was overcome by the addition of a little cobalt blue which yielded the green to be seen with much early Worcester. The value of a method which depends on factors of this kind is obviously suspect.

*

Another test for the nature of a porcelain body is provided by the decoration. Porcelain is often painted in colours which are, necessarily, metallic oxides because they need to be exposed to a considerable degree of heat to develop them and fix them permanently.

31

Ceramic colours are divided into two main classes, those which are painted directly on to the body before the glaze is applied (underglaze colours), and those which are painted over the glaze (overglaze, onglaze, or enamel colours). Enamel colours are fired on in a 'muffle' kiln at the lower temperature of about 750 degrees Centigrade. Underglaze colours have to bear the full heat of the kiln – about 1,250 degrees in the case of soft porcelain, and about 1,450 degrees in the case of hard porcelain. Of the underglaze colours in use before 1800, cobalt oxide was used in Europe, and both cobalt and copper in China, although the latter appears much more rarely. Cobalt blue, which ranges in colour from a greyish blue to a pure sapphire, was extensively used in the Far East and in Europe for that range of porcelain commonly referred to as 'blue-and-white'.

The overglaze colours are usually oxides of copper, iron, and manganese. It will be noticed that such colours on a feldspathic glaze stand out from the surface somewhat thickly, whereas the same colours on soft porcelain glazes sink in, are more or less level with the surface, or, in a few extreme instances, have sunk below it. Unlike the hard porcelain glazes, the lead glazes of the soft variety melt at a considerably lower temperature than the body itself. In the enamelling kiln the glaze is partially remelted and softens sufficiently for the colouring oxides to sink into it.

This property of soft porcelain glazes frequently causes well-marked defects to appear if an attempt is made to fire on enamel colours after any considerable space of time has elapsed since manufacture. Since it has been a not uncommon practice for forgers and fakers to remove a sparse decoration with acid in order to provide a surface on which to paint in more sumptuous and valuable styles, this is distinctly useful, because signs of refiring are generally fairly obvious.

Some remarks on the various colours used are desirable. Copper oxides are undoubtedly the most useful pigments in the ceramic artist's palette. They give a whole series of blues and greens, including a brilliant turquoise when used on a kind of glaze containing alkaline substances. If the oxygen in the kiln is replaced with carbon monoxide, the kiln is said to have a 'reducing' atmosphere. Copper then yields a red which is termed a

32

'reduced' copper colour. The Chinese added wet wood to the furnace to provide the necessary carbon monoxide, which is a gas that results from the slow combustion of a substance made predominantly from carbon. It can, for example, be produced by strongly heating – not burning – ordinary coal. The resulting product is coal-gas which contains a large quantity of carbon monoxide. Chinese *flambé* glazes contain both reduced and unreduced copper colours, usually vivid reds streaked with blue.

Iron oxides give a range of colours varying from pale yellow to black according to the manner of use. They also yield a red of bright rust colour – *iron red*, and, in some circumstances, a distinctive green, of which the Chinese celadon glaze (see p. 62) is an example.

Manganese oxide yields, usually, a purple colour somewhat similar to permanganate of potash. This, on Chinese porcelain, is sometimes called *aubergine*, and resembles the colour of the ripe fruit. In conjunction with a glaze containing lead it also gives a peculiar brown.

Tin oxide was employed in some English and French porcelain glazes to opacify them. Added to the glaze it converts it to a milky opaque white. It was used, in the first place, to provide the characteristic glaze of that class of earthenware known as *maiolica*, *faïence*, or *delft*, in which the glaze resembles a coating of hard white enamel. It was also used occasionally to provide a white overglaze pigment.

Rose red – the *famille rose* colour of the Chinese – was obtained from colloidal[1] gold mixed with chloride of tin. In colour it ranges from rose, through purple, to violet, according to the degree of heat applied to it.

These remarks can hardly apply to the nineteenth century since colour-chemists developed a large range of both underglaze and overglaze colours. Green from chromium oxide is an example. This was not used before about 1802, and is a peculiar opaque yellowish-green unlike the earlier colours.

Pigments of these kinds were also used to colour glazes. The technique is to be seen at its best in Chinese porcelain of the Sung period. The colours used in this way are neither over nor

1. Divided into particles too small to sink in the liquid of suspension.

under the glaze, but suspended in it. The technique, of course, is somewhat different from that used in enamel colouring, since the pigment had to develop under the full heat of the kiln. Iron was much the more frequently used in this way.

Coloured grounds were often used on European porcelain, and on the later Oriental wares. Underglaze blue was the first pigment to be used in this way, if we except certain Chinese examples of the Ming dynasty which were in the nature of forerunners.

Blue grounds were given various names. *Gros bleu* and Mazarin blue are both underglaze colours, and differ little one from the other. *Bleu de roi* was an enamel blue introduced at a slightly later date. These terms, incidentally, are sometimes confused. Cobalt blue applied in powder form underglaze was called powder-blue, or blue *soufflé*. The latter term was derived from the Chinese practice of blowing on powder colour through a bamboo tube with a silk screen at the end of it.

Overglaze colours were also used for ground-laying, and often sank into soft porcelain glazes in the manner already discussed. These grounds were usually employed in conjunction with white panels which received enamelled decoration, termed 'reserved' panels, or 'reserves'. Since the edge of the coloured ground was often a little ragged, gilding was used overglaze to disguise this fault, and to divide the reserves from the ground.

In Europe, grounds were mostly either brushed or sponged on in the early period, and are therefore inclined to be applied unevenly. Ninteenth-century wares, on the contrary, will usually show an evenly laid ground.

Gold was frequently used to embellish enamelled decoration. The earliest gold was applied with size, and has mostly yielded to time, although traces often remain. At a later date, gold ground up in honey and fired on came into general use. This is dull, with a rich and sumptuous effect frequently heightened by chasing. The mercuric gilding process, which gave thin gold of a brassy colour, was developed towards the end of the eighteenth century.

A type of decoration first employed in England, and not often used outside that country, is the transfer-print. This appears to have been invented by an Irish engraver, John Brooks, about 1753, although there are other claimants to the honour.

An engraved copper plate was inked with ceramic colour and a print taken for it on paper. Whilst the ink was wet, the paper was pressed on to the porcelain surface, leaving behind an impression of the design in monochrome, most often in black overglaze or blue underglaze. An attempt was made to print in polychrome at Liverpool during the eighteenth century, but surviving specimens are few. Transfer-printing in polychrome, however, was frequently used during the nineteenth century.

Transfer-prints are of two kinds, those which are complete in themselves, with the usual hatching and shading of an engraving, and those which are outlines merely, intended for later colouring. The former were sometimes coloured over, but this is quite easily detected, and can be regarded as the work of an 'outside decorator' (see page 276).

Towards the end of the eighteenth century, engraving by a 'stipple' process became popular. The process is well seen in the work of the engraver, Bartolozzi, whose prints have not uncommonly survived. Prints on porcelain in this technique were transferred to the glaze on 'bats' of soft glue – hence it is often referred to as 'bat printing'. If an example of this kind is examined carefully, it will be seen that the design is made up of a multitude of small dots or stipples, somewhat analogous to the appearance of a photograph in a newspaper. A low-powered magnifying glass will make this clear.

*

The glazes upon which these colours were used are feldspathic in the case of hard porcelain, and of lead glass in the case of the soft variety.

All soft-paste glazes are types of glass which were applied in powder form. The usual method employed was to grind the glass to powder and suspend it in water. The ware, which had previously been fired unglazed, was dipped into the mixture, the particles of glass thereupon adhering to it. A low temperature firing then melted the particles and spread the glass in an even layer over the surface.

Porcelain left in an unglazed state is referred to as *biscuit*, *bisque*, or Parian ware, and there was a fashion for porcelain of this kind in the eighteenth and nineteenth centuries. Its use was, for the most part, confined to figures. Parian is the nineteenth century version of the earlier *biscuit*.

During the nineteenth century chemists evolved new glaze substances. Lead was dangerous to the health of the work-people, and considerable research was undertaken into substitute materials. The first patent for a leadless glaze was taken out by the Coalport factory about 1820.

*

Ceramic figures and vessels are formed in a number of ways. No doubt the potter's wheel is too well known to need description in detail, but I would strongly recommend the student of old porcelain to spend an hour or two watching a good 'thrower' at work, or, better still, to try his hand at 'throwing' some simple bowls. The experience will be invaluable. Even when vessels are made in other ways, the influence of the wheel can usually be seen, and quite often the ultimate shapes are based on wheel-thrown forms. Obviously any ceramic object shaped on a wheel must be of circular section. In the case of certain vases with orifices too small to admit the hand of the potter, or even to take a tool satisfactorily, it will be found that the throwing has been carried out in two separate parts, afterwards 'luted', or cemented, together with fluid clay slip. Frequently the joint between the two parts can be detected.

The lathe is a development of the potter's wheel. This is one of the most useful and ubiquitous of machine-tools, finding its most important application in the turning of wood and metal, but when a pot had dried to 'leather hardness' – that is to say, to about the same degree of pliability as leather – it was often mounted in a lathe and, by means of suitable tools, either pared down to reduce its thickness, or, in some cases, decorative ornament was incised into the body.

Extensive use has always been made of moulds for the formation of ceramic vessels. These were of various materials in the early period, but since the first part of the eighteenth century

have almost entirely been of plaster of Paris. A master model
was first made in clay or wax by a modeller, and a plaster mould
taken from it. The body was then either pressed into the mould
– and, in this way, took the shape required – or slip-casting
was used. By the latter method the paste was diluted with water
to the consistency of cream and then poured into the mould.
The porous plaster walls absorbed water from the slip, leaving
behind a thin layer of firm porcelain body. When the desired
thickness had been attained, surplus slip was poured off, the cast
being left to dry to leather hardness before the mould was finally
removed. This method was especially suitable for elaborate and
complicated things.

At an earlier date moulds were made from clay and fired to
give them permanence, the resultant mould being porous and
absorbent in the same way. Moulds of this kind, however, had
to be simple, because clay is prone to warp during the firing
process. Block-cutting, that is to say the cutting of wooden
moulds in *intaglio*, was practised in England, particularly during
the early part of the eighteenth century, but wares made in this
way are usually primitive.

Such methods as the jolley, principally used for quantity production of plates and dishes, it is unnecessary, for our present
purpose, to discuss in detail.[1]

Figures were first modelled in clay or wax, and then *dissected*
by cutting them into a number of separate parts – arms, legs,
torso, and head. These pieces were moulded separately, and
casts or 'squeezes' taken from the moulds. The moulded com-
ponents were put together by a workman called a 'repairer'.
The act of putting figures together was called 'repairing', and
has nothing to do with mending broken porcelain. Bases were
moulded separately, and the same figure can sometimes be
noticed on different bases.

Inspection of a completed figure can often give much information about the difficulty or otherwise which the factory experienced with the type of body they were using. Where it can be
seen that care was taken to avoid unsupported parts, or to

1. These are fully described by Ernst Rosenthal, *Pottery and Ceramics*
(Pelican Books).

support such things as an out-thrown arm, especially in cases where the support is inappropriate to the pose, it can safely be assumed that the body was difficult to fire successfully and liable to collapse and warp in the kiln. This can be well seen in some early or primitive specimens from European factories. In some cases figures have sagged out of perpendicular, even though some such addition as a tree trunk was used to lend support. The hard-paste body allowed a great deal more latitude than the soft, and this will be the more obvious if early figures of both these kinds of porcelain are examined.

Additions to figures, vases, and service ware were either moulded, or modelled, and applied. Such things as handles to cups and jugs were luted into position with clay slip, and applied decoration ranges from little prunus sprigs added to early service ware, to the elaborate attributes to be seen on the bases of figures, as well as to such things as knops in the form of birds which we commonly find on the covers of vases. It is rare to find a figure which has been completely moulded without the application of some hand-modelled parts. It is equally unusual to find a figure which has been completely modelled by hand, but a few simple things, particularly those from early English factories, must have been made in this way.

*

Throughout this volume reference will be made to a number of styles, or fashions, in art. These are described below, and the terms are henceforth used without further definition.

The characteristics of a style are to be seen in the modelling of figures, particularly in the bases. Vase forms, and the decorative ornament applied to them, can usually be placed in well-defined categories, and the subjects of painted decoration, and the manner in which they are used, can frequently be revealing. The palette used for colouring varied with style and period.

Baroque is the earliest European style to be seen in porcelain. It is in evidence from the first period until about 1740, although the latter year must not be regarded as rigidly transitional. Originally a revolt against the classicism of the Renaissance, the *baroque* style is to be seen in every branch of the decorative arts from about 1600 onwards. In painting, the works of Rubens and El Greco may be cited as characteristic examples. In architecture, whilst it sometimes touches the vulgar and the theatrical, *baroque* exhibits an attractive liveliness and exuberance. The staid supporting columns of the classical style, for example, are twisted to resemble barley-sugar sticks. Vast staircases reveal painted vistas similar to a stage back-cloth, often because the architect's imagination outran the amount of money available. The sober statuary of Greece and Rome became alive with exaggerated and mock-heroic gesture.

At its best it is characterized by a tremendous vitality, as well as the use of unusual and theatrical angles of view. Nevertheless, it is symmetrical, and exhibits a certain balance which is lacking from the following *rococo*. In porcelain, *baroque* decoration was usually carried out in a strong palette, and washes of solid colour were used for the painting of figures, the use of floral motifs for this purpose being, generally, somewhat later. The term is employed occasionally in reference to the work of the latter part of the Ming dynasty. No connexion is implied, beyond the fact that, as in Europe, much work of the late Ming period was in a somewhat theatrical idiom in direct contrast to the classicism of the Sung styles.

The *Régence* style is not often mentioned in discussing porcelain. It falls between *baroque* and the following *rococo*, and partakes of both to some degree. It was current between 1715 and 1730, and can be regarded either as transitional, or as an early form of *rococo*.

The *rococo* style is often said to typify best the spirit of European porcelain. The impact of the fashion for Chinese decorative styles on the earlier *baroque* was probably the greatest single factor which led to its rise into popularity, and shells of one sort or another and rockwork bases (*rocaille*), which were popular decorative themes in the 1740s, contributed to its development. Essentially, *rococo* is French, and it can be seen in Continental porcelain from about 1730, coming somewhat later in England. In porcelain, and in the decorative arts generally, Bavarian *rococo* is an interesting development (see Nymphenburg). The style is characterized by many small

39

a

b

c

Fig. 1. Styles in porcelain
(a) *Baroque*. (b) *Rococo*. (c) Neo-classical

flourishes, and an asymmetrical scroll-work which is often of an elaborate nature. These can be delicate and airy, particularly where the style is well understood, but, at its worst, in some of the wares of the English Derby factory, for instance, and in the later nineteenth-century repetitions it is merely meaningless and vulgar. The scroll-work is particularly in evidence on the bases of figures, in contrast to the plain bases of the *baroque* style.

The *neo-classical*, or *Louis Seize*, style was in evidence from about 1765 until the early part of the nineteenth century. Essentially a revolt against the wilder and more elaborate modelling and the gross over-decoration of the later *rococo*, it reintroduced the severe and simple lines of Greece and Rome. In ceramics the pottery forms of these earlier civilizations, which were then becoming known from excavations at Pompeii and elsewhere, were fairly closely copied, and classical subjects suggested by those appearing on Italian red-figure vases were employed, side by side with the development of a contemporary rendering of these ancient subjects. Wedgwood's jasper wares may be cited as examples of the neo-classical style carried to its logical conclusion. The Greek *krater* was especially used as a vase form, but the *oenochoe*, the *lekythos*, and the *hydria* were hardly less popular. The finer forms, such as the *skyphos* and the *kylix*, were rarely or never used.

Actually, the *Louis Seize* style proper retains elements of the *rococo*, and was the precursor of the neo-classical, but in porcelain they are often so merged as to be indistinguishable. The terms are, therefore, virtually interchangeable. Although Louis Seize did not succeed to the throne until 1774, the style is usually regarded as commencing about ten years earlier.

The *Empire* style we owe to the Napoleonic Wars. It developed from the neo-classical, and is principally in evidence in France from about 1800 to 1820. The influence of the Egyptian Campaigns can be seen in the use of sphinxes as decoration. The *Regency* style in England is somewhat similar in many ways, although the term is more often applied to furniture than to porcelain. Eagles were frequently used in both, and elaborate painting was the rule. Eagle-like birds, used during the

41

eighteenth century, are more usually intended to represent the phoenix.

The *Biedermeier* style is more or less synonymous with early Victorian in England, although its Continental manifestation was, usually, of a higher order. It is undistinguished, heavy, and inclined to be ornate.

It is difficult to see anything worth calling a style in most of the decorative art of the later part of the nineteenth century. Virtually everything is derivative, and nothing emerged from the hodge podge which can be regarded as more than a passing fad.

About 1890 we have *l'art nouveau* – known in Germany as *Jugendstil*. This lasted until about 1910, and whilst it would, perhaps, be invidious to fix responsibility for it on one person, the whimsies of William Morris were, in part, to blame for its emergence. Fortunately, its course was comparatively soon run. It is approximately synonymous with the expression, *Edwardian*.

Derivations from the Orient have, generally, received no especial name which needs to be defined at this point. Mention ought to be made of the *Kakiemon* style which had its beginnings in Japan at the end of the seventeenth century. It is characterized by asymmetricality, much empty space, and, in the original, distinguished drawing. The derivations are of variable quality, but the palette usually approaches that of the originals fairly closely (see page 111).

The *Imari* style is also Japanese, and was based on native textiles and brocades. It is slightly later than the Kakiemon types.

Baroque, *rococo*, and *neo-classical* can be seen compared in outline sketches on page 40. A Kakiemon pattern is shown on Plate 53B.

*

The chapters which follow will provide a considerable amount of detailed information about the wares of various factories and centres of production, even though space does not permit more than a bare outline of the more important facts. In very few instances has there been documentary evidence in existence sufficient to provide these facts, and a note of some of the ways in which the story has been pieced together may be useful to anyone proposing to carry out research.

Knowledge of early Chinese wares has been drawn from two principal sources – from native writings, and from excavations.

Literary references are of variable importance and trustworthiness. Safest of all are those which are more or less contemporary with the manufacture of the type of porcelain in question. Less useful are those which were compiled later from earlier writings, because these often contain examples of copying from original sources without practical experience of the porcelain itself, and, as will later emerge, most Chinese writings on the subject of porcelain are likely to be as obscure, in such circumstances, to a Chinese as to a European. Nevertheless, these can be valuable where they bring together information from several sources, more particularly in cases where the original manuscripts have been lost. In the field of ancient literature, both Oriental and Occidental, we owe much to later compilers who worked from manuscripts in existence in their time, but which have since been lost or destroyed. It is not, perhaps, always realized how many Greek writers are known to us only from the works of later compilers.

Excavations are the most revealing, and in many cases contribute important evidence of the greatest assistance in helping us to judge provenance and period.

The widespread custom of burying a man's possessions with his corpse not only provides specimens of pottery and porcelain for the collector and the Museum, but, in many cases, gives much valuable evidence as to the form and decoration of the craftwork of the time. Obviously, in some cases, the objects thus inhumed can be considerably older than the actual date of burial, but they cannot have been made later than the burial date if the grave has been undisturbed. A note of caution is necessary, however, in cases where excavations have not been carried out under responsible supervision. Instances of graves being 'salted' with objects of antiquarian interest are not unknown, and have led to such absurdities as the placing of a comparatively late type of Chinese pottery in the tombs of Egypt. An amusing instance, noticed by H. V. Morton in a tour of the Near East, was the inclusion of an English 'red devil' motor-cycle mascot in a Museum Collection. It was catalogued as probably North Assyrian, and regarded as a representation of the god Baal, the period being given as the ninth century B.C. The coupling of this snook-cocking figure with the god Baal might not be so very wide of the mark, and although we may give a comfortable chuckle of superiority, it is as well to remember that similar opportunities for error in attributing early Oriental works of art and craft lie in wait for the European.

Excavations on kiln-sites, where the actual kiln can be uncovered along with the quantity of 'wasters' and broken fragments which always accumulate wherever pottery is made, provide clinching evidence of the highest possible value, but, quite frequently, such excavations have been carried out for no other reason than commercial profit, and the correct inferences may not have been drawn from discoveries made.

When we turn to European porcelain, we find the evidence varies considerably in value and extent. The Meissen factory is fairly well documented, and its earlier work was copied extensively by other factories. In cases where we can assign a date to the introduction of an innovation at Meissen, we are also in a position to suggest the earliest possible date at which the fashion or style could have been copied elsewhere. Due allowance must be made, however, for the inevitable time-lag, and thus it is that we find Meissen fashions of the 1740s copied at some of the early English factories ten or fifteen years later.

Of the greatest possible assistance are documentary pieces – those which have inscriptions, dates, or signatures of one kind or another. Even when the date is missing, it is often possible to find some way of using an inscription or a signature. For instance, if we know when an artist was born and when he died, then we can assign limits during which a signed piece must have been made. If we have greater information about his life than this, then it is often possible to use it to fix the date even more closely.

Engravings were employed extensively as a source of inspiration for porcelain paintings, figures, and groups of figures. These engravings can often be identified, and, in such cases, may bear a date, or there may be some other way of estimating when they were executed.

Early English porcelain is very badly documented. Nevertheless, research workers have built up a large volume of knowledge based on such things as contemporary newspaper advertisements, rate-books, old sales catalogues, letters, parish records of births, deaths, and marriages, the discovery of 'wasters' on kiln-sites, the pairing of specimens with their Continental inspirations, and even from comparative study of a large number of specimens. One signed example, for instance, has often helped to ascribe a large number of unsigned specimens to an artist.

An excellent example of this is provided by the researches of the late Major W. H. Tapp into the life of the Irish miniature painter, Jeffryes Hamet O'Neale. His monograph on this artist, published in 1938, has enabled us to attribute a large number of important things in Worcester and Chelsea porcelain, the painter of which was at one time unknown, as well as providing a portrait of the man who was formerly little more than a signature on a few Worcester vases. Incidentally, this work will provide the reader with an excellent example of the methods by which research of this kind is conducted.

The student of English porcelain has received considerable assistance from such scientific methods as chemical analysis, and the use of ultra-violet radiation. Within certain limits, factories adhered to proven formulas, and chemical analysis will often help to establish the factory at which a specimen was made. Certain things fluoresce in a manner which is peculiar to a factory or a period, and ultra-violet radiation is now frequently used as a routine method of examination. Further advances on these lines can confidently be expected in the future. Continental and Chinese porcelain have not yet been studied in this way, but it is likely that this will be done eventually.

I have already mentioned engravings as a source of inspiration for paintings and for figures. Books containing botanical illustrations were often used, and drawings from Aesop's *Fables*, to be seen on English porcelain from Chelsea and Worcester, were taken from an edition illustrated by Francis Barlow.

The theatre was a common source of inspiration. The Italian Comedy – an improvised play performed by companies which travelled throughout Europe – is perhaps the best known example of the kind. The characters of Harlequin, Pantaloon, Punchinello, Pierrot, Columbine, the Doctor, the Lawyer, and so forth, are too well known to need detailed description here, but they can all be seen in porcelain from many factories, principally from those of Germany and England. The English theatre was well to the fore as a source of figure models particularly. Peg Woffington, Kitty Clive, David Garrick, and other well-known players, usually in character, are among the better-known examples. Others obviously had their origin in theatrical entertainment, although the source is now somewhat difficult to trace.

The student who takes interest in the methods by which attributions are made will find that no information about the period of his studies is entirely worthless, and much which appears, at first sight, to have no connexion whatever, will later provide a useful key to dating and attribution. For instance, a knowledge of eighteenth-century politics will provide information about the portrait figures of John Wilkes made at Derby, and vessels inscribed *Wilkes and Liberty* should be fairly easy to place in their right compartment so far as date is concerned.

Some of the Jacobite symbolism is a little less obvious. These adherents of the House of Stuart were proscribed, and it is not always easy to detect things intended for their sympathizers. It is possible that some early English porcelain decorated with oak-leaves may refer to the fact that Charles escaped by sheltering in an oak-tree, and this is a fairly well-known Jacobite emblem. Derogatory references to the House of Hanover occur on pottery, but I do not know of an instance to be seen on porcelain.

This necessarily brief sketch is intended to give the student an outline of the methods commonly employed for the purpose of investigating the history of porcelain, and of attributing specimens to the place of manufacture, as well as estimating the approximate age. It also suggests ways in which research may be conducted. It is difficult to do basic research on Continental and Oriental porcelains without living in the countries in question, but careful study and comparison of specimens can often throw fresh light on unsolved problems.

*

It is not to be expected that so frail a substance as porcelain could, in every case, survive the passage of the years without some accidental damage, and there are relatively few entirely perfect specimens existing which were made before 1800.

Documentary specimens, that is to say specimens which, for one reason or another, throw light on porcelain history, need to be treasured whatever their condition.

Under this heading we may include specimens signed by the artist, those bearing a rare mark, those known to have been discovered during a particular excavation, things which have descended in a family connected with early porcelain manufacture or otherwise notable, specimens with armorial bearings, pieces referred to specifically in old documents, and those which bear a date.

Fragments with especially fine decoration should be kept, but generally this observation refers rather more to certain kinds of pottery.

Items of service ware which are cracked but brilliantly decorated are preferable to uncracked things with rubbed decoration. Chips are not too important in an inconspicuous position. They are almost inevitable, particularly if there is fragile applied decoration.

Hands and fingers are frequent casualties, and when they have been replaced with well-modelled composition substitutes, no great harm has been done. Elaborately restored specimens are undesirable unless they are of more than usual rarity. On the other hand, if a figure has been broken and put together cleanly without overmuch restoration, the damage is not so serious. After all, some allowances must be made for the accidents of two centuries, and Swift has some apposite remarks on the behaviour of eighteenth-century serving-maids. Moreover, it is only within the last one hundred years or so that many of these things have been collected and treasured.

There is a foolish prejudice among some collectors against

figures which have had the head broken off and replaced. If the repairs have been well executed and there is little or no restoration, no more harm has been done than a similar accident to an arm, of which little notice is usually taken.

Restorations are usually carried out in a plaster-like substance which is painted and varnished to resemble porcelain. In order to disguise the repair, most restorers carry the painting over on to the glazed porcelain surface to some extent. It is advisable to put such work into the hands of experts. Too often, in the hands of inexperienced people unused to fine work, the overpainting is spread widely over the surface to disguise lack of competence, and, in the case of service ware, unnecessary and unsightly rivets and bands are employed. The Chinese and Japanese make a virtue of necessity by covering repairs with gold lacquer, and there is much to be said for this method in suitable cases. It is better confined to Oriental porcelain, however.

Expert restorers have files of reference photographs which ensure that restorations are accurately carried out, and there are few models which they have not seen at some time or another. Occasionally, it may be necessary to turn to one of the larger museums for information as to the exact nature of the missing part. Rarely, the restoration must be conjectural.

Restoration, in the case of porcelain, is a well-established practice both with collectors and museums, and is, of course, perfectly legitimate. It is essential for the student to know how to detect restored areas, however, and some of the usual methods are noted below.

Ultra-violet light is much the most useful apparatus for the purpose. The repaired areas fluoresce a brilliant yellowish-white which is immediately obvious. Latterly, in an attempt to defeat this kind of examination, one or two restorers have sprayed the whole surface – restoration and porcelain alike – with cellulose acetate varnish. This exhibits an even yellowish-white fluorescence, and it is impossible to gauge the full extent of the repair, but it does suggest very strongly that the damage is greater than the owner would willingly have known. Cellulose acetate varnish of this kind can be wiped off immediately with a cotton-wool pad damped with acetone.

If an ultra-violet lamp is not available then careful examination with a strong glass will give all the information required, the difference between paint and glaze being apparent.

The point of a needle will slide over glaze, but will cut into paint and varnish in a manner immediately obvious.

Restoration is not limited to figures, chips in service ware being filled, and cracks overpainted. Undoubtedly porcelain looks very much better if properly restored in this way, provided the amount of restoration is not excessive, and there is no disfiguring overpainting of the glazed surface.

Cracks and similar small defects were often overpainted with enamel colours by some of the European factories during the eighteenth century.

PART I

The Porcelain of the Orient

*

CHAPTER ONE

China

HISTORICAL BACKGROUND

THE history of China has received such scant attention from the Western world that it is desirable that a consideration of Chinese porcelain should be prefaced by some brief remarks on salient facts and dates against which the achievements of the potter will be viewed.

Chinese civilization is often credited with an antiquity far greater than the facts will support. The earliest known Chinese pottery – the Neolithic types of Kansu Province – cannot be regarded as earlier than about 3000 B.C., at which time the civilizations of Sumeria and Egypt, as well as that of the Indus Valley, had reached a point of considerable complexity. There is every reason to think, in fact, that the pottery of this period is not without Sumerian influence, and the fact that Kansu is the gateway to China from the west seems to suggest that Sumeria may have been the starting point of this phase of Chinese culture, just as, at a somewhat later date, a relationship with Pacific art becomes apparent.

Chinese civilization is remarkable for its continuity. Long after Sumerian towns had crumbled into dust, and the Arabs had despoiled the tombs of the Pharaohs, the Chinese dynasties rose and fell, the Chinese peasant tilled his land, and the Chinese potter spun his wheel. During the Han dynasty silk was exported to Rome, to the delight of the courtesans of the Imperial Court and the despair of the moralists, and, by the T'ang period (A.D. 618–906), ships plied between Egypt and the Far East by way of Basra.

China is taken to include, in its widest sense, Manchuria, Mongolia, Eastern Turkestan, Tibet, and the Eighteen Provinces – an area about twice the size of the United States. Much of it is desert and grazing land, but the great river valleys are fertile, although the rivers rise and flood the land disastrously at intervals. Porcelain kilns were located, for the most part, in the more easterly of the Eighteen Provinces, that is to say in Kuangtung, Fukien, Kiangsu, Chekiang, Kiangsi, Honan, and Chihli. The climate of these varies from rigorous in northern Chihli to tropical in southern Kuangtung.

The Han dynasty (206 B.C.–A.D. 220), possibly the most brilliant in China's long and varied history, was founded by a peasant, Liu Pang, who led a successful revolution against a tyrant in 206 B.C. It was during this period that the pattern of provincial government, which lasted (with some interruptions) until modern times, was laid down.

About 100 B.C. the Emperor Wu embarked on a military career, in course of which he acquired vast new territories. As so often happens, trade followed the flag, and when the new territories had been pacified and assimilated, Chinese travellers undertook long exploratory journeys westwards. Some reached Bactria on the northern frontier of India.

Bactria corresponds to the modern Balkh in Afghanistan. It was first conquered by Cyrus in 540 B.C. and made part of the Persian Empire. It later fell to Alexander of Macedon, when, under Seleucus, it became a province of the Macedonian Empire. It is from here that Greek art influenced both Northern India and China. The sturdy Bactrian horse was speedily introduced into China, and the value of the twin-humped Bactrian camel, with its ability to withstand the intense cold of the interior deserts, is obvious. These animals are frequently represented in pottery during the T'ang period.

The most famous of the Han travellers was Chang Ch'ien, and about his name many legends have been woven. One tells of him sailing a log down the Milky Way. But certain it is that he travelled in other of the Greek provinces as well as Bactria, and he is reputed to have brought back information which led to the opening of trading relations with India.

The China of Han times is referred to by Pliny the Younger as Seres – that is to say, Silk – and the Chinese have records of gifts received from An Tun – probably Marcus Aurelius Antoninus. The great caravan route through Persia was the medium by which goods were exchanged between these two empires.

During the first century A.D. strong measures were instituted against the nomadic Huns. These Huns had constituted a serious threat to the integrity of the northern Provinces for centuries, and the Emperor Huang-ti built the Great Wall as a protection against their destructive raids in the third century B.C. The new measures forced these tribes to turn westward, and, under the leadership of Attila, they penetrated Europe as far as Orléans in 451, leaving behind a swathe of depredation across half the world.

The Han dynasty collapsed in course of time, principally as the result of palace intrigue. It was succeeeded in A.D. 220 by a troubled period known as the Six Dynasties, which lasted until 581. This period witnessed the growth of Buddhism in China, although its initial introduction took place during the latter part of the first century A.D. The growth was not without opposition, the Emperor T'ai Wu decreeing that all foreign gods be utterly erased from the land and their worshippers put to death. These set-backs, however, were of a temporary nature, as later history will show.

Towards the close of the fourth century, after a period of civil war, a Tartar Kingdom was established in the Northern Provinces which took its title, Wei, from a previous dynasty of that name. This separation, known as the period of the Northern Wei, lasted until 535. The Tartars came from the region of Lake Baikal, north of the Gobi Desert and in the southern part of Siberia. They absorbed the native culture fairly completely, a phenomenon to be noticed on other occasions on which the Chinese have been over-run by foreign conquerors. But they were also responsible for the protection of Buddhism, and a considerable School of Buddhist sculpture arose under their influence. The simultaneous growth of this religion in the South eventually healed the breach between the two factions.

Apart from the sculpture referred to, this period was not particularly notable for achievements in the realm of art and literature, probably because of long-prevailing unsettled conditions. The introduction of such religions as Nestorian Christianity, Zoroastrianism from Persia, Manichaeism – a fusion of Christianity and Mithraism – Judaism, and Mohammedanism, met with limited acceptance, and they were allowed to exist side by side with Buddhism and Taoism which commanded by far the greater number of adherents. A Jewish colony was founded in China in 1163, and persisted as a separate entity until the nineteenth century. The first written record of the presence of Nestorian missionaries is dated 751. At this time flourished the General, Kuan Yü. He was later deified during the reign of the Ming Emperor, Wan Li (1573–1620), as Kuan Ti, God of War, and is the occasional subject of porcelain figures.

Of the short-lived Sui dynasty little need be said, except to record its existence between A.D. 581 and 618. It gave place to the T'ang dynasty, which is one of the most important in Chinese history, although the Chinese probably regard that of the Han as a period of greater achievement. Particularly is the T'ang period noted for a renaissance of the arts, and, whilst this volume, being concerned only with porcelain, refers to T'ang times with little detail, it is noted for its fine pottery, and especially for the magnificent series of figures of men and animals excavated from graves of the period. These frequently show traces of Greek influence and, less often, of Indian art which was brought to China by Buddhist missionaries.

The boundaries of the Empire reached out to the very borders of Persia. These were the days of Hārūn ar-Rashīd [1] fifth 'Abbāsīd Caliph, and of his son, the Caliph Mu'tasim. Hārūn is probably best known for his appearance in many of the tales and legends of *The Arabian Nights' Entertainments*, but the importance of his reign in shaping the history of both the Western and Eastern worlds is rarely mentioned. His Empire was immense, possibly larger than that of Jinghiz Khan. If, as seems possible, Charlemagne was, to some extent, under his suzerainty, his sphere of influence reached to the waters of the Atlantic. For part of the time the Eastern Roman Empire was his vassal, and it was not until his death that the decay of the vast 'Abbāsīd Empire became an accomplished fact. His wife, Zubeide, is reputed to have built the city of Kashān, and Mu'tasim founded a pleasure resort at Sāmarrā, some sixty miles up the Tigris from Baghdad, in 838. Sāmarrā was virtually abandoned in 883, and

1. Aaron the Upright (764–809).

left to decay, but amidst its ruins have been excavated numerous T'ang wares in a fragmentary state, including some undoubted specimens of porcelain. The date of manufacture can, therefore, be fixed with some accuracy as not later than 883.

An exceptionally important reference is cited by Arthur Lane (*Early Islamic Pottery*). This records that 'twenty pieces of Chinese Imperial porcelain, the like of which had never been seen at the Caliph's court before' were sent by Ilī ibn-Isa, governor of Khurāsān, as a gift to Hārūn ar-Rashīd. Two thousand other pieces were sent in addition. The author goes on to point out the significance of the distinction made between Imperial and export wares. These will be further discussed in their place.

It was during the T'ang period that Japanese scholars came to China to study, thus laying the foundation for much cultural interchange between the two countries in the centuries which followed.

The end of the T'ang dynasty was a period of strife of a kind which ushered the fall of Chinese dynasties throughout history. In the arts may be observed a certain decadence characteristic of the end of dynasties the world over, and, in due time, the T'ang Emperors gave place to the Sung. The intervening Five Dynasties lasted merely for fifty-three years. The Sung period commenced in 960 and continued until 1279.

The Sung dynasty is the first we shall consider in detail for its porcelain, since it is during this period that porcelain begins to fall into well-marked categories. The examples of the earlier periods are often of unknown origin.

The Sung dynasty was founded by General Chao K'uang-yin who was hailed Emperor by his army. His first tasks were to reunite the Chinese Empire, to obtain the allegiance of contending war-lords, and to provide peaceful and settled conditions. He solved the problem of the war-lords by exchanging land for arms, but his success in other directions was for some time limited, and border warfare was almost continuous. The efforts of an able statesman, Wang An-shih (fl. 1068–76), produced more stable conditions by somewhat unorthodox methods, but the history of the whole period is a tale of internecine strife, culminating in the invasion of the Mongols under Jinghiz Khan. Despite this, the dynasty was, perhaps unexpectedly, rich in philosophers, artists, and men of letters, and the Sung style is particularly well-defined in porcelain.

The predatory hordes of Jinghiz were drawn from the deserts of Mongolia. They were, originally, nomads, and lived by hunting and tending herds. Their constant struggle with adverse climatic conditions gave them a toughness and a ferocity as fighters which made them irresistible, and this dynamic power, unleashed and canalized by Jinghiz, carried them – within his lifetime – into the ownership of an empire unchallenged for size in the history of the world at that time, except, perhaps, for that of Hārūn ar-Rashīd.

By 1280 China was part of the Mongol Empire under Kublai Khan, later to be followed by others of the same house. It was to the Court of Kublai that the Venetian, Marco Polo, travelled in 1275, and the Emperor is widely known by reason of the fragmentary poem by Coleridge which begins –

> In Xanadu did Kubla Khan
> A stately pleasure-dome decree :
> Where Alph, the sacred river, ran
> Through caverns measureless to man
>   Down to a sunless sea.

Xanadu is a form unknown in China, but it may be a variant of *Shangtu*, not far from Peking, where Kublai held his court and received Marco Polo.

The dynasty founded by Jinghiz is known as that of the Yüan, and lasted, in effect, from 1280 until 1368, although parts of China had been subjugated to Mongol rule almost from the beginning of the thirteenth century.

Even those of my readers whose interest in things Oriental has hitherto been of the slightest will have read of Ming porcelain. Usually the collector of such things is depicted by the novelist as somewhat precious, with long tapering fingers caressing bowls of untold worth. This is a complete misunderstanding of the nature of Ming porcelain, and the collector is a character who does not exist outside the mind of the novelist. Later, the porcelain of the period will be discussed in detail; at present it is sufficient to record that the Ming dynasty was founded by Hung-wu, who became Emperor in 1368 as the result of a successful nationalist revolt against the Mongol reigning house.

The new dynasty was Chinese, the monarchy absolute, and the system of land-tenure a reversion to feudalism. Its inception was marked by civil war, and the art of porcelain-making did not begin to flourish afresh until the time of the fifth Emperor, Hsüan Tê. From then onwards the potter shows increasing command of the technical aspects of his craft, but the artistic value is somewhat uneven and variable. Ming porcelain is certainly more prized in the West than it is in China, but it is interesting to see that Western taste in Chinese art is, with the increase in understanding, beginning to follow the native taste much more closely. Especially is this so in the preference for Sung wares, as well as in the appreciation of those of the T'ang and Han periods.

The Mings passed away in due time, the principal cause of their downfall being the imposition of excessive taxation. Comparison is superfluous. They were replaced by the Manchus who came from Manchuria. The garrisons of Tartar troops, which were placed in important centres of population at the time, were never withdrawn, neither did they mingle noticeably with the other inhabitants. Their descendants occupied a place apart almost down to the present day. The dynasty is, perhaps, more widely known as the Ch'ing (Purity), but both names are in common use.

The first Ch'ing Emperor to reign over China as a whole was Shun Chih, who ascended the throne in 1644, but the dynasty is especially notable for the reigns of K'ang Hsi (1662–1722), Yung Chêng (1723–35), and Ch'ien Lung (1736–95). During this period much fine-quality porcelain was manufactured, including some specially designed for export to Europe. There was an increasing tendency to decorate excessively, but the products of these three reigns, which include the kind of Chinese porcelain best known in Europe, are discussed in greater detail hereafter.

The House of Ch'ing came to an end in 1911 with the establishment of the Chinese Republic. Wares of recent manufacture which have been exported to Europe in the last few decades show little that is noteworthy, and are mostly copies of the older styles.

In the Appendix to this book will be found a list of the Chinese dynasties, together with the names of the principal Emperors.

(i) THE ORIGIN OF PORCELAIN

I have referred in the Introduction to the difference between Chinese and European porcelain, and, before proceeding further, it would be as well to discuss the Chinese definition of this material in a little more detail.

The Venetian traveller, Marco Polo, in writing of his journey to the Court of Kublai Khan, uses the word *porcellana* to describe certain wares which he saw in process of manufacture. There seems little doubt that he selected the word because of the resemblance between the glaze of the ware and shells of the *genus porcellana* which have a highly polished and variegated surface. There is no suggestion that the question of translucency was even considered.

But the term did not come into general use in Europe until the sixteenth century, and was first applied to Ming wares, the wares of the Sung and Yüan periods, except for certain celadons, being then unknown. Ming porcelain is both white and translucent. Coloured decoration is usually of the nature of applied enamels, coloured glazes being somewhat rarer. It is not surprising, therefore, that whiteness and translucency were fastened upon by Western potters as those qualities which differentiated porcelain from either stoneware or pottery.

The Chinese refer to porcelain in its widest sense as *tzŭ*, by which may be understood a substance which gives a resonant note when struck. There are some variations on the term, such as *pai-tzŭ*, which signifies that the substance in question is white as well as resonant. The appreciation of this point is essential to a discussion of the origin of porcelain.

The body of Chinese porcelain is a mixture of *kaolin* and *pai-tun-tzŭ*. In powdered form *pai-tun-tzŭ* is used for glazing, and there are reasons for thinking that it was first employed for this purpose about the third century B.C., certainly before its use in the body of the ware. These early essays in its use as a glaze, in conjunction with a hard-fired greyish-coloured body, have been termed proto-porcelain, and there is little doubt that such wares were made in the early part of the Han dynasty. The existence of stonewares of this kind which can undoubtedly be called *porcellanous* at so early a period is a matter of observation, as they have been found in graves in company with characteristic Han products in bronze, jade, and other materials.

The first literary reference to a translucent substance appears to be in the early part of the T'ang dynasty when 'false jade' is mentioned. Much more definite are the words of Suleiman, a traveller who was probably an Arab or Persian merchant belonging to a trading caravan. He wrote, in 851 . . . 'the Chinese have a fine clay of which they make drinking vessels as fine as glass, one can see the liquid contained therein, though they be made of clay.' This statement has been confirmed by the excavations at Sāmarrā already mentioned. It is unlikely that anything excavated here could have been made after about 883, and among the fragments brought to light were some examples of a translucent ware.

These references provide us with evidence as definite as we need to assign the production of a translucent porcelain to the early part of the T'ang dynasty at the latest.

It is, of course, hardly necessary to say that translucency depends, to some extent, on the thickness of the ware. Even a translucent porcelain will be opaque when a certain thickness is exceeded. The actual measurements have been given by Gustaf Lindberg [1] as between 5 and 6 mm. for the early varieties, and 8 mm. for the finer Ch'ing porcelains.

Throughout this chapter the Chinese definition of porcelain as a resonant material is accepted. The European definition will, for the most part, be accepted in writing of European wares. To confine the meaning of the terms to translucent ware alone would lead to the omission of a number of important Chinese varieties, and this would be both unwise and undesirable.

1. Gustaf Lindberg, 'Porcellanous Ware', *Ethnos*, 1947, 3.

(ii) T'ANG PORCELAIN

Of the porcelain made before the beginning of the Sung dynasty it is impossible to do more than generalize. The Sāmarrā porcelains are represented in the British Museum collections by some fragments of white and creamy-white translucent ware.

Somewhat earlier in the T'ang period comes the fine stoneware made in the Yüeh Chou district of Shensi Province, and this is the earliest of the celadon group. Yüeh ware was for long unidentified, although the late R. L. Hobson [1] advanced the speculation as early as 1915 that it was a type of celadon – a suggestion which did not at first find general agreement.

The word *celadon* needs explanation, since it is inaccurately defined in some older works. The name is probably a corruption of Sālāh-ed-dīn (Saladin), Sultan of Egypt, who sent forty pieces of this ware to Nūr-ed-dīn, Sultan of Damascus, in 1171. It is often suggested that the derivation is based on the colour of the costume of a character, Céladon, in *L'Astrée,* a seventeenth-century French romance. The costume is said to have been a greyish-green in colour, but the celadon glaze of the Chinese varies from the putty colour of the Yüeh celadons, through shades of olive and grey, to the jade green to be seen in the later examples from Ch'u Chou.

The colour of celadon glazes, in all their variety, is due mainly to the presence of ferrous or ferric oxides, and it is common to find either a gradual and even change of shade, or discoloured patches, in the glaze of a specimen. These variations are principally due to the amount of oxygen and carbon monoxide present in the kiln atmosphere during firing.

Yüeh ware is first mentioned in the eighth century, and on a number of occasions thereafter, but in the absence of exact knowledge these literary references do not help. For instance, Lu Kuei Meng, a T'ang poet, says that Yüeh bowls 'despoiled the thousand peaks of their *ts'ui* colour', which is virtually meaningless to us, even when we know that *ts'ui* is the colour of kingfisher

1. R. L. Hobson, 'Yüeh ware and Northern Celadons', *Transactions of the Oriental Ceramic Society*, 1936–7.

feathers. The student of Chinese ceramics is beset with these difficulties of translation superimposed upon poetical and inexact description whenever he endeavours to link existing specimens with contemporary references.

Yüeh is in some respects similar to a group of wares generically known as Northern Celadons. The latter have been found at fairly widely scattered points in the Northern Provinces, and have a dark olive-green glaze. They are mostly distinguished for handsome floral decoration, either carved or moulded.

The major differences between Yüeh ware and the Northern Celadons as enunciated by Hobson are, firstly, in the colour, which is lighter in Yüeh and inclined to a putty shade. Secondly, Yüeh carving in the decoration is bolder, although the somewhat thicker and bubbly glaze of the Northern Celadons sometimes tends to obscure the depth of carving. Thirdly, the Yüeh wares have a splayed foot. Lastly, Yüeh specimens almost always show signs of having rested on little piles of sand in the kiln, whereas this feature is absent in the Northern wares. Additionally, Yüeh decoration is *always* carved, whereas that of the Northern group is sometimes moulded. Both types have a hard greyish stoneware body. The Northern group is here represented by a bowl shown in Plate 4. Fragments of Yüeh ware in profusion were found at Sāmarrā.

Some of the ware known as *ying ch'ing* belongs to the T'ang dynasty, although the name, which means *shadowy blue*, is a comparatively recent invention of the Chinese dealer. *Ying ch'ing* porcelain is translucent, with a glaze which – in early pieces – is bluish-grey or bluish-green. The later Sung pieces usually exhibit a purer blue, but the colour is always pale. The body, where not covered with glaze, is a reddish biscuit colour. Thicker pieces of the type are opaque, and fractures will show a texture somewhat resembling fine sugar. It is usually decorated with floral motifs, either carved or incised. *Ying ch'ing* ware is very widely distributed, but the original kiln-sites appear to have been located in Kiangsi Province, although the type may also have been made elsewhere. It has been recovered in quantity from Sung graves.

There is evidence that some of the more elaborate specimens

purporting to be Sung are forgeries made in recent times. Certain ewers have been singled out for suspicion, and my own opinion is that *ying ch'ing* generally needs careful examination and consideration.

Although the appearance of some of the more primitive pieces leaves little doubt that they can reasonably be assigned to the T'ang period, it is impossible to be entirely certain on the point without additional evidence such as would be provided by excavation on a site like Sāmarrā. Vases likely to be of the period are decorated with small, somewhat crudely modelled figures, characteristically T'ang.

Two wares, known from literary references, *Ju* and *Ch'ai* porcelains, were both at one time tentatively identified with *ying ch'ing*. Of these, Ju has been convincingly identified, and is later discussed. Ch'ai is still unknown. It belongs to the short period of the Five Dynasties (907–960), and was made for a few years only. Its colour, says a Chinese commentator, was 'blue as heaven after rain, seen through rifts in the clouds'.

The white porcelain of the T'ang period is related to the Ting ware later discussed. Bases are of the flat T'ang type, and the glaze often has 'tear-drops' where it has run irregularly and gathered into globules.

There are also a number of hard-fired porcellanous stonewares, more or less resonant, the commonest being those with a dark brown or black glaze. The greater part of T'ang wares, however, are in a soft pottery body easily cut with a knife, and this is covered with a soft lead glaze instead of the hard feldspathic glaze of the stoneware.

T'ang porcelain is much scarcer than pottery of the same period. It is not possible to give definite rules for differentiating between Sung wares and those of the earlier period. Form is, generally, a good guide, but manufacture of particular styles did not stop short at the end of a dynasty, and there are transitional and persisting types. Many Sung glazes stop in a roll of perceptible thickness, almost as though thick treacle had been poured over the piece and frozen suddenly into its final position. T'ang pottery glazes are thin and seem to merge almost imperceptibly into the body. T'ang stoneware and porcelain glazes do not possess this property in so marked a degree: neither do they resemble the thicker Sung glazes in this respect.

A foot-ring is something which belongs commonly to the Sung period, T'ang bases being flat. It would be dangerous to say, however, that a foot-ring necessarily proclaims a Sung origin. The line of demarcation, in many cases, is somewhat vague, but it is rarely necessary to reach a definite conclusion on the point.

The unnecessary ante-dating of Sung porcelain to the T'ang period is to be avoided, but, equally, there is the possibility of underestimating the achievements of the T'ang potter in this field.

(iii) THE SUNG DYNASTY

In the long history of Chinese art, the outstanding position of the Sung period is something which needs no emphasis, and it was at this time that the ceramic art reached its zenith. The finest wares of the later periods cannot bear comparison with them, and they represent something unique in the ceramic history of the world. The artistic importance of Chinese ceramics begins slowly to decline from the end of this period, and although the downward curve was at times arrested, it was always on the level it had then reached. There are no more peaks of attainment which come within measurable distance of those of the period under discussion. To some extent this is due to the emphasis placed on decoration during the later periods. The white porcelain developed during Yüan and Ming times at Ching-tê Chên provided a magnificent vehicle for painted decoration, and the temptation to use it excessively was often too great to be seriously resisted. Sung wares, on the contrary, depend entirely on form, and on the colour of the glazes, and in both these respects the potters of this period have never been surpassed. There are, writing generally, small differences in the body of the various wares, the principal point of differentiation being usually in the colour and the nature of the feldspathic glazes applied to the body. These glazes are of variable translucency. Minute bubbles and particles of unvitrified material suspended in some of them cause a scattering of light which renders them more or less opaque.

The wares are numerous, and not all are of equal importance. Six are of such outstanding beauty that they have been aptly termed *classic*. *Ju yao*,[1] made at Ju Chou in Honan; *Kuan yao*, made first at K'ai Fêng Fu (Honan Province) and later (after (1127) at Hang Chou; *Ko yao* and *Lung-ch'üan yao*, made at Lung-ch'üan in Chekiang; *Ting yao* made at Ting Chou in Chihli; and *Chün yao*, from Chün Chou in Honan, complete the six.[2]

Important, but somewhat lacking in the finer qualities of those above mentioned, are the wares of Tz'ǔ Chou in Southern Chihli, the black and brown glazed types from Honan, and the *ying ch'ing* already discussed. *Tz'ǔ Chou* ware is notable for some fine painted decoration. The Yüeh types continued to be made, and can to some extent be identified with the classic wares.

Literary references to *Ju* ware are many. It was made at an Imperial factory which commenced production in 1107 and closed in 1127. In a work of this nature it is not possible to discuss it in detail, but the reader is referred to the commentary by Sir Percival David[3] for information on this exceedingly rare kind. This includes translations of all literary references of any merit, as well as illustrations of its characteristics. The colour is a fine pale lavender, the glaze closely crackled, and on the underside of the base may be found a ring of small oval spur-marks left by the kiln-supports, referred to by a Chinese commentator as 'small supporting nails'. The number of examples in European collections is extremely small.

Kuan is another Imperial ware, exceedingly rare, and of the highest importance. The kilns at K'ai Fêng Fu at which this was made were established at the beginning of the twelfth century and were closed in 1127 when the Court fled southwards. They were re-established at Hang Chou, the new seat of government.

Chinese commentators speak of a 'brown mouth and iron foot' which refers to the colour exhibited by the body at these points,

1. *Yao* is equivalent to the English *ware*.

2. Some authorities omit *Lung-ch'üan* from the classic wares. Others include this and *Yüeh*.

3. Sir Percival David, 'A Commentary on Ju Ware', *Transactions of the Oriental Ceramic Society*, 1936–7.

and the Hang Chou examples were probably made in a darker body than the earlier examples. The glaze varies in colour between lavender and grey, with perhaps an occasional inclination towards blue and green, although examples of this kind have not been identified with certainty. Most likely specimens have either a widely- or a closely-meshed crackled glaze, often emphasized by the application of brown or black pigment. The glaze is virtually opaque, and of a richness associated with the best Sung wares. Chinese sources have many descriptive phrases for the finer glazes, of which 'massed lard' is one of the most typical.

Ko yao was, by tradition, made by the elder of two brothers Chang, and *ko* can be translated as *elder brother*. The type has a very dark stoneware body, and a greyish-white glaze with a closely-meshed crackle, the lines of the crackle usually being emphasized by reddish-brown or black pigment. *Ko yao* was extremely similar to the Southern Kuan types, and Chinese sources seem agreed that the clay was imported from Hang Chou. The Chinese connoisseur believes that the *Ko* glaze contains masses of minute bubbles which cannot be distinguished in the Kuan glaze, and in this way separates the two. This, however, is a fine point about which it is possible to hold more than one opinion, and some Western authorities are inclined to doubt the existence of the brothers Chang, and to regard them as the invention of a writer of the early part of the Ming dynasty.

Points of this kind were slowly being resolved by excavations on kiln sites in China, sherds and 'wasters' providing proof of the kind of wares made at the particular place. At the time of writing, however, these excavations by foreigners have come to an end, and it is impossible to foresee when they will be resumed.

We are on much safer ground in discussing the celadons made at Lung-ch'üan. From these kilns came most of the green glazed celadons. The body of the greater part of the surviving examples, that is to say the heavier and stronger kinds, is greyish in colour. Occasional examples which are both thinner and whiter can be faintly translucent in places. The foot-ring of most Lung-ch'üan celadons, where unglazed, is dark red in colour owing to contact with free supplies of oxygen in cooling, which converted the iron in the highly ferruginous clay into ferric oxide. An inclination to brown can usually be seen at the rim where the glaze is thin.

The glaze is somewhat more translucent than that of the wares already discussed, and this tempted the potter to decorate the body with carved and incised designs which are visible through it. Other specimens have moulded decoration left unglazed, which burns to a dark red in colour in the same manner as the foot-ring, and provides an effective contrast to the green glaze.

Kinuta seiji is a Japanese term meaning 'mallet' celadon, so called from a famous vase of mallet shape which has a blue-green glaze of a kind much prized in Japan. The *tobi seiji* 'buckwheat' celadon) has a green glaze splashed with small brown spots at intervals and is also, as the name suggests, highly regarded by the Japanese.

Some of the fragments found at Sāmarrā resemble Lung Ch'üan wares sufficiently to make it probable that the kilns were working in T'ang times. A number of the Lung Ch'üan potters moved to Ch'u Chou at the beginning of the Ming period, and it is thought that kilns persisted here until the early part of the Ch'ing dynasty. The Ming wares are generally inferior, and are not usually difficult to separate from the earlier. The later celadon glaze of Ching-tê Chên was used over a white porcelain body, and the practice of imitating the Sung carved designs by painting on the body in white slip before glazing can probably be placed to the latter part of the Ming dynasty at the earliest.

Celadons were greatly prized in China and Japan, and in the Near East. The Chinese admired them for their resemblance to jade, which they greatly esteem. There was a widespread belief in the East that celadons possessed the power to reveal the presence of poison in food, either by breaking, or by changing colour. Because much of it was shipped from the port of Moulmein, on the Gulf of Martaban, the Persians referred to it as *Martabani* ware, and copied it in a soft pottery body. In India it received the name of *ghori* ware, derived from Afghanistan, the seat of the Ghori kings, which was on the caravan route to Northern India. Occasional pieces found their way to Europe where they were much prized. Archbishop Warham bequeathed a bowl of celadon to New College, Oxford, in 1530.

There are a number of celadons of importance, apart from those made at Lung Ch'üan. The Northern Celadons have received some attention in the preceding section. These may have emanated from Korea, and Korean wares are later discussed separately. The wares of Sawankhalok are likewise separately treated. Within the limits mentioned, the colour of celadons is extremely variable, comparatively small alterations in the composition of the kiln-atmosphere effecting corresponding changes in the colour of the glaze.

Ting yao has already been accorded passing mention in the discussion of T'ang porcelain. The kilns were situated at Ting Chou (Chihli Province), and were working from T'ang times onwards throughout the Sung dynasty, although it did not attain a reputation for fine wares until it came under the patronage of the Court.

Ting is a type of Sung porcelain which is almost always translucent. The translucency is orange in colour, and it varies between this and opacity in the thicker parts. Generally, the glaze of the finer variety called *pai ting* (white Ting) is inclined to collect in drops, on the exterior of bowls particularly. These have been called 'teardrops' and are regarded as evidence of genuineness, although their absence, by itself, does not necessarily condemn. The colour of this variety is a fine ivory-white,[1] and a particular point to be noticed in the bowls is the raw or unglazed rim which is often bound by a copper or silver band. Such pieces were fired mouth downwards in the kiln, a somewhat primitive method which was used also by some other kilns, including early bowls of the *ying ch'ing* type.

Chinese commentators also refer to *fên ting* (flour Ting) and *t'u ting* (earthen Ting); the latter has a yellowish glaze and a coarser body, and both varieties are inferior to *pai ting*. There are also literary references to brown, black, and red Ting. Of these kinds, only black Ting has been identified, and I only know of two specimens in this country, one in the Burrell Collection in Glasgow and the other in Bristol's Schiller Collection.

1. The later Ch'ing copies are chalk-white in colour.

The later has three ball-shaped feet, a unique feature. Ting decorative *motifs* are mostly floral, the finer specimens being carved or incised, the lesser moulded.

The kilns are reputed to have moved south in 1127, but specimens of Southern Ting have not been separated with any measure of certainty.

It is impossible to discuss the numerous coarser white wares made elsewhere during the period in detail, but some examples of a fine quality came from kilns at Chü-lu Hsien. These have a coating of white slip over a greyish body. The overlying glaze has a closely-meshed crackle. Forms are of the simplest, and the products of these kilns can be placed among the finer Sung wares.

Chün yao, from Chün Chou in Honan Province, is a type somewhat more favoured by the Western connoisseur than by the Chinese. The Chün kilns certainly supplied bulb bowls, flower pots, and stands, to the Court, and to this extent it can be regarded as an Imperial ware. Actually, the colours of the finer Chün glazes are superb if a little more showy than those from other kilns. They are of varying shades centred around a lavender-grey, often either splashed or suffused with a colour which varies between crimson and purple.

The glaze itself is thick and contains myriads of tiny bubbles. Partings of the glaze which look like small cracks in the surface, usually shaped like a V or Y, are called by the Chinese 'earthworm tracks', and are regarded as a sign of genuineness. These marks are ordinarily to be seen in the interior, and need close inspection to find them. The surface is often minutely pitted at intervals as though some of the bubbles had burst on the surface.

The body, a hard-fired porcellanous type, is of the ferruginous colour often to be seen on Sung wares, and the rim inclines somewhat to the same colour when the glaze is thin.

Flower pots usually bear numerals (from 1 to 10) incised into the base. These indicate sizes.

Plate 7A is unusually interesting. It throws light on the methods of manufacture employed by the Sung potter, and shows that Chün ware was fired in protective cases of fireclay.

These cases are technically known as saggers (or, less often, seggars).

In this particular case a fine bowl has adhered to the sagger, and is, therefore, a waster. The cause of the damage was excessive heat apparently applied locally to the base of the sagger, since the glaze is of an excellent colour.

'Soft Chün' (*shu t'ai*) has a similar glaze, so far as colour is concerned. It is, however, denser and more opaque, and minutely crackled. The colour can incline to a marked turquoise which is not to be seen on the more important variety. The body is buff in colour and sandy. The Chinese call it *ma chün*, after a potter named Ma who is reputed to have been its originator. Most of it is obviously of the Ming period, even the earliest examples being very doubtfully Sung.

Fatshan Chün comes from the area around Canton in Kuangtung Province. The body is porcellanous, and of a reddish-brown colour. The glaze is usually thick and dappled with various colours which range from a Chün type to a dark brown. A somewhat crude kind of celadon comes from this district, often in the form of figures and shrines with the flesh left unglazed and burned to a dark reddish-brown. Kuangtung stoneware generally is unlikely to be earlier than the Ming period and most of it is quite modern, that is to say of the nineteenth century.

Other specimens which more or less resemble *Chün yao* come from Yi Hsing in Kuangtung Province. Some of these imitations are remarkably close. Copies were made at Ching-tê Chên in a white porcelain body. Many of these were made to the order of the Emperor, Yung Chêng (1725–35), and bear his incised mark on the bottom. In some cases this has been ground off, the white porcelain body thus exposed being appropriately painted over. These are not usually difficult to detect.

Chien yao came from Chien-an in Fukien Province. The tea-bowls made here are especially sought after by the Japanese, who have given them the name of *temmoku*, and were used in the Tea Ceremony (*cha-no-yu*). They have also been copied by the Japanese.

The body is a hard-fired stoneware, very dark in colour. The glaze is exceptionally thick, and usually ends in a roll near the base. The glaze colours are either black or near-black, mottled and streaked with brown. This is referred to as 'hare's fur' marking; and silvery spots, often spaced out with a certain regularity, can be noticed on one rather scarce type of Chien ware which is referred to as the 'oil spot' glaze.

Other black glazed wares, some extremely fine, came from unidentified kilns in Honan Province. The glaze is somewhat thinner, and varies from the variegated kind to be seen on *Chien yao* to a lustrous and even black.

The kilns of Tz'ŭ Chou, now in Chihli Province, made a kind of ware which is somewhat different from the varieties already described.

The body is coarser and greyish-white in colour. Usually the piece was given a preliminary coating of white slip, over which was placed a clear transparent glaze. Much greater use was made of added decoration than is commonly seen on Sung wares.

Decoration was painted in black or brown slip, broadly and with great skill. One variety is decorated by incising the design through the white slip to the body beneath (*graffiato*). A rare type is covered with a brown glaze which is treated in the same way. The few reasonably certain specimens of Sung wares painted (very slightly) in enamel colours probably came from here, but whilst there are literary references to the use of underglaze blue, and this colour had been used in Perisa since the ninth century, the earliest examples of which we can be certain belong to the Yüan period (see Plate 8). Tz'ŭ Chou decorative *motifs* are usually floral.

Some extremely large pieces came from these kilns, and unusual forms, such as pillows, can be seen occasionally, although most are later than Sung.

The foundation of these kilns may conceivably go back to the T'ang dynasty; they were working until recent times, and may, in fact, still be working. The identification of Sung examples, therefore, is not always easy or certain.

(iv) THE YÜAN DYNASTY

The wares of the Yüan dynasty are mainly transitional. The greater part of surviving Yüan products are celadons of one kind or another, and the contact with the Nearer East and the West, which developed under Mongol suzerainty, has distributed these wares widely.

Yüan wares are especially apt to be more elaborately and less happily decorated than those of the preceding period, and an acquaintance with both Sung and early Ming pieces will usually enable Yüan specimens to be recognized, because their function as a bridge between the two will be apparent.

Of the porcelain we have already discussed, celadons were still being made at Lung-ch'üan, and possibly at Ch'u Chou. A type of Ting, inferior to Sung productions, was probably still being made. Tz'ŭ Chou wares were continued, and the more elaborately decorated pieces can probably be given a Yüan dating. The carved brown-glazed type may properly belong here.

Ching-tê Chên, later discussed in more detail, may have been making white porcelain at this time, and the vase decorated in underglaze blue shown in Plate 8B is very similar to another in existence which actually bears a Yüan date as part of the decoration.

Cobalt blue was introduced during this period, and Chinese commentators speak of 'Mohammedan blue' (hui ch'ing) which can be taken to refer to Persian sources. There were extensive cobalt deposits in Baluchistan. It has also been suggested, with some evidential justification, that the earlier blue may have come from Sumatra, perhaps the su ni p'o referred to in the quotation on page 77, and that supplied during the Chia Ching period (see page 78) may have come from Yunnan in the extreme south-west of China.

The use of Near Eastern metal-work as a source of inspiration for forms begins to be obvious in this period, and forms generally are more florid and elaborate than the simpler Sung types. Spouted ewers are either late Sung or Yüan.

(v) THE MING DYNASTY

Ming porcelain is notable for two innovations, the movement away from Sung severity, and the greater value placed upon painted decoration. It is remarkable, too, for the growth of the manufacturing centre of Ching-tê Chên, near Nanking. Nanking was the earlier Imperial Capital. This was removed to Peking in 1421.

The story of Chinese porcelain from this time onwards is little more than a history of Ching-tê Chên, there being few centres of importance elsewhere. The earliest wares were decorated in underglaze blue, and although it is impossible to be certain of the attribution, there are a few pieces in existence which seem likely to belong to the reign of the Emperor, Hung Wu (1368–98). The reign of Yung Lo (1403–24) is principally remarkable for bowls of egg-shell thickness which are so fragile that they have been termed by the Chinese, *t'o t'ai* – that is to say, bodiless. These are especially interesting as providing evidence that the early Ming potters had attained a high degree of competence in handling their materials.

The body of the usual kind of early Ming porcelain is of fine grain, white in colour, with a faint tinge of reddish-brown at the unglazed foot-ring, due to the accidental presence of iron. The earlier glazes are thick, sometimes uneven, and with an appearance – well described by a Chinese commentator – of 'massed lard'. 'Pin-holes' in the glaze are fairly common, and the glaze has a bluish tone which could equally be due to traces of cobalt or of iron. Some glazes show what the Chinese call a 'chicken skin' effect. It looks somewhat like the skin of a plucked chicken, or of orange-peel, but, of course, to a much slighter degree. The same effect is commonly to be seen on later Japanese porcelain glazes where it is more marked.

The 'finish' of most Ming porcelain lacks the almost machine-like precision of the wares of the Ch'ing period, but something must be allowed for intended use. Export porcelain would necessarily be heavier and stronger, and, since it was made for foreigners, of poorer quality. The finer Ming wares are finished

74

with much greater exactness than those intended for rougher usage.

Blue-and-white porcelain is extremely difficult to place in point of time, although certain individual pieces can be attributed with a high degree of certainty. Controversy on the point is frequent, and sometimes heated, and much confusion has been caused by the Chinese custom of copying earlier examples and adding the appropriate reign-mark. Let it be said that the object of this was not to confuse Western scholars and collectors, but to pay tribute to the wares of their ancestors. Thus, a bowl in a style recognized to be that in use during the reign of the early Ming Emperor, Hsüan Tê, and bearing his reign-mark, may be genuinely of the period, but it could be a sixteenth-century copy, or a much later Ch'ing copy, and it needs close acquaintance with the wares of all these periods before the subtleties whereby they may be distinguished begin to clarify in the mind. Although these points are impossible to describe satisfactorily in the absence of an opportunity to demonstrate with actual specimens, the more important public collections usually show an adequate range of archaizing pieces.

W. B. Honey, in an essay on the subject, puts the position clearly when he writes: ... 'the first Chinese blue and white was *presumably* [my italics!] primitive in technique ... and it is natural to wish to assign an early date to specimens showing these characteristics. But they may be due to common or provincial make rather than earliness, and no Chinese examples have come to light which can be proved to date before the fourteenth century.'

Very little of the finer kinds of blue-and-white porcelain was exported, although, as witness the Palace collection at Istanbul, this cannot be regarded as an invariable practice.

Apart from blue-and-white, the reign of Hsüan Tê was noted for the use of underglaze copper-red – the *chih hung*, or 'sacrificial' red. This extremely difficult colour was obtained from an oxide of copper in the presence of a kiln atmosphere heavily charged with carbon monoxide. It was reproduced again in the Ch'ing dynasty, although perhaps with not the same brilliance, but Western potters were unable to use it until the nineteenth century. Most examples in Europe belong to the Yung Chêng period (1722–35), and are reproductions of early Ming pieces. Stem cups with three red fish or three red fruits are probably the best known of a rare type.

Yellow, green, and red enamels were almost certainly used during the Sung period. I have seen a number of likely specimens. The *wu ts'ai*, or five-colour decoration, was first used in the Hsüan Tê period, and the enamels were thickly applied. Iron-red, a brownish yellow (somewhat similar to that used on T'ang pottery), green, and a turquoise blue, together with cobalt blue underglaze, make up a characteristic Ming palette which, from Chinese references, seems to have been in use at this time, even though examples of reasonably certain attribution are very few.

Another class, well known in later examples, is the *san ts'ai*, which is a three-colour palette. These colours are actually washes of soft lead glazes instead of the feldspathic glazes in ordinary use. They were kept from mingling, either by *cloisons* of clay threads, or else by more or less elaborately carved and pierced work (*ling lung*), the effect of the former being reminiscent of some earlier T'ang varieties. Pieces decorated in this style usually have one colour as a background which predominates – either turquoise-blue or dark green – the other colours being yellow, *aubergine*, or dark blue. They are not infrequent, although it is unlikely that any belong to the Hsüan Tê period.

Apart from the 'sacrificial' red already mentioned, some other monochrome glazes were used at this time. Dark blue and yellow are both mentioned by native writers. Oil-gilding is also mentioned in the *T'ao Shou*[1] which, with the *Po wu yao lan*[2], is an important source of information. Both leaf-gold, and that applied with a brush, have been noticed, the second being the later process of the two.

From references it would seem that some pieces were made with *an hua* or 'secret' decoration which was first used in the

1. A discussion of pottery by Chu Yen. Published 1774.
2. By Ku Ying-tai, published about 1625. Contains much information of value on Ming porcelain.

reign of Yung Lo. The design was lightly incised into the body with a needle-point before glazing, and can only be seen when the specimen is held to the light. A similar effect was obtained by painting the design in white slip on a white body before glazing. Later, elaborate designs with somewhat deeper incisions were deliberately revealed by covering with glazes of contrasting colours.

The reign of Ch'êng Hua (1465–87) was a fruitful one, and some fine wares were produced. The blue-and-white, however, was not of the same quality. The author of the *Po wu yao lan* gives his opinion as follows:

'In my opinion the Ch'êng *yao* blue-and-white does not equal that of the Hsüan *yao*, but the coloured ware of the Hsüan court is inferior to that of the Hsien Court [i.e. of Ch'êng Hua]. The reasons are that of the blue of Hsüan ware is *su ni p'o* [perhaps Sumatra, see page 73], and this was exhausted after that reign, so that in the Ch'êng Hua period only the ordinary class of blue was used, and that the colours [i.e. enamels] of the Hsüan *yao* were deep and thick and piled on and consequently not very beautiful, while those of the Ch'êng *yao* are rather thin and subdued in colour and produce a pictorial effect.'[1]

Very few specimens of blue-and-white exist which are at all likely to be of this date, although some decorated in a rather pale blue have been assigned to it. The 'Rock of Ages' pattern was probably introduced about this time. It is formed of somewhat stylized waves with rocks rising therefrom. It can be seen in a debased form as a border pattern on Isnik (Turkish) pottery of the late sixteenth century, and was also copied in Europe on early wares, both *delft* and porcelain.

The Ch'êng Hua enamelled wares, however, are well known and of exceptionally fine quality. It is for these that the reign is noted. About this time the practice of applying enamels directly to the *biscuit* (*émail sur bisque*) instead of on to the glaze was first adopted. Enamels applied in this way are apt to be somewhat darker in colour than those used on a glazed surface.

The following reign of Hung Chih (1488–1505) is chiefly remarkable for yellow of fine quality, described as the yellow

1. Quoted from Hobson, *The Wares of the Ming Dynasty*.

of the sunflower and the yellow of steamed chestnuts. No doubt the latter was a paler variety. These references intend, most probably, a yellow used predominantly as a coloured ground or a coloured glaze rather than an enamel, and there are a number of such pieces in existence which can reasonably be referred to this reign.

The reign of Chêng Tê (1506–21) is of distinct importance. Not only was the production of the highest quality, but it now becomes possible to assign specimens to a period with a much greater degree of certainty. There was, for instance, a notable revival of blue-and-white, possibly due to the acquisition of fresh supplies of Mohammedan blue, a supposition made the more likely by the existence of pieces bearing Arabic inscriptions. Chêng Tê wares decorated in blue are scarce, but they can be recognized by the fine quality of the colour.

The following reign of Chia Ching (1522–66)[1] shows a blue-and-white porcelain with an intense dark violet blue. This is noticeably less scarce than examples from the earlier reigns discussed. The use of Mohammedan blue continues until the reign of Wan Li (1573–1619), but its use during this latter reign is infrequent, and native supplies appear to have been used thereafter.

An extremely effective Chêng Tê decoration, copied later in the reigns of the Ch'ing Emperors, K'ang Hsi (1662–1722) and Yung Chêng (1723–35), has a yellow ground with an incised dragon coloured with green enamel.

San ts'ai decoration is used effectively during this period, from which date most of the finer extant specimens. Occasional examples with a coloured ground and a decoration of a dragon in relief in white *biscuit* have been recorded.

At this time, trade with Europe and the Near East increased greatly, and many pieces found their way Westwards by one route or another.

The reign of Chia Ching (1522–66) is notable for the failure of the material used for 'sacrificial' red which was replaced by iron-red (*fan hung*) used overglaze. This colour, occasionally

1. Not to be confused with the Ch'ing Emperor, Chia Ch'ing, 1796–1820.

referred to as tomato red by Occidental writers, has a marked iridescence around it on most genuine specimens, probably due to some chemical interaction with the glaze.

Much polychrome ware (*wu ts'ai*) was made, as well as incised designs covered with a deep blue glaze, and gilt decoration over a similar glaze. Another class is decorated predominantly with red and green enamels.

The reign of Wan Li (1573–1620) is the last of importance in the Ming period, and it also saw a marked decline in the power of the Empire. Apart from numerous conflicts with the Tartars, the Japanese invaded Korea in 1598, and internal troubles were violent and prolonged.

Large fish-bowls were mostly made in this reign, and the story is told of potters who were given orders by the Palace for bowls of such immense size that their manufacture was regarded as impossible, until one sacrificed his life for the others, who were in imminent danger from the executioner, by plunging into the flaming kiln. This caused the bowls to emerge perfectly fired and flawless. A somewhat similar story is told of the 'sacrificial' red which remained unattainable until a potter threw himself into the blazing kiln. The latter version has the merit of some scientific basis, since the combustion of the body would provide the necessary excess of carbon monoxide needed to induce this colour.

It must, of course, be appreciated that a considerable amount of superstition collected around these various processes. For example, it was said of Ts'ang Ying-Hsüan, the director of the Imperial kilns at Ch'ing-tê Chên from 1683 to 1726, that 'the figure of God was often seen in the middle of the furnace, either painting designs on the porcelain or shielding it from harm, so that it came out perfect and beautiful'.

Large quantities of blue-and-white were made during the period of Wan Li, and much of it found its way Westward. It is not at all uncommon in Europe today, and many of the shapes show signs of having been made for Western use. Much of it is in a body which is thin, hard, crisp, and resonant, and unlike the earlier Ming varieties, although its introduction probably pre-dates the reign of Wan Li by a few years. This was largely made for export, and most Wan Li porcelain to be seen here is of this kind.

Decoration in relief was continued, and pierced decoration (*ling lung*) which was done by piercing the thrown pot before firing was carried to new lengths of elaboration.

A combination of polychrome enamels with underglaze blue was frequently used, and was the precursor of the *famille verte* of the next dynasty. A large bowl of this transitional type is illustrated in Plate 11.

It is probable that the *flambé* glazes dealt with at greater length in describing the wares of the following period were first made about this time, and may have been discovered accidentally during attempts to reproduce the earlier underglaze copper red, continually the subject of experiment.

In some respects the wares of this reign are transitional, and the further development of many of the varieties noticed may be seen in the reign of K'ang Hsi. The years of the last Ming Emperors do not contain anything significant for our present purpose, and most of the work done was principally transitional in style. Much was inferior in quality, but some excellent work was done in wares painted with blue underglaze.

The varieties hitherto discussed were made, mostly, at Ching-tê Chên, and insufficient is known of porcelain made elsewhere to enter into a discussion of its nature in a work of this kind. Most specimens are difficult to date within even wide limits, just as they are difficult to assign to a particular kiln-site with any exactness.

There was, however, one centre of production at Tê Hua in Fukien Province which was working in the latter part of the Ming dynasty. The porcelain made here is often referred to as *blanc de chine* and can be of the highest quality and of great translucency. The glaze has been aptly described by R. L. Hobson as 'like milk-jelly'. The colour ranges from cream-white to chalk-white, and those of the former colour are likely to be earlier, although this cannot be regarded as definite. Most of the wares which can readily be identified are small statuettes or figurines, finely and crisply modelled, and the early examples often suffer from fire-cracks at the base, of the kind which can sometimes be seen in some early European soft porcelain figures.

Most frequently represented is a Buddhist female deity, Kuan Yin, usually seated but sometimes standing, but other deities, such as Kuan Ti, God of War, as well as figures of sages and dignitaries, are to be seen. Somewhat rare are figures in European costume, and these mostly belong to the eighteenth century. Figures are generally quite small, but I have seen one example of a standing figure over two feet in height.

Some of the figures have detachable heads, and hands have often been added separately. On some examples, holes have been pierced for the insertion of human hair, principally for moustaches.

Bottles, dishes, furnishings for the writer's table, little libation cups, and so forth, are all to be seen. Ordinarily these are in white porcelain, and it is at least arguable whether the few coloured examples were painted contemporarily. The balance of evidence is against it when an otherwise early example is under consideration.

Celadons were made both at Ch'u Chou and at Ching-tê Chên. It has been said that the presence of an unglazed ring, coloured brownish-red, at the base indicates manufacture during the Ming period so far as those made at Ch'u Chou are concerned. This accords with the observation of other Ming characteristics. Many examples have incised and carved floral designs of a kind also to be seen on Ming painted wares. Celadons painted in white slip underneath the glaze belong to this period and later.

'Kiangnan Ting' is a cream-glazed ware, somewhat resembling the earlier Ting, which was also made during the following Ch'ing period. The type was probably made at a number of places, and cannot be assigned to any one kiln-site with certainty.

Ming specimens from Tz'ŭ Chou are not infrequent, although in later wares from these kilns the line of demarcation between pottery and porcelain is extremely vague, and they would be better classified as pottery.

There is a reference from Chinese sources to the kilns at Chün

Chou during the reign of Hsüan Te, but no certain identification of its wares has been made.

The kilns of Kuangtung were active, mainly with the type of ware already discussed, and those of Yi Hsing were making, among other things, red stoneware teapots, highly modelled, and known in the West as *boccaro*. This name was originally given to scented red pottery from Mexico, but later applied to wares from Yi Hsing imported into Europe in the seventeenth century, and in great demand for brewing the new drink of tea.

(vi) THE CH'ING DYNASTY TO 1796

During this period the variety of ware made was truly enormous. Ching-tê Chên increased greatly in importance and influence, and an event of the first magnitude to the ceramic historian is provided by the letters of a Jesuit missionary, Père d'Entrecolles, dated September 1712 and January 1722 respectively.

These letters provide us with a complete description of the art of porcelain-making as it was then carried on. They begin with the mixing and preparation of the clay, and continue through all the various processes of formation and decoration. They tell of a mass-production system which was almost modern in its completeness. The decoration, for instance, was analysed, each workman being responsible for a part, one man tracing outlines, another colouring, and so forth. Naturally this method would not be used for the finest wares, but there is no doubt that some extremely good work was done on this co-operative basis.

As a centre of manufacture Ching-tê Chên may go back to Han times, although it did not become of importance until the eleventh century when a Sung Emperor, Ching Tê, patronized it, and gave it his name. With some set-backs it continued to increase in importance and size from that time onwards. In the reign of the Ming Emperor, Hung Wu, the Imperial kilns on Jewel Hill were founded, and the town continued to expand until, in the time of d'Entrecolles, it contained over a million people who consumed ten thousand loads of rice and a thousand hogs daily. At that time there were at least three thousand kilns within the confines of the city, and, at night, the glare of its furnaces could be seen for many miles round.

In this section the wares made during the reigns of K'ang Hsi, Yung Chêng, and Ch'ien Lung, will be discussed. Those of the nineteenth century are dealt with separately. It is extremely difficult to draw lines of demarcation between reigns so far as the type of ware produced is concerned. The attempt has often been made in the past, an example being the assignment of the first use of *rose* enamel to the reign of Yung Chêng, but there is no doubt that the colour was well known in the period of K'ang Hsi. It must be understood, therefore, that such assignments are sometimes arbitrary.

Moreover, in view of the enormous export trade which had by then grown up with Europe, it is necessary to discriminate between export wares, which are often artistically inferior, and those in the Chinese taste. Later, I shall describe a certain class of porcelain decorated with European subjects, but there are other things decorated with Chinese subjects which should properly be regarded as not in the true Chinese taste, but made for export. These have generally inferior decoration, which is often a meaningless juxtaposition of decorative *motifs* suggested by Western merchants. The section on the symbolism of Chinese decoration will make this point clearer. The so-called 'Mandarin' type from the Cantonese studios is an example.

It is, perhaps, best to start the discussion of the period with blue-and-white. An extremely large export trade had been in existence since the days of Wan Li, mostly in the hands of the various East India Companies. The advent of K'ang Hsi saw also the development of processes whereby native cobalt oxide could be refined to a brilliant sapphire blue of the utmost purity, without trace of red. The body was close-grained and of fine quality, the glaze clear and even, and the potting precise. The body was remarkable for a whiteness which is the more obvious when it is set against earlier and later wares, the glazes of which are usually tinged with blue probably due to slight traces of iron.

The polychrome wares show some differences from those of the late Ming period. The best known in Europe are grouped under the headings of *famille verte, famille jaune, famille noire,* and *famille rose*,[1] of which the green family, called after the predominating brilliant green enamel, is the earliest. Most of the decorative styles which can be grouped under these various families are export wares. The *verte* family is a combination similar to the Ming five-colour palette, but the underglaze blue of the Ming and transitional wares is replaced by an overglaze blue enamel which, on early specimens, is usually surrounded by a small area of glaze with a matt surface, the enamel having affected the glaze in this way. This provides a useful test of genuineness. The Ming turquoise was discontinued at this time on polychrome porcelain.

The *verte* palette was often used in panels in conjunction with a powder-blue (*chui ch'ing*) ground. This ground was also used in conjunction with panels painted in underglaze blue. The powder-blue ground – often called in Europe, blue *soufflé* – was used later by European potters, and was applied by blowing the colour through a tube in powder form. Complete covering with powder-blue with an over-decoration of gilt traceries is not unusual. The colour can vary somewhat, a deep purple-blue being called Mazarin blue by the French, but the Mazarin blue of the European potter is usually a rich cobalt. Incidentally, since Cardinal Mazarin died in 1661 it is difficult to account for the name.

Of the reds, the underglaze copper-red was again in use, although the earlier specimens do not have the same excellence of colour as can be observed both in the Hsüan Tê pieces and the later Yung Chêng copies. It is used by itself, or in conjunction with underglaze blue.

Sang de bœuf is a copper-red glaze which exhibits patches like the coagulation of ox-blood in parts, principally at the shoulders of vases and near the base. The best specimens have been attributed to a family of potters, and named *Lang yao*. The use of copper as a colouring material is somewhat chancy, the colour varying according to kiln atmosphere. Later, when these furnace transmutations (*pien yao*) were better understood, the *flambé* effects came under fairly close control. Peach-bloom is a reduced

1. We owe these, and similar terms, to the fact that the earliest European literature of the subject was in French.

copper glaze of pink, mottled with deeper red, as well as with slight markings in green and brown. This glaze is much prized, and was used only for such small pieces as water-pots.

Coral-red was made from iron oxide, and corresponds to the Ming tomato-red which is slightly darker in shade. It was used both in polychrome decoration and as a ground colour, the latter being usually later than the K'ang Hsi period.

Mirror-black (*wu chin*), a lustrous and brilliant glaze, was used as a monochrome, with, generally, a little gilding. It is related to the earlier blacks and browns from Honan, and is distinct from the *noire* ground in which the black is washed over with a film of green enamel. The ornate *famille noire* class have a black ground in conjunction with decoration in *verte* enamels, and are very highly valued, although it is not easy to see why. Apart from their rarity, they have little to commend them.

Brown is frequently used, often as a ground with panels decorated in colours. *Café-au-lait* is a warm brown, often used in bands with intervening decoration in blue underglaze. Silver was also used on a brown or black glaze. This may not always be easy to recognize, as the silver has sometimes oxidized. Very gentle cleaning with a silver polish of good quality usually restores the colour.

The so-called Imperial yellow is a lead glaze, dark and slightly brownish in colour. *Famille jaune* refers to the use of yellow in conjunction with polychrome decoration in *verte* enamels. An egg-yolk yellow, as well as an opaque antimony yellow used as an enamel, can be observed during the period, and a mustard-yellow ground colour is covered with a closely-meshed and even crackle.

Rose, an opaque pink enamel, was an innovation imported from Europe and mostly used on export wares. The Chinese called colours of this kind *yang ts'ai*, that is to say, *foreign colours*. The first tentative use of this enamel may be referable to a date as early as 1685, and the more usual assignment of early examples to the reign of Yung Chêng may therefore be inaccurate. The usual *famille rose* class of commerce, however, was not made until after the death of K'ang Hsi, and usually belongs at least to the Ch'ien Lung period.

Turquoise and blue derived from copper and used as monochrome lead glazes are Ming types made in the Ch'ing dynasty. A pale lavender-blue (*clair de lune*) was obtained by adding a trace of cobalt to a clear feldspathic glaze, and is used in conjunction with a controlled crackle, coloured with black and brownish-red pigment, mostly for pieces of restrained form with Sung affiliations.

Greens of several shades were used as monochromes. *Lang yao* green is possibly the result of wrongly firing a copper-red – probably the *sang de bœuf* already referred to. Apple-green is an unusual example of an enamel used as a monochrome. It is a transparent green applied over a grey crackled glaze. Other shades of green recorded include cucumber, sage, and camellia leaf, although the first has not been identified with certainty.

The technical development of the Ming *san ts'ai* class produced wares enamelled on biscuit, some examples of which have, in the past, erroneously been given a Ming dating, although, no doubt, the method was used in late Ming times.

The reign of Yung Chêng is perhaps most notable for the development of the *rose* enamel as well as for close copies of Sung wares. Much of this class of decoration is for export, although some examples are in the Chinese taste. A dark *rose* opaque enamel was used as a monochrome, and on the backs of dishes – the noted 'ruby-back' type. We begin to hear of the enamelling studios of Canton at about this time, and many of the 'ruby-back' dishes were painted here. Later, the Canton studios became noted for debased, over-decorated, and overcrowded patterns of little merit, particularly the so-called 'Mandarin' patterns copied avidly by some nineteenth-century English potters. Canton was one of the ports of shipment to which porcelain destined for Europe was sent, and was in close touch with foreign merchants and accustomed to their requirements. The founding of enamelling studios here was, therefore, a logical development.

So far as archaizing wares are concerned, the Sung copies of this period often had the Yung Chêng reign mark (*nien hao*) incised in the base. This has subsequently been ground out from some specimens to enable them to be passed off as belonging to the Sung period. Ju, Kuan, Ko, Lung Ch'üan, and Ting were all copied. Some celadons of the period had a little cobalt added to the green glaze, which took on a bluish tinge in consequence.

The so-called Ku-Yüeh Hsüan ware belongs to this period or perhaps a trifle later. The name means *Ancient Moon Pavilion*, and the style is notable for an asymmetry which is almost Japanese, and brushwork in the European manner.

Hua shih (slippery stone) or 'soft' paste porcelain is an unusual variety. Père d'Entrecolles wrote that it was (in 1722) a rare and expensive variety composed of eight parts of *hua shih* to two of china stone (*pai-tun-tzŭ*). D'Entrecolles identified *hua shih* with soapstone or steatite, but an American writer has stated categorically that an analysis revealed no trace of magnesium oxide. Porcelain made with soapstone will always show some magnesium oxide on analysis, as can be well seen in analyses of English soap-rock porcelains. The same writer suggests that *hua shih* may have been pegmatite, a coarsely crystallized granite. As I know nothing of the properties of this substance as an ingredient in the manufacture of porcelain I merely record the suggestion. Obviously, if such pieces contain no magnesia, they cannot have been made from soapstone.

Actually this ware is light in weight and finely potted. *Hua shih* was sometimes used in the body, sometimes only in the glaze. Specimens of the former which I have examined appear to be softer than the usual Chinese porcelain of the period, despite both Hobson's and Honey's opinion to the contrary. This is a point which might well bear re-examination. Of course, the terms 'soft' and 'hard' porcelain have never been closely defined, which may, in itself, be the cause of some difference of opinion on the point.

Pieces of this kind are painted in underglaze blue, and are nearly always small, although the British Museum has a vase with a 'steatitic' wash over the body which is seventeen inches in height. *Hua shih* was not used in the body of this specimen.

Porcelaine laquée burgautée is porcelain painted over with black lacquer, with designs inlaid in mother-of-pearl. This, as decoration, is indefensible on artistic grounds although the effect is not so unpleasant as might be expected. Lacquer colours were sometimes used to decorate white porcelain from Tê Hua, with disastrous results. It is doubtful whether such decoration is contemporary. One prefers to think it a nineteenth-century practice.

Imitations of the Persian Gombroon ware, in which the walls are pierced with small holes of the shape of a rice-grain, subsequently filled with glaze (from which the Chinese name, 'rice-grain'), are not uncommon.

The *flamé* glazes (*pien yao*) became especially popular towards the end of the reign of Ch'ien Lung. These have a lustrous glaze, usually crimson with purple and turquoise splashes and streaks. Vases are often of considerable size, and show every sign of the various effects having been under complete control.

The imitations of such materials as jade, the lacquer already mentioned, wood, rhinoceros horn, and many more, prove the skill of the potter in handling his material without altogether commending his taste.

A description of Ch'ing wares of the period would not be complete without reference to Chinese porcelain with European decoration. This takes a number of forms. The so-called 'Jesuit china' has European engravings of religious subjects meticulously copied in black, almost line for line. Some slight thin gilding is usually added. Mythological subjects were also copied in the same way, and a few rare examples of decoration of Masonic significance are known. The Chinese rendering of these subjects is often amusing, and the distinctive Chinese idiom in drawing is never absent. Polychrome decoration, usually in the *famille rose* palette, is somewhat rare, but includes careful copying of Watteauesque figures and scenes. Of course, enormous quantities of the erroneously named 'Oriental Lowestoft'[1] flooded into Europe towards the end of the eighteenth century. This class consists of table-services, with vases somewhat rarer, mostly decorated with armorial bearings of the original owner. All these were painted at Canton to special order, and many amusing and mostly apocryphal stories are told of Chinese errors in copying coats of arms and inscriptions. Large punch-bowls decorated with hunting-scenes are among the most effective

1. This ludicrous error is further discussed on page 256.

specimens of this type of Chinese porcelain. Mention should also be made at this point of Chinese porcelain decorated in Europe, commonly in Holland, of which more will be said under the appropriate heading.

(vii) THE NINETEENTH CENTURY AND LATER

The reign of Chia Ch'ing (1796–1820) has little to show that is new, and the wares are hardly more than repetitions of Ch'ien Lung styles. The tendency to over-decorate is marked.

By the accession of Tao Kuang in 1821, the deterioration, artistically, is obvious, and many of the wares have a glaze of inferior quality with the same kind of 'muslin' surface as can be seen on Japanese porcelain. The *rose* and *verte* palettes are often combined in a manner hardly pleasing. *Graviata*, in which the body is first decorated with incised scrolls and then coloured over the glaze with enamels, is a late Ch'ien Lung novelty used during this period. There is also much porcelain decorated in a fussy and meticulous manner. Here and there, some examples of good quality in both form and decoration can be noticed, although these are mostly repetitions of earlier things.

The reigns of Hsien Fêng (1851–61) and T'ung Chih (1862–73) have little to commend them, and the same applies principally to the period of Kuang Hsü (1874–1908). Such glazes as *sang de bœuf*, apple-green, *famille noire*, and peach-bloom were repeated, but are hardly deceptive.

The Imperial Factory at Ching-tê Chên was burned down in 1853 during the internal dissensions of the times, but was rebuilt in 1864. It is still producing.

Much over-decorated ware was shipped from Canton during the early part of the century, where it had been enamelled. Snuff-bottles, and little miniature pieces, were commonly made during the earlier reigns.

(viii) DECORATION

Before proceeding to discuss decoration it is important to say something about the Chinese language, of which bracketed examples have already been given. This is peculiar, because it has a vast number of written characters which are derived from primitive pictograms. For example, to express the *idea* of brightness, the characters for sun and moon are juxtaposed, thus : 明

These characters, like the Egyptian hieratic script, have now been stylized until it is difficult to see in them any kind of pictorial representation, but there is no doubt of their origin. Actually, the characters shown represent the spoken word, *ming*, which forms part of the Ming dynasty reign mark, of which a typical example is given hereunder :

Hua	化	Hua (4)	(1) Ta	大	Great
in the	年	nien (5)	(2) Ming	明	Bright (dynasty)
reign of	製	hao (6)	(3) Ch'êng	成	Ch'êng

that is to say, made *in the reign of Ch'êng Hua of the Great Ming (dynasty)*. The characters are read from the top right downwards, and it is typical of the reign marks to be found on porcelain.

This is comparatively simple, but the complications start here. 名 means *fame*, and is also, in the spoken language, *ming*. 命 indicates *life or fate*, and is once again, *ming*. The number of vocables in comparison with the number of characters is much too small to give one to each. This is partly overcome by the use of tones (five in Old Mandarin) which help to determine the meaning of the word. For example, *ming* in the sense of *bright* is spoken with the lower even tone, in the sense of *life or fate* it is given the departing tone. This peculiarity is the origin of many humorous stories in which the European student of the language inadvertently insults a Chinese whilst intending to be complimentary.[1]

This brief explanation is necessary so that the reader can appreciate some of the curious plays upon words which become possible, and which are used as porcelain decoration.

For instance, a bat (*fu*) on porcelain represents happiness,

1. Obviously the foregoing is a simplification which is sufficiently accurate in principle for our present purpose.

which is also *fu* (Fig. 2). The written characters are different, but the spoken words are the same. To make a gift of a bowl decorated with bats is to wish happiness to the recipient. Five Bats represent the Five Blessings – longevity, wealth, serenity, virtue, and an easy death.

Fig. 2. The Bat (*fu*)

This kind of verbal symbolism can, of course, be used in conjunction with symbolism of other kinds. For example, the pomegranate is emblematic of a large progeny because of the enormous number of seeds contained within the fruit. With the peach (longevity), and the Buddha's Hand citron [1] happiness, it forms the Three Abundances, or the Threefold Blessing.

Longevity is represented in various ways. The pine, for example, symbolizes it because it is evergreen. The stork, itself credited with a wealth of years, represents longevity for this reason, as does the tortoise. The character 壽 *Shou*, which means long life, is used as decoration in a number of ornamental forms (Fig. 3). The peach, also *shou*, is used in conjunction with the bat to represent long life and happiness, *fu shou*.

The swastika (or gammadion) drawn in the opposite way to the Nazi symbol, thus 卍 means 'ten thousand' but is usually a longevity symbol. There may have been an esoteric meaning involved in its use at one time, since the swastika was, possibly, a sky prop in more primitive times – somewhat analogous to the Greek myth of Atlas who carried the sky on his shoulders. There are early Chinese myths which refer to the pillars

Fig. 3. A form of *Shou*

of the sky having been broken and repaired, and symbols of this kind are almost universal. The chance of it being used with this meaning by the Chinese within the period discussed in this book, however, is remote.

1. A curious fruit with finger-like appendages, sometimes modelled, sometimes painted.

Symbols with what may be called a religious meaning include the *yang-yin* – the male-female principle which signifies the duality of nature. The *Pa Kua* – the Eight Trigrams – are often used in conjunction with it. These represent natural forces – heaven, wind, earth, water, fire, thunder, vapour, and mountains – and are commonly written in circular form (Fig. 4).

The three principal religious sects of China are the Confucianists, the Taoists, and the Buddhists. The first are followers of K'ung fu-tzŭ – Latinized as Confucius – who expounded a humanist system of ethics, at the heart of which is the Doctrine of the Golden Mean, the cultivation of a spirit of reasonableness, admirably crystallized by Lin Yutang in the phrase, *A is right, and B is not wrong either*. This, probably the most civilized (if the least religious) of all religious systems, is not by any means so widely held in China as the other two,

Fig. 4. The Eight Trigrams. In the centre the *yang-yin* symbol

being, perhaps, more generally followed among the middle and professional classes. The *Analects* are available in an English translation. Mêng Tzŭ (Mencius) was a distinguished teacher and philosopher who largely followed the system of K'ung fu-tzŭ.

Taoism – the Way – was taught by Lao-tzŭ who is often represented on porcelain. The supernatural and mystical element occupies a much more important place in Taoism, many of the myths and legends of China originating here.

Buddhism is not, of course, a native growth, and here again the supernatural element looms large. Buddhist *motifs* are frequently to be seen, and mention has already been made of the popularity of Kuan Yin (Kuan Shih Yin), the 'Taking-away-fear Buddha', who is more or less synonymous with the Taoist goddess of the North Star, Tou Mu. Both these goddesses are central figures in their respective religious systems.

Confucianism does not provide many subjects for porcelain decoration – Kuan Ti, God of War, is one of the few deities to be associated with this sect, K'ung fu-tzŭ himself being regarded as no more than human, although attempts have been made to deify him within recent times. The prunus, pine, and bamboo represent K'ung fu-tzŭ, Lao-tzŭ, and Buddha (Fo) – the Three Friends.

Taoist gods are legion, and it would be a lengthy excursion to examine them in any sort of detail. Lao-tzŭ (Shou Lao) is frequently represented, alone, and in company with the Eight Immortals (*Pa Hsien*). He can be recognized easily by his unusually enlarged and protuberant forehead. Of the Eight Immortals, Chung-li Chüan was a fat man holding a feather-fan and the peach of longevity; Lü Tung-pin was skilled in fencing and carries his sword, Chou-yao Kuai (Devil-slaying sabre), and a fly-whisk; Li T'ieh-kuai is a lame beggar with a stick or crutch, and carrying a gourd; Ts'ao Kuo-ch'iu is shown with his tablets of admission to the Sung Court which are sometimes erroneously described as castanets; Lan Ts'ai-ho is supposed to have been either a woman or an hermaphrodite, and he-she is popularly represented as a gardener with flower-basket and spade; Chang Kao (Lao) is occasionally represented seated on a mule, sometimes facing the tail, and carries a peach, a feather, or a bamboo tube drum; Han Hsiang Tzŭ carries a flute; Ho Hsien Ku is a maiden immortal who holds either a peach or a lotus.

These eight are an extremely popular subject for decoration on porcelain, and they are modelled as sets of figures, with Shou Lao in addition.

Less frequently represented, but popular, is Hsi Wang Mu – Golden Mother of the Tortoise. Formed from the West Wind, she is the passive or female principle (*yin*), the *yang* being Mu Kung, god of the Immortals, who was formed from the East Wind. The creation of the universe sprang from the interaction of these principles. The mountain home of Hsi Wang Mu is said to have been visited by the Emperor Mu Wang of the Chou Dynasty, whose travels about the Empire drawn by his famous eight horses are often celebrated by Chinese artists.

The Isles of the Blest were a frequent subject. *Pa Hsien kuo lai* (The Eight Immortals crossing the sea) depicts them on their way to these islands which are situated in the Eastern Seas. During the voyage the Immortals demonstrated their power over the elements by riding on the surface of the water on their emblems, Chung-li Chüan using his feather-fan, and so forth. The Immortals often covered immense distances seated on clouds, which was, in fact, their normal method of transport.

In the Islands grew the *ling chih* fungus, another longevity symbol. The deer often carries a *ling chih* in its mouth, and is a Taoist symbol meaning longevity, as are the hare, stork, and tortoise. Similar in shape to the *ling chih* is the *ju-i* (which means 'as you wish'). This : ⌒‿⌒ is frequently used in many ways, and forms the basis of the 'connected cloud' pattern.

The three star gods of Happiness are Fu Hsing, who carries an infant and a peach; Lu Hsing, who carries a staff with a *ju-i* head; Shou Hsing, who has a scroll attached to a long staff and carries a peach. The last named somewhat resembles the Japanese Fukurokujiu.

The Buddhist Deity, Kuan Yin, has already been mentioned. The Eighteen Lohan (Arhats) are disciples of the Buddha used both as figures and as painted decoration. A magnificent life-size ceramic statue with this subject is in the British Museum. Pu-tai Ho-shang (synonymous with Hotei, god of Contentment, from Japan) is usually represented seated, with a protruding belly. Bodhidharma was a Buddhist apostle who remained for nine years in China in contemplation. He is usually represented in the act of crossing the River Yang-tse on a reed, an incident of his return journey from India.

The *pa chi-hsiang* or Eight Buddhist Emblems are illustrated below (Fig. 5). They are (a) *Lun*, a flaming wheel – the 'Wheel of the Law'; (b) *Lo*, a conch shell, a wind instrument used at religious ceremonies; (c) *San*, a state umbrella; (d) *Kai*, a canopy; (e) *Hua*, the lotus, the most frequent of all Buddhist symbols, an emblem of purity; (f) the vase; (g) *Yu*, a pair of fishes, also symbolic of connubial felicity; (h) *Ch'ang*, the endless knot.

Monkey, the central figure in a popular Buddhist romance (by Wu Chêng-ên who lived in the Ming dynasty) superbly translated by Arthur Waley, is infrequently represented in porcelain. Tripitaka (Hsüan Tsang or Hsüan Chang), an important figure in the same story, was presented by the Emperor with a white horse (*pai ma*) to carry him to India in search of scriptures, and this appears in porcelain.

The Lions of Buddha (Fo), sometimes miscalled Dogs of Fo (Fig. 6), are often represented in decoration and modelled as figures. Erroneously they are also referred to as kylins – an en-

Fig. 5. The Eight Buddhist Emblems

tirely different animal. The lions are temple guardians, and the male is modelled playing with a ball, the female with a cub or cubs. Smaller versions are usually joss-stick holders.

The *kylin* (properly the *lin*, or *ch'i-lin*) (Fig. 7), is a mythical creature compounded from the head of a dragon, a scaly body, deer's hooves, a bushy tail, and a single horn. It was an amiable beast, despite a ferocious appearance, and was reputed to be too gentle even to tread on living blades of grass. Its appearance always portended some auspicious event, one being seen, for example, at the birth of K'ung fu-tzŭ. Relatively speaking, the true kylin is not often used as decoration, and still more rarely modelled as a figure. I have seen a joss-stick holder from Tê Hua.

Fig. 6. The Lion of Fo

The *t'ao t'ieh* mask is principally used on vessels of bronze form, often in the form of moulded handles. The origin of this curious decoration is very obscure, and the name has been translated as 'gluttonous ogre'. It is often used as a warning against avarice. I am inclined to think it may have been intended, when first used, as a representation of a tiger-mask, probably that aspect of the striped head as it breaks through the tall jungle grasses.

The tiger (*hu*) is found in China, and is fairly widely distributed. The Chinese regard him as lord of the land animals, and a somewhat more recognizable tiger-mask is used in the same manner as the *t'ao t'ieh*, sometimes with a ring in its mouth. The tiger symbolizes military prowess, and is often used to scare off evil spirits. The White Tiger symbolizes the West in the Four Quadrants, the others being the Dragon (East), the Phoenix (South), and the Tortoise (North). The

Fig. 7. The Kylin

same animals are sometimes used to represent the Four Seasons.

The tortoise is supposed to convey, by the markings on its

shell, some clue to the mysteries of the universe, and the Eight Trigrams are probably derived from this source. It is also known as the Black Warrior and represents Winter.

The Phoenix (*fêng huang*) (Fig. 8) is synonymous with the Japanese *ho-ho* bird. It is the symbol of the Empress, just as the five-clawed dragon represents the Emperor. The *fêng huang* is sometimes called the Vermilion Bird, represents Spring from the Four Seasons, and is always an auspicious symbol.

The Dragon (Fig. 9) takes several forms. *K'uei*, an archaic dragon, is principally found on early bronzes and jades and has little interest for our present purpose. *Ch'ih lung* is a slightly

Fig. 8. The Phoenix

later kind of dragon which occupies a midway position between the earliest *k'uei* and the sort of dragon most often used. A frequent form in which this beast is represented is shown in Fig. 9. Dragons are often found, single or in pairs, in conjunction with a symbol called the *flaming pearl* which may, in fact, be intended for the sun. The dragon is emblematic of Spring, a Spirit of the Waters, and has symbolized the Emperor from earliest times. Dragons with four or three claws represent lesser members of the Imperial household and high officials. Unlike its appearance, it is generally a mild and beneficent creature, although certain Buddhist dragons (*nagas*) are evil.

The Dragon is said to have nine resemblances: 'its horns resemble those of a deer; its head, that of a camel; its eyes, those of a devil; its neck, that of a snake; its abdomen, that of a large cockle; its scales, those of a carp; its claws, those of an eagle; the soles of its feet, those of a tiger; its ears, those of an ox'. Some have no ears, the creature 'hearing through its horns'.

In Spring it ascends to the skies, in Autumn it disappears into the flood. The Blue Dragon (*ch'ing lung*) is a Taoist Temple guardian.

Many explanations of the origin of the dragon have been put forward. It probably sprang from the alligator, common in some Chinese rivers.

The Dragon, Phoenix, *Ch'i-lin*, and Tortoise, are the Four Supernatural Creatures (*ssŭ ling*).

The Twelve Animals of the Zodiac are the dragon, hare, tiger, fox, rat, pig, dog, cock, monkey, goat, horse, and snake. Each

Fig. 9. An early form of Dragon

year, month, day, and hour is associated with one of these animals. The moon is symbolized by a hare on its hind legs pounding the Elixir of Life in a mortar, or by a three-legged toad. The sun is represented by a three-legged bird (a raven?) within a circle.

Kuei Hsing, distributor of literary degrees, is represented with the face of a demon, holding a writing brush, and riding on the back of a fish-dragon. The fish-dragon is a symbol of literary endeavour. Poets and sages are frequently depicted amidst mountainous scenery, often crossing bridges over mountain streams, which is a favourite theme with Chinese painters. The *Po ku* (Hundred Antiques) are a collection of instruments and implements mostly used in the arts and sciences – musical instruments, brushes and water-pots for writing, and so forth. The *Pa pao* (the Eight Precious Things) form part of this group (see Fig. 10).

Occasionally, illustrations of historical subjects and scenes from popular romances are used, but unless there is some means of identification, and the reader is well acquainted with Chinese literature, these will usually prove almost impossible to identify, although this by no means destroys their effectiveness as decoration.

Figures of elongated girls (*mei jên*) appear in panels, and are the origin of the Dutch *Lange Lyzen*, the 'Long Elizas' to be

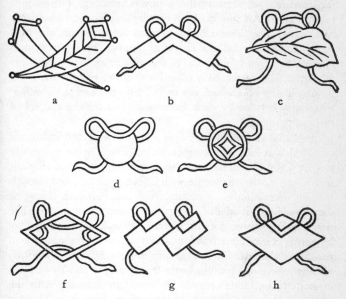

Fig. 10. The Eight Precious Things
(a) Rhinoceros horn cups. (b) Musical stone of jade. (c) The artemisia leaf (also used as a mark). (d) A jewel. (e) A coin. (f) A painting. (g) A pair of books or tablets. (h) Symbol of victory.

seen on eighteenth-century English porcelain, and especially popular at Worcester.

Meanders and diaper patterns need not detain us. The most important is the *lei-wên* – the 'cloud and thunder' fret – which is a very ancient *motif* to be seen on early bronzes, and later used as porcelain decoration. The earliest form is as follows: ⊚. Later use is much more rigid and precise : ⊡

As might be expected, the Chinese have an elaborate flower symbolism. Certain flowers typify the seasons and the months, usually according to the month in which they bloom. The flowers associated with the months are: the plum, January; the peach, February; the tree-peony, March; the cherry, April; the magnolia, May; the pomegranate, June; the lotus, July; the quince, August; the mallow, September; the chrysanthemum, October; the gardenia, November; the poppy, December. There are a number of lists of this kind, all of which differ somewhat from each other. The flowers of the seasons are the plum, the tree-peony, the lotus, and the chrysanthemum. The white prunus blossom is a *motif* used on K'ang Hsi vases and ginger-jars which has been extensively copied ever since. Usually the background is of a blue which has aptly been described as pulsating, irregularly divided by dark lines to suggest the cracked ice of the Spring thaw.

The bamboo (found in China in both wild and cultivated varieties) is a longevity symbol which, from the Sung dynasty onwards, is probably the most frequently represented of all plant forms. It is a favourite theme with Chinese painters, and is much used as decoration on porcelain. Also, we find such things as small wine-pots modelled as sections of the bamboo-cane. The narcissus, cultivated for the Chinese New Year Festival, may have been introduced from the West at some time anterior to the Sung dynasty. The *ling chih* fungus (*Fomes japonicus*) already mentioned grows on tree-trunks and is also an emblem of immortality. It is occasionally found in company with the artemisia leaf. The latter is often used on the bottom of vases and bowls in place of a mark. The lotus is always associated with Buddhism, being the seat of Gautama himself. Kuan Yin is also frequently seen on a lotus seat. The peony represents love, and symbolizes the beauty of women. The chrysanthemum is to be seen as early as the T'ang dynasty on bronze mirrors. Anything but the most conventional representation of such useful plants as the millet is virtually unknown in Chinese art until the introduction of Buddhism into that country.

The peach is frequently used not only as painted decoration, but such things as small water-pots are modelled in peach form, and *Monkey*, already mentioned, is sometimes depicted with the Peach of Immortality which he stole from the garden of Hsi Wang Mu. The Buddha's Hand citron (*Citrus medica*) is a symbol of wealth. The pomegranate is usually represented as open, showing its seeds.

This very brief note of some of the flowers and fruits to be found on Chinese porcelain could be expanded to much greater size without doing more than touch the fringes of the subject.

Insects are not often used, but cicadas can be seen occasionally, often in a formalized version at the base of vases where they have been regarded as leaves, and called by some the 'stiff-leaf' pattern. The cicada is an ancient device to be seen on the old ritual bronzes, and in jade. Jade cicadas of the Han period are usually 'tongue' jades – that is to say, jades placed on the tongue of a corpse to seal the mouth against the entry of evil spirits.

Fish, mostly of the carp family, are used together with aquatic plants, and are often superbly drawn. Ducks and water-fowl in the same setting are a favourite theme.

Chinese characters are used decoratively, and fine calligraphy plays an important part in Chinese art appreciation. Arabic script appears occasionally on dishes and such things made for export, and is used for the same purpose.

Writing generally, it is difficult to assign a date to Chinese porcelain entirely on the basis of the *nature* of the decorative *motif*, particularly after the beginning of the Ming period. The *way* in which it is handled and the colours used are, of course, often extremely revealing. Most of the themes mentioned in this section can be found alike on Ming and Ch'ing porcelains. Elaborate figure-compositions are not often seen before the end of the Ming period.

The human figure is rarely used in decoration on Sung porcelain, and the appearance of a figure subject on an early piece usually indicates at least a Yüan date. Sung decoration is almost always carved, incised, or moulded, and floral *motifs* are the most frequently used, simply and without elaborate border ornament. The dragon is more often to be seen on celadons than elsewhere, sometimes in conjunction with a simple scroll border. For the most part, however, decorated pieces are outnumbered by those examples which depend simply on form and the colour and quality of the glaze for their effectiveness.

Tz'ŭ Chou floral decoration, whether incised, carved, or painted, is often quite elaborate in comparison with most other things of the period, but is always restrained and usually handled with an artistry missing in the later wares from the same source.

There is usually a quality of precision and 'tightness' about Ch'ing painting which is missing from the free style of the earlier things. Whether or not this is an improvement is a matter of personal taste, and there it must be left.

(ix) DATING CHINESE PORCELAIN

Writing generally, the one way in which Chinese porcelain should *not* be dated is by reference to such date marks as may appear on the bottom of the specimen. Sometimes these are correct, but just as often they are false. If my reader examines catalogues of Chinese porcelain he will notice some examples listed as *Mark of* (for example) *Ch'êng Hua* and others as *Mark and reign of Ch'êng Hua*. The former expression is usually intended to convey that the period of manufacture is doubtful, and probably later than the mark would indicate. It must be said at once that this use of marks had no fraudulent intent, but was a sign

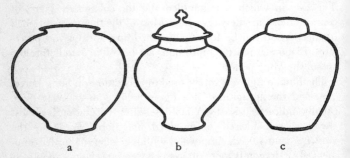

Fig. 11. The Evolution of Form
(a) T'ang (b) Ming (c) Ch'ing.
For a Sung version see Plate 6.

of appreciation of the earlier wares. Naturally, some of these things were made for less than honest reasons. It was, for instance, far from unknown for a Court official with an acquisitive eye to have a duplicate made of one of the Palace pieces, and to exchange them when opportunity offered.

At the end of this book will be found a list of the commoner Chinese date marks. It is, perhaps, a little difficult to keep the reign marks in mind without reference to a list, but this book is of pocketable size, and the dynastic marks are easily remembered, thus:

| Great | 大 | Great | 大 |
| Ming | 明 | Ch'ing | 清 |

Sung marks are rare, and it is unnecessary to quote them.

Wares of the Sung dynasty, and reproductions of them, are easily recognized by their distinctive form and methods of decoration, and the greatest danger is the archaizing wares of the Yung Chêng period and later, although some remarks have already been made on their detection. Particular attention should be paid to a study of form, since later pieces are usually accused by divergencies from characteristic Sung forms, as well as by differences in the glaze.

It must be remembered that early potters, both European and Chinese, drew their raw materials from natural sources in a comparatively crude state, and lacked the necessary chemical knowledge to refine them to modern standards. Thus, the results were affected by impurities present. For this reason subsequent copyists have undertaken a virtually impossible task, because they do not know what the original impurities were or in what quantities they were present, and chemical analysis cannot help them to reconstruct the original formula.

To obtain the same results as the Sung potter it would be necessary to use materials from the same sources in much the same way. Early potters, particularly, consistently drew their raw materials from the same source, and this is, in some industries, still the method used today. Certain of the effects to be seen in the earlier Chinese wares are due to impurities in the materials, and there is not the slightest doubt that, with some wares, the actual result of each kiln firing was unpredictable, more especially in the matter of the colour of the glaze. This, of course, does not apply equally to all wares. Those of the Tz'ŭ Chou type, for instance, would be much less difficult to reproduce, and some celadons have been copied effectively.

Obviously the finest safeguard is a close acquaintance with originals of merit and certain attribution, and I repeat here a word of advice which I have offered on other occasions. If the eye is to be educated adequately it must be in a position to see these things constantly, and it is not usually an expensive matter to acquire a few pieces in a damaged condition which can be used for comparative purposes. These should be left about where they can be seen constantly, and a point will eventually be reached where all but the cleverest reproductions will be automatically rejected.

The line of demarcation between Sung and Yüan wares is not very sharply drawn. A tendency to floridity of form is usually to be observed, but some considerable experience in handling actual examples is necessary before it is possible to separate Sung and Yüan examples with any degree of assurance. The Ming period, on the other hand, is in many ways a little easier. To arrive at the *earliest* possible date at which a thing *might* have been made does not usually present much difficulty. The problem is to say whether it is of the period, or made later. The whole ques-

Fig. 12. Some bottle and vase forms

(a) An early bronze-form. Chou dynasty. (b) T'ang dynasty. (c) Form used with various glazes. Sung and early Ming dynasties. (d) Form usually associated with the 'mallet' or *kinuta* celadons. Sung dynasty. (e) Form usually associated with the *ying ch'ing* glaze. Sung dynasty. (f) A fourteenth-century type, the profile being somewhat exaggerated. Yüan dynasty. (g) Another fourteenth-century form, sometimes associated with early blue and white decoration. Yüan and early Ming dynasties. (h) Typical early Ch'ing bottle form. (i) Bottle of the late seventeeenth and eighteenth centuries. (j) Bottle of the double gourd type. Ch'ing dynasty. In a somewhat coarser form, this shape was made at Arita and Kutani around 1700.

These outline drawings, and those to be seen in Figure 11, are intended to show the manner in which specimens may be dated by reference to the form. This necessarily has to be considered in conjunction with the other factors present, but the student ought to pay close and particular attention to this point because many otherwise excellent copies are exposed by subtle variations from the earlier form.

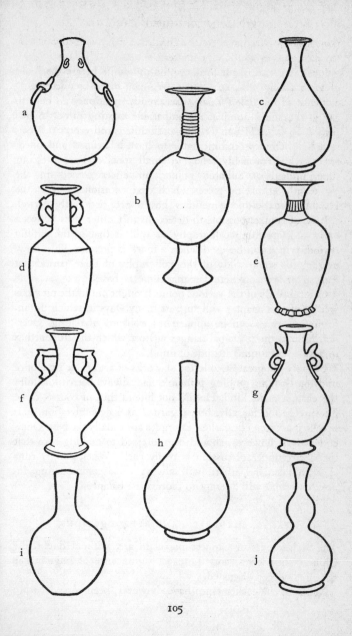

tion is one of frequent controversy, and it is distinctly unwise to take any firm stand in the matter.

It is, as yet, difficult to date blue-and-white before the reign of Chia Ching with confidence. We can, of course, accept the evidence of the dated Yüan vase already mentioned to help to assign the small number of comparable existing pieces to this period. So far as Hsüan Tê blue-and-white is concerned, this was said by a Chinese commentator to have a 'heaped and piled' effect, which probably refers to small spots of darker colour superimposed at suitable points, an effect copied in the eighteenth century on pieces which were occasionally given the Hsüan Tê mark, and sometimes those appropriate to the period.

It is, of course, possible to detect distinct differences between early and late Ming calligraphy, as well as that of the Ch'ing period, which can be used when a mark is present. This, however, needs some study of the calligraphy of these periods, at least so far as it applies to date marks on the bases.

Careful study of the various points brought out in the previous section of this chapter will suggest many ways in which the information given can be applied to problems of dating. Over-optimism is the principal danger against which the student has to develop a cautious attitude of mind.

Possibly the greatest collector of works of art of our time once told me that his guiding principle had always been to acquire the earliest of its kind. He did not intend this, of course, to be interpreted too literally, but, regarded as a generalization, it is excellent advice. The earliest examples are usually the best. One's endeavours, however, should be addressed to making sure that the object under discussion is really early. When supply runs short of demand, there will always be accommodating individuals who will attempt to redress the balance.

FAKES, FORGERIES, AND REPRODUCTIONS

The arch-forgers of Chinese porcelain are, without doubt, the Chinese themselves, and the exact significance of reign-marks has already been discussed.

Many of the earlier types have, however, been copied within

recent years with an entirely fraudulent intent. Some are sold to unsuspecting tourists, and, in the past, a certain number have found their way into Hong Kong to be brought back to England by incautious purchasers. The fact that genuine pieces have sometimes been bought in this way, and sold in England at a good profit to the buyer, probably keeps the trade in existence. But for the novice to dabble in these things, and to accept the description of a dealer of unknown reputation, is often an easy and hardly agreeable way of losing money. It is well known among the makers of these forgeries that they are easier to sell in the Far East than in Europe, where the standard of knowledge among collectors and the established dealers is extremely high.

The expert is usually able to detect forgeries with comparative ease because, over a long period, he has studied genuine examples until he has reached a point where small differences become obvious. A copy of an enamelled piece often reveals itself in the quality of the drawing. To a Chinese the difference between a nude by Ingres and one by Etty would not be immediately apparent, although he could acquire the ability to discriminate with study and experience, but the difference would be discerned immediately by a European, even if he were unversed in the study of painting. This applies equally to Chinese painting, and although the essential differences in style are not apparent to the untutored European eye, experience reduces the element of uncertainty by bringing a greater comprehension of the idiom.

Insistence on too great a degree of perfection is always dangerous, since many of the genuine examples have suffered somewhat in the course of centuries, and it would be foolish to reject a rare piece simply because it had suffered a little damage which does not seriously affect the qualities of form and decoration. The demand for perfection usually finds someone ready to supply it, if not legitimately, then by more dubious means.

Such aids to identification as the 'halo' to be seen around the Ming tomato-red, and a similar 'halo' around the blue enamel of the K'ang Hsi period, are often useful. Although K'ang Hsi pieces have been noticed on which the blue enamel does not exhibit this effect, I have never known or heard of a reproduction on which it could be seen, and this is an example of an idiosyncrasy which it is difficult for the forger to copy.

Many excellent reproductions of the later enamelled wares are made in Europe. Samson of Paris, for instance, has done some good copies of Chinese armorial porcelain – a kind much sought in the United States – which can usually be detected by the colour of the glaze, by the foot-ring, and by the appearance of the unglazed body at this point. The brushwork often copies the peculiar Chinese idiom in rendering European subjects quite cleverly, but it is rarely entirely convincing. The Herend factory, founded by Moritz Fischer, produced many excellent imitations of enamelled wares, including those in the *verte* style, some of which can be very deceptive.

The base and foot-ring, more often than not, is the place where most forgeries fail to follow the original, and this has led to a rare type of forgery in which a genuine piece, decorated perhaps in underglaze blue, is 'skinned' by grinding off glaze and decoration, subsequently reglazing and enamelling in a more costly manner. Vases are the things most often treated in this way, and since the interior glaze cannot be removed, the junction between old and new can be detected. If well done, this can be extremely dangerous, since the porcelain and the foot-ring are both perfectly genuine. The painting should proclaim its European origin, and only the expensive and exotic types of decoration are worth faking in this way. Since these things are rarely among the best of Chinese porcelain, most collectors ought not to be exposed to this kind of temptation.

Certain types of underfired Chien wares are refired at the proper temperature, and exhibit a glassy, polished, appearance, totally out of keeping with that of untouched specimens. I have known the same thing to be done with an underfired Chün bowl with similar results. These, of course, are genuine specimens, and can be regarded as fakes rather than forgeries. They are decidedly not worth including in a collection, save as curiosities.

Of course, here and there are forgeries which will deceive the most expert, but they are few and far between in the realm of porcelain. Pottery tells a somewhat different story, virtually undetectable forgeries of the unglazed T'ang tomb-figure being legion. The glazed figures cannot be copied so convincingly.

Unfortunately, in the past, a great deal of excavation of a haphazard kind has been carried out by native dealers who have concealed the source of their 'finds'. Whilst this may be an obvious commercial precaution, it does no particular service to ceramic scholarship, and a specimen with a history attached is a decided acquisition, more particularly if the excavation has been carried out under European supervision.

CHAPTER TWO

Japan

(i) THE KILNS

JAPANESE porcelain has been somewhat neglected in recent years. This is undeserved because, at its best, it can easily hold its own with most Chinese productions of the Ch'ing period. The Japanese are partly to blame for the neglect. Porcelain made for export has been of such inferior quality, artistically, that it has been easy to conclude that such wares are a fair measure of the whole. On the other hand, porcelains decorated in the native taste, such as those painted by the Sakaida Kakiemon family, and the wares of old Kutani, often have much greater feeling for the material and its possibilities than is to be seen from eighteenth-century Ching-tê Chên.

Somewhat naturally, Japanese porcelain owes much both to China and Korea. In the thirteenth century, Kato Shirozaemon visited China to study the art of making pottery. These early pieces were mostly made for the *cha-no-yu* (Tea Ceremony), but as they are of earthenware they need not detain us here. The Japanese began making porcelain shortly after 1500, and the secret is traditionally said to have been brought from Ching-tê Chên by Gorodoyu-go Shonzui during the first half of the sixteenth century. The first kilns were established at Arita in Hizen Province,[1] and the finest specimens from here fall into two well-marked categories, those in the style of the Sakaida Kakiemons, and those which have been called 'Imari'.

Twelve members of the Sakaida family have been recorded, the first working in the early part of the seventeenth century, the last being born in 1879.[2]

The first member of the family, born in 1596, in the beginning painted only in underglaze blue, but is said to have learned the

1. Sometimes *Hishū* on modern maps. It is part of the island of Kyūshū.
2. For detailed information consult Soame Jenyns, *The Polychrome Wares Associated with the Potters Kakiemon*, Trans. O.C.S. 1937–8.

secret of enamelling in colour in 1644, and the process remained the private preserve of the family for some years. Before this date, a rather pale underglaze blue was in use, the colour being imported from China. Much ware of this kind was made in the forms of contemporary European *faïence* and metalwork for export, and it is not uncommonly confused with seventeenth-century Chinese porcelain decorated in the same way.

The Dutch were given a trading monopoly in 1641, and proceeded to ship these Japanese wares to Europe. Later, they persuaded the potters to use brocades as inspiration, thus beginning the overcrowded decoration, so much at variance with the spirit of the Kakiemon style, which has been called 'Imari', after the port of shipment some miles from Arita.

'Imari' wares are painted in a number of colours, of which a blackish underglaze blue and a strong dark red predominate. They are often excessively and poorly gilded. A debased form of 'Imari' was extensively shipped to Europe during the latter part of the nineteenth century. These patterns were also copied by the Chinese when their success in Europe was observed, and the earliest examples of this class from China were made around 1700.

The Arita productions need to be examined fairly closely because they had considerable influence on European decoration, as will later be recorded. The well-known 'Quail' pattern, still used today and popular during the eighteenth century at Bow, Chelsea, and Worcester in England, as well as at many Continental factories, was originally a Kakiemon pattern. So, too, was the 'tyger and wheatsheaf' which the Japanese acquired from Korea. The so-called 'Hob in the Well' pattern of Chelsea (Plate 53B), which was derived from the Sung legend of the boy, Ssŭ-ma, who saved a small friend from drowning in a large fish bowl by breaking it with a stone, is typically Kakiemon in style. Mr Jenyns, in his excellent paper on this subject, mentions that this pattern was also used at Worcester, but there are no surviving examples, and even Chelsea specimens are exceedingly rare.

Not only were Kakiemon and 'Imari' decorations copied in Europe, but characteristic Arita shapes were also employed.

Octagonal dishes and bowls, and the octagonal, hexagonal, and square section vases of the European factories, were derived from this source. These shapes appear to have been adopted originally because of the difficulty of firing the natural mixture of kaolin and *petuntse* which was used. Although they will warp in the kiln as easily as wares of circular section, they show it less. These wares were given a light firing first, and then glazed and given the full firing. After the first firing the body was absorbent, and this property of absorption gave a 'muslin' surface to the glaze, somewhat akin to the Chinese 'chicken-skin' but much more obvious. This can occasionally be useful in differentiating between Chinese and Japanese wares in cases of doubt.

The Arita palette was copied in Europe with great fidelity, and it is not at all impossible to confuse the two at first sight, although the confusion does not survive close inspection. The usual Arita colours are iron-red, a bluish-green, light blue, and yellow, with (rarely) some gilding. The bluish-green is not found on Chinese wares, and the Japanese red is thicker and darker. Arita specimens with the blue underglaze are probably earlier than those having an enamel blue. Later examples, around the beginning of the nineteenth century, are decorated in a reddish-brown, purple, black, yellow, and a blue which inclines to lilac.

The keynotes of Kakiemon decoration are simplicity, a great feeling for the value of the white porcelain surface which is balanced very effectively with the painted areas, and a carefully judged asymmetry which is typical of Japanese art as a whole (Plate 53B).

Kutani (Kaga Province) seems to have been at work from mid seventeenth century. These kilns were noted for brilliant colouring in a blue which is almost a Prussian blue in tone and intensity, green, yellow, and a characteristic manganese purple which is analogous to the Chinese *aubergine*. *Ko Kutani* has a red patterned background with reserved panels painted in enamel colours. *Ao Kutani* has decoration predominantly in green enamel with the pattern drawn in black outlines. The productions of these kilns are of extremely fine quality as to decoration, although the porcelain is often inferior. It is rare and highly valued, both in Europe among the knowledgeable, and in Japan.

Old Kutani was made up to about 1750, but there were many attempts to revive it during the nineteenth century in Kaga Province.

A factory at Okawachi (Okochi) not far from Arita was founded in the middle of the seventeenth century by Nabeshima, Prince of Kaga, with the aid of Korean potters. Much of the factory's production was for his use, and early decoration was mainly in the Kakiemon style, although a pale underglaze blue, a combination of red and blue reminiscent of some sixteenth-century Ming wares, and a celadon with a closely-meshed crackle on a red stoneware body, have also been noted. The body varies from a stoneware to a fine porcelain.

The Mikawachi pottery did not become important until mid eighteenth century. Most of the porcelain made here was for the Prince of Hirado.[1] The wares were usually small and of fine quality, and decorated in pale underglaze blue. Small figures – fish, dragons, ducks, etc. – were made here, as well as celadons.

Kyoto produced a great deal of porcelain from the eighteenth century onwards, mostly in imitation of Sung celadons and the Ming red and green style.

Seto, in Owari, is the place of origin of most of the enormous and hideous Oriental vases which plague the auctioneer. Sometimes as tall as three and a half feet, they were admired at the height of the enthusiasm for pseudo-Japanese art in the latter part of the nineteenth century, but are now unwanted and un-saleable. Imitations of *cloisonné* enamel were also made here, as well as a certain amount of blue-and-white of no more than average quality.

Much ware from Seto, Kyoto, and Satsuma was decorated in Tokyo for export. The designs are debased, overcrowded, and unworthy of attention, lacquer often being used in conjunction with enamel colours. The best of these things can show some finely detailed work which is an excellent example of misapplied ingenuity. Generally porcelain in the true Japanese taste is of fine quality, but that decorated for export has little to commend it.

The recognition of Japanese porcelain depends partly on the

1. A small island off the coast of Hizen Province.

ability to recognize the Japanese flavour in decoration, a faculty which comes with acquaintance with the art of the country. The potting is inclined to be somewhat cruder than that of the Chinese, and firing defects more noticeable. The enamel colours are often stronger and darker, although underglaze blue is sometimes paler, and sometimes of a dark blackish tone – the latter to be seen in the later export wares principally. The 'muslin' surface of the glaze is fairly widely distributed over the various kilns.

(ii) THEMES OF DECORATION

Whilst at first sight, to the novice, Chinese and Japanese decoration may be a little difficult to separate, a study of the two will simplify the task. Many of the themes are similar to those used in China – with a difference which will become more obvious with the acquisition of experience.

The two principal religions of Japan are Buddhism and Shintoism. The Chinese reverence for family and ancestors is extended, in Shinto, to the worship of the State and of the Emperor. The doctrines of K'ung fu-tzŭ were adopted by the Shintoists in the third century, although in a distorted form.

The Buddhist Kuan Yin becomes Kwannon in Japan; her position in the hierarchy of heaven is approximately the same. She is probably Japan's most popular divinity. The Arhats, or Lohan of China, become the Rakan of Japan. They are sixteen in number, and usually have shaven heads surrounded by a nimbus. They can only be distinguished one from the other by their accompanying attributes which it is unnecessary to detail here.

The gods of Good Fortune are frequently used, and are roughly analogous to the Eight Immortals. Jurojin is god of longevity, who carries a staff and a fan. As with Chinese decoration, the bamboo, prunus, and pine are emblems of longevity and sometimes accompany him. He is approximately equivalent to Shou Lao. Fukurokujiu appears to be a variation on the same theme. He has a vast cranium and carries a stick from which hangs a roll of manuscript. He is frequently accompanied by a crane, a deer, or a tortoise – all longevity symbols. Yebisu is lame and often represented as struggling with a fish. Hotei is fat, and derived from the Chinese Pu tai Ho-shang already described. He is god of Contentment. Corpulence is an admired quality, both in China and Japan. Daikoku is god of riches. He holds a miner's hammer, and is seated on a bag of rice which is often being gnawed at one corner by a rat. Bishamon is god of good fortune and longevity. Benten is a goddess. Usually she carries a stringed instrument.

Demons and mischievous imps abound, and can usually be recognized by their extreme ugliness and malevolent expressions.

The dragon is not so popular as in China, but is still frequently used. Usually the Japanese dragon is three-clawed, although four or five claws are not unknown. He possesses much the same qualities as in China. The tiger is not a native of Japan, and mostly appears in decorations derived from the mainland, the Kakiemon 'tyger and wheatsheaf' pattern, for example, being copied from Korea. The *ho-ho* bird appears frequently, and is similar to the Chinese *fêng-huang*. The *ch'i-lin* becomes the *kirin*, and is not often used: the significance is the same as in China. The tortoise is used occasionally, again for much the same purpose as on the mainland, and the Lions of Fo are depicted similarly as either playing with a ball (sometimes said to be the Sacred Gem), or with cubs.

The chrysanthemum is the most important of flowers, appearing in decoration very frequently – usually in a stylized geometrical version. It is an Imperial badge. Badges of rank (*mon*) were used by the nobility and higher officials much as Europeans used armorial bearings.

The peony is another flower which is often seen, and which is also used as a *mon*. The lotus, as in China, is the Buddhist emblem of purity, and the Buddha is occasionally depicted as seated on a lotus. The prunus is often used, as are the willow, pine, bamboo, cherry, and peach. The appreciation of flowers is an important part of Japanese life, and the art of flower-arrangement is a cult which has spread to Europe in recent years. It is not surprising, therefore, to find that floral decoration is extremely popular. Trees, too, are constantly delineated by Japanese artists.

The Japanese use the rat, ox, tiger, hare, dragon, snake, goat, monkey, cock, dog, and boar to denote the hours, and at one time the day was divided into twelve two-hourly periods, from 11 p.m. to 1 a.m. being known, for example, as the Hour of the Rat. The rat is a favourite theme, rarely seen in Chinese art. The hare appears, pounding his Elixir, and is an emblem of the moon, and of longevity. The three monkeys with hands over eyes, ears, and mouth to denote that they see, hear, and speak no evil are not a modern device, despite the fact that they are mostly seen in crude export pottery models worth, perhaps, a few pence. They are not much used as decoration, however, and only then in comparatively modern times. The bat appears, but the name (*komori*) has no such significance in Japanese as it has for the Chinese. The cock is used very frequently, the crane is a longevity symbol, and herons, peacocks, pheasants, and ducks are all popular.

Carp, often leaping up a waterfall, are fairly common. Insects are sometimes kept as pets, and frequently delineated in one form of art or another.

Unlike the Chinese, the Japanese occasionally use the female nude in native decoration, although I have yet to see it on porcelain. The Chinese, of course, use it on subjects copied from European engravings, such as the *Judgement of Paris*.

Decorative themes taken from legend and literature are legion and for the reader interested in pursuing the subject the works of Lafcadio Hearn, the New Orleans reporter who became a naturalized Japanese, will provide information with entertainment.

Works of art in the true Japanese taste are not much known in Europe, and deserve a higher place than they have been assigned in recent years. The nineteenth-century adulation of Tokyo-decorated Satsuma pottery has nothing whatever to do with Japanese art, and the suggestion that the latter is mostly derivative is a mistaken one, probably based on the difficulty experienced by the novice in separating Chinese work from Japanese.

CHAPTER THREE

Korea (Chosen)

KOREA has formed a cultural link between China and Japan
for many centuries, and Korean porcelain is usually sufficiently
distinctive to be fairly easily recognized.

The two main periods are the Koryu (Korai) dynasty (918–
1392) and the Yi dynasty (1392–1910). The capital during the
earlier period was Song-do. It was removed to Seoul in the fourteenth century.

During the Koryu dynasty the principal productions fall
under three distinct headings: a porcelain with a creamy glaze,
somewhat akin to Ting wares; a translucent porcelain of the
ying ch'ing type; and celadons with a glaze of green or bluish-
green. There are some early examples of the latter type, which
can be regarded as proto-porcelain, in a hard grey body. It is
difficult to be sure whether or not some of these wares were
actually made in Korea, or whether they were introduced
from China, and, except in the case of some clearly defined
varieties, attributions as between Korea and the Northern Provinces are sometimes doubtful.

Northern celadons are sometimes claimed for Korea on very
slender grounds. There is record of Korean celadons having
resemblance to the wares of both Yüeh Chou and Ju Chou.[1]
Since these do not resemble each other closely, it is a little difficult to see exactly what was meant. Ting type wares were mentioned by the same commentator, and since Ting wares have
been recovered in some quantity in Korea, presumably they were
a popular importation.

Peculiar to Korea is the *mishima* decoration, in which pieces
covered with a celadon glaze are also inlaid in black and white
clays. The design was first incised into the surface of the raw
clay, the coloured clays afterwards being rubbed into the incisions, the whole being glazed and fired. The name is said to

1. Written by Hsü Ching, a Chinese traveller in Korea, about 1167.

have been derived from the radiating characters of certain almanacs made at Mishima in Japan.

Belonging to the latter part of this period are wares painted with floral scrolls, aquatic birds, trees and grasses, flying birds amid cloud scrolls, and so forth, in a brownish-black pigment, the technique being somewhat akin to that of Tz'ŭ Chou.

The early part of the Yi dynasty is notable for a continuation of the *mishima* technique. A white porcelain was made from about the sixteenth century onwards. It was heavy, clumsily wrought technically, and often opaque. The glaze is greyish in colour or, less often, greenish blue. A blue of a blackish tone was commonly used in decoration with sometimes a red or brown of uneven quality. Despite imperfections, these wares are often of considerable stature artistically, the early specimens being painted in a remarkably effective free style.

Korean forms show considerable differences from the general run of Oriental ceramics. Cups and stands are fairly common; spouted vessels, often based on the gourd, have a singular elegance; and metalwork was used occasionally as an inspiration. Highly-modelled spouted vessels are unusual but not excessively rare. They are probably contemporary with the Yüan period.

The *mei ping* [1] form was frequently used, and lobed forms are not unusual. All these varieties are seen with carved and incised decoration under the glaze, usually of floral scrolls. Bowls form a considerable body of extant Korean wares, although they are not usually the most interesting. Little boxes with covers in porcelain are found both in the *ying ch'ing* type and in the Ting type porcelains.

Unlike most Chinese wares, those from Korea usually have spur marks on the base where they were supported in the kiln. Others show marks of having been stood on piles of sand. The bases are nearly always completely glazed over.

The *mishima* decoration has been copied in Japan in recent times.

1. A vase having a bulbous body and a very short narrow neck with a small aperture. Used for single sprays of prunus blossom.

CHAPTER FOUR

Sawankhalok and Annam

WARES of a Chinese type were uncovered in the ruins of Sawankhalok, the old capital of Siam. Celadons were the commonest wares to be recovered in this way, either painted or plain. Painting is carried out in black or brownish underglaze pigments. *Potiche*-shaped covered jars are fairly common. The glaze is a pale green, inclining to brown, but some examples show a bluish tinge. Glazes usually have an accidental crackle which shows no sign of control.

Wares in imitation of the Chinese recall the tradition that Chinese potters came to Siam during the Yüan period.

The body of Sawankhalok wares is greyish-white in colour, burnt brown in exposed places. Dishes have been noted with an unglazed ring on the base which marks the method of support in the kiln. These things are difficult to date with any kind of accuracy, but reference to related Chinese types seems to show that it is reasonable to regard some examples as contemporary with the Sung period.

Annamese wares were decorated somewhat in the Chinese manner in a greyish underglaze blue. The body is usually coarse and without refinement, although I have one example with decoration based on a Hsüan Tê *motif* which is much more finely potted than one would ordinarily expect. Brownish celadons are ascribed to this source. The glaze varies between thick and thin, and the thicker variety is inclined to run into drops.

Indo-Chinese wares are somewhat difficult to identify, even for the specialist. W. B. Honey summarizes the available information in his *Ceramic Wares of China and other Countries of the Far East.*

Care should be taken not to confuse Chinese wares decorated in the Siamese idiom for export with specimens actually made in Siam. Chinese wares of this type are often cruder than those intended for home consumption.

PART II

European Porcelain

*

CHAPTER FIVE

Germany and Austria

HISTORICAL BACKGROUND

THIS chronicle of the history of porcelain must next turn to Germany, because it was here that the true nature of Chinese porcelain was first discerned and discovered.

Ships had brought porcelain from China and Japan for many years before Johann Friedrich Böttger commenced the collaboration with Ehrenfried Walther von Tschirnhausen which was to lead to the discovery of the Chinese secret.

The Court of Augustus the Strong, Elector of Saxony and King of Poland, took much greater interest in Far Eastern porcelain than was good for the health of the Treasury. It caused von Tschirnhausen, a Saxon nobleman who was a chemist as well, to describe China as 'the bleeding bowl of Saxony'.

Augustus, himself, was a prolific spender of his country's revenues. Apart from a family of over three hundred and fifty children – which caused him to be named 'The Strong' – he collected Chinese and Japanese porcelain avidly, often paying enormous sums for single specimens. It is said that he spent one hundred thousand thalers in the first year of his reign, and, upon one occasion, gave the king of Prussia a regiment of dragoons in exchange for a set of forty-eight vases. Exaggeration often changes fact to legend, but it was obviously a matter of some moment to his unfortunate subjects that a way should be found speedily of satisfying at least one of their ruler's propensities at a somewhat lower cost.

Augustus had many competitors for the shipments of porcelain as they arrived. Kings and princes vied with each other for the finest pieces, whilst the nobility scrambled for the remainder. At first, the fashion was for blue-and-white porcelain belonging either to the late Ming period or to the reign of K'ang Hsi. This was extensively copied by the Dutch potters of Delft in a tin-glazed earthenware which has since become known as *delft*. The first factory erected in Saxony was actually for the manufacture of *faïence*, which is a kind of *delft*. These copies, however, lacked the vital quality of translucency which was, in the eyes of the Western collector, of the utmost importance, and for many years the method whereby this could be attained was sought eagerly by experimentalists throughout Europe.

As I have recorded, the problem was resolved in two essentially different ways, of which the Saxon followed the Chinese method closely, both as to technique and materials used.

Von Tschirnhausen began his researches about 1694. He had had some previous success in melting a variety of refractory substances which needed higher temperatures than were generally attainable at the time. About 1704 he met Johann Friedrich Böttger, then engaged in the more than ordinarily hazardous occupation of attempting the manufacture of gold from base metals, and in the search for the Philosopher's Stone.

Frederick of Prussia, who sought money for the purpose of waging war, took so much interest in the researches of young Böttger, then barely nineteen years of age, that he found it embarrassing, and fled from Berlin to Saxony into the ungentle arms of Augustus. The latter, perhaps, was less belligerent than Frederick, but, for his own purposes, he was at least as greedy for gold. He gave Böttger the dubious honour of a military escort to Dresden.

Böttger was there provided with the facilities he needed, and was instructed, under threat of numerous pains and penalties, to make gold. No doubt he was, by this time, convinced of the futility of his researches, and attempted to escape from his dangerous position. He was arrested, and placed under the supervision of von Tschirnhausen.

Together, the two had no better fortune, and, in 1705, the patience of Augustus was exhausted. Böttger was clapped into gaol to sharpen his wits, but his alchemical knowledge was too useful to waste. He was brought back, and given to von Tschirnhausen as an assistant in his porcelain researches. Apparently, he felt this new assignment to be undignified, because he placed over the door of his laboratory the following inscription:

Gott unser Schöpfer hat gemacht
aus einem Goldmacher einen Töpfer.[1]

Perhaps Augustus would have tired of Böttger to the point of shortening him by a head. But von Tschirnhausen died in 1708, leaving no alternative but to continue with Böttger, or to risk the loss of the money already invested in the enterprise.

The first discovery was a red stoneware imitation of that from Yi Hsing, of which more will be said in due course, but the obvious necessity was for a white clay which would retain its colour in the kiln, as well as a fusible rock similar in its properties to *petuntse*. The first clay of this kind came from Kolditz, but proved unsatisfactory and unpredictable in use. Later, a clay from Aue, near Schneeberg, was employed with better results, the large deposits here continuing in use until well into the nineteenth century.

The story is told of Johann Schnorr, an ironmaster of Erzgebirge, who, whilst riding at Aue in 1711, noticed that his horse's hooves were turning up a white clay. This, he thought, might make a cheap substitute for the hair-powder which was then fashionable. A sample of this earth – henceforth known as *Schnorr'sche weisse Erde von Aue* – was sent to Böttger for examination, who found it distinctly more tractable than the Kolditz clay. Precisely the same story has been told of William Cookworthy of Plymouth, who made the first true porcelain in England, and whilst the arm of coincidence may be long, both ought to be accepted with some reserve.

(i) THE MEISSEN (DRESDEN) FACTORY

The first specimens of an unglazed white porcelain seem to have been made in 1708 from the Kolditz clay, although it was not possible to glaze it until the following year. Additionally, the design of the kiln to reach high temperatures essential to the manufacture of porcelain gave much trouble. In 1710, however, a factory was established for the manufacture of porcelain, under the title of the Royal Saxon Porcelain Manufacture, at Meissen,

1. God, our Creator, has turned a goldmaker into a potter.

some twelve miles from Dresden, although the first intention was to erect it in the City itself.

Although porcelain had been made, and the factory established, by 1710, Böttger's troubles were by no means over, and he proved unequal to the task of managing the undertaking. Michael Nehmitz, who had been continually hostile to him, was given charge of the factory. It is said that the secret of the body was given to one Court official, and that of the glaze to another. This was calculated to avoid its total loss in the event of Böttger's death, whilst preventing its communication as a whole to any one person, who would then have been in a position to start his own factory elsewhere. These precautions, however, availed little. By 1719 Christoph Konrad Hunger and Samuel Stölzel had both arrived in Vienna with the secret, and proceeded to assist Claudius Innocentius du Paquier to establish a porcelain factory. Hunger moved on to Venice in 1720, and thus the chain of factories making porcelain in the manner of Meissen grew and developed.

The earliest decoration at Meissen was in enamel colours. These were thick, and inclined to be 'dry' in appearance. They included a good rose-pink, a turquoise, and a brownish-red. There was, in fact, a fairly comprehensive palette in use, but despite the fact that there were rich deposits of cobalt ore in Saxony, underglaze blue eluded the Meissen colour chemists for some years after the invention of porcelain. The earliest essays in this direction were poor in quality and of a blackish colour. The first really good blue did not come along until 1725, and Böttger, who died in 1719, did not live to see it.

These early years were far from easy. Frequent disputes marred the factory's growth, and, after Böttger's death at the age of thirty-seven, conditions were such that even the survival of the factory seemed doubtful. Augustus stepped in and appointed a Commission, which made a number of changes in the factory directorate. This had an almost immediate effect, and a revival began which lasted until 1756.

These were the great days of Meissen. Johann Gregor Höroldt, an enameller, miniaturist, and engraver, was given charge of the painting shop in 1720. Adam Friedrich von Löwenfinck, a painter of some skill, was apprenticed in 1726 at the early age of thirteen years. One of Höroldt's relatives, Christian Friedrich Herold (or Heroldt) became a factory artist about the same date – at least the relationship has been assumed, despite the slightly different way in which each spelled his name. Incidentally, both names are quite often Anglicized as Herold. Johann Georg Heintze, who eventually became one of the factory's most important decorators, began work about 1725. He was frequently in trouble because of his 'outside decorating' proclivities, which are discussed later under the heading of *Hausmalerei*.

Some of the early figure modelling was undertaken by Georg Fritzsche, who was already employed in 1712, and whose work has only doubtfully been identified; Johann Gottlob Kirchner, a troublesome young man who arrived in 1727; and Johann Christoph von Lücke, an ivory carver, who was employed for a short time only.

The great Johann Joachim Kändler, whose name is a household word among students of porcelain, and who will be frequently mentioned in the pages which follow, was appointed in 1731. Johann Friedrich Eberlein became his assistant in 1735, and Peter Reinicke was appointed in 1743.

This brief mention by no means exhausts the list of notable artists, but refers only to those who are best known.

Augustus the Strong, who had undertaken personal direction of the factory in 1731, died in 1733. He was succeeded by his son, who became Augustus the Third of Poland. The Directorship of the factory then fell into the capable hands of Count Heinrich von Brühl, who continued in this capacity until 1763.

The year 1745 saw the factory under the control of the Prussian Army, but the occupation was temporary, and no serious damage was done. In 1756 the Seven Years War began, and Frederick occupied Dresden in September of that year. This time the factory did not come off so well. Frederick was covetous, and attempts were made to move it to Berlin to augment the factory there. This was unsuccessful, and it was later 'sold' to Karl Heinrich Schimmelman. After numberless intrigues, work was started once again, and part of the output devoted to table-services and such things for Frederick.

The Prussian grip on the factory relaxed in 1763, and a new Commission of management came into being. In the form set up, however, it lasted but a few months, since both Augustus and Count von Brühl died in the same year, and the Commission had to be reconstituted. Christian Wilhelm Ernst Dietrich, Court Painter, was appointed principal of the Dresden Academy of Arts, and the factory artists were sent on a tour of European factories to search for inspiration. Kändler was still chief modeller, but Michel-Victor Acier was brought from France in 1764, and installed beside him on equal terms in an attempt to meet competition from Sèvres, Vienna, and other Continental factories, which had taken advantage of the Prussian occupation to make inroads into markets where Meissen had hitherto been supreme. Acier held his position until 1779, and was mainly responsible for the eventual introduction of the neo-classical style.

The time between 1763 and the appointment of Count Camillo Marcolini as director in 1774, is known as the Academic period – sometimes called the 'Dot' period in reference to the mark employed at this time. Marcolini commenced work at a difficult period in the factory's history, when strong competition from Wedgwood's newly-invented cream-ware had to be faced.

Dresden was once more in enemy hands in 1813, and the city suffered severely as a result. It recovered with difficulty, but production began to decline artistically with the advent of the *Biedermeier* style (1815–40). This, a heavy, somewhat ornate style designed to appeal to the *bourgeois* tradesman, was followed by a revival of eighteenth-century styles in a debased form, to which belong the Dresden Shepherdesses so popular in Victorian England. These were brought to England at the time by the ton, and would be much more common today had they not been bought avidly by American interior decorators in the years immediately following the Second World War.

In 1865 the factory was transferred to a new site near Meissen. The end of the First World War saw some revival of old glories, principally due to the work of a modeller of uncommon skill, Paul Scheurich. Little is known of it during the war of 1939–45, but token amounts of new manufacture have since been imported into England.

At this point it would be desirable to say a word on the question of the name given to the porcelain. In England it has usually been called 'Dresden', just as in France it has always been referred to as 'Saxe'. In Germany, on the other hand, the term, 'Meissner Porzellan', is always used. I am not in favour of a purist attitude to these things, but I think we would do well to follow the Germans, especially so far as the earlier wares are concerned. During the first period porcelain of magnificent quality was made which has hardly been excelled anywhere in Europe. But the nineteenth century, as in England, saw a production which was entirely commercial and markedly inferior.

The term 'Meissen' should be reserved for wares made and decorated at the Royal factory, 'Dresden' being used for the small factories and decorators' studios which operated in and around the city from about 1770 onwards.

The Wares before 1731

Before the invention of porcelain in Europe, the table-ware of the rich had been mostly of silver or *faïence*, the poor using either common earthenware or pewter, or even dipping into a communal trencher. Oriental porcelain was particularly prized for decorative purposes, and for some considerable time was too precious to use for matters of utility.

Mention has already been made of the red stoneware which was the first fruit of Böttger's labours. Although this cannot be regarded as more than porcellaneous, it was the hardest substance of its kind produced, and could be engraved and polished on the wheel of the lapidary in the same way as semi-precious hardstones.

Thus we get such pieces as the teapot in the Victoria and Albert Museum which has been cut into hexagonal facets. It is not surprising to find that Böttger did, in fact, attempt the manufacture of artificial stones of the semi-precious variety, such as agate, onyx, and so forth, from clays of variegated colour.

Baroque forms based on contemporary silver were much used for the red stoneware under the influence of the Court goldsmith, Johann Jakob Irminger. The 'thrown' pieces were made under the direction of Peter Eggebrecht, an expert potter from Holland, and the engraver's wheel was employed to cut in armorial bearings and decoration of this nature. It is difficult today to be sure whether or not such engraving is contemporary, plain pieces having been thus decorated in recent times to enhance their value. Small relief ornament was moulded separately and applied. These mostly took the form of acanthus leaves, or small masks – such as lion-masks – all sharply moulded.

Occasionally, primitive enamel colours were used as decoration, but these on the red ground presented by the stoneware are not particularly effective. Possibly the least interesting, artistically, are those things – principally vases – which have been decorated in lacquer colours. I have already noted this practice as existing in China. Since no second firing was necessary, it may have been used for cheapness, or because the enamelling kiln had an adverse effect on the surface. It is noteworthy that the porcelain of Tê Hua, which is occasionally decorated in this way, is hardly ever decorated with enamels before the nineteenth century. This suggests that there may have been some difficulty in applying enamel colours to this glaze, 'cold' colours being used instead. The English porcelain factories frequently used 'cold' colours on porcelain figures in the early years, principally because of the difficulties experienced in firing enamels on to the glaze.

The two main classes into which red stoneware can be divided are those of a red, or reddish-brown, colour, and those with a blackish surface due to overfiring. These are red beneath the black. A few existing pieces seem to have been taken directly from teapots made at Yi Hsing, and from Chinese porcelain figures. The simplicity of modelling to be seen in many of the figures from Tê Hua, more particularly the seated Kuan Yin, made this kind of moulding comparatively easy.

Some pieces have been mounted in gold and silver, a common practice in Europe with treasured porcelain from the earliest times onwards. Elias Adam, an Augsburg silversmith, was responsible for some of the finest work of this kind. Less happy are those specimens set with stones, such as the turquoise and the emerald. I have noticed one porcelain figure of a hare of about 1740 which had a collar set with rose-diamonds, but this is extremely unusual.

Ivory-carvings were the inspiration for some figures in this medium. Particularly to be noted are amusing and distinguished Italian Comedy figures, some things derived from Roman sculpture and from that of Bernini, and a statuette of Augustus striking an attitude.

The output of the red stoneware was on a comparatively large scale, and the manufacture was probably continued side by side with that of porcelain for some years after the introduction of the latter. It is essential to mention Plaue-an-der-Havel, where red stoneware was made from about 1713. This manufacture was started by a runaway workman from Meissen, one Samuel Kempe. Occasionally these are difficult to separate from Meissen examples, and, to judge by sale prices, have sometimes been valued as highly. Kempe is said to have later gone to Bayreuth.

Böttger's white porcelain is somewhat reminiscent of the stoneware in general form, although, because of the covering glaze, the lapidary's art could no longer be used. The earliest pieces, in which alabaster was used instead of *petuntse*, were not highly translucent, and 'moons' appear occasionally. The colour has been well described as having a 'smoky' appearance, and a creamy-yellow was also fairly common. The glaze was thick, even, and 'bubbly', probably owing to the fact that it was fired on separately, and the 'bubbles' have been used as a method of separating porcelain of this period from that of the earliest Vienna manufacture in which they do not ordinarily appear. Generally, however, the difference between the work of the two factories is sufficiently great for the distinction to be made in other ways.

A fairly wide range of enamel colours was used on Böttger porcelain from the earliest times. Underglaze blue was not employed until 1725, although a few earlier and relatively unsuccessful experimental pieces are known. Both gold and silver were used decoratively, although the latter has usually oxidized to black.

Applied decoration, particularly the acanthus leaves already mentioned, was used freely, and the moulding was often heightened with touches of enamel colour. A 'mother of pearl' lustre which is pale purple in colour was first employed during the period, very occasionally as a ground colour.

Some amusing and interesting figures were produced. The 'Pagoda' figures are probably the most frequently seen. Made about 1715, they depict a squatting Chinese with a grinning, open, mouth, and they may have been intended for incense burners. Dwarfs, derived from grotesque engravings by Jacques Callot,[1] are comical caricatures which we may owe to Georg Fritzsche.

Böttger died in 1719, and Johann Gregor Höroldt was given charge of the painting shop. It has been established that he came from Vienna, brought by the returning prodigal, Stölzel, and that he had learned the craft of enamelling at this factory. Höroldt speedily added some new colours to the Meissen palette, and improved on those of his predecessor. His iron-red, for instance, is a brilliant colour distinct from Böttger's rather brownish-red. His work is extremely difficult to identify with certainty, and it is probable that his position allowed him very little time for painting. It seems that, for the most part, he confined himself to devising decorative schemes and to overseeing their execution.

The finest work of this period was based on Chinese and Japanese styles. Decoration in the manner of the Kakiemons was carried out in a palette which corresponds fairly closely to that of the original. Numbers of large vases were made and decorated in the Oriental style for the Japanese Palace, which Augustus had bought to house his collection. These sometimes bear the Royal Monogram, *AR*, which was copied in the 1870s by a certain Madame Wolfsohn of Dresden, an outside decorator and faker whose work is noticed in more detail hereafter.

Possibly the most amusing of the decorative styles initiated by Höroldt are the *chinoiseries* – little pseudo-Chinese figures, pagodas, and monsters – which are among the best things to come from Meissen at this period. They appear to have been

1. Taken from *Il Calotto Resuscitato*. Amsterdam. 1716.

first produced about 1720, which is a trifle earlier than the date usually suggested. They are sometimes unframed, sometimes surrounded by a simple border, or, at a slightly later date, with an elaborate border pattern of gilt ornament in the *baroque* style referred to as *Laub- und Bandelwerk* – leaf- and strap-work. A few of the finer examples have been attributed to Höroldt, partly on the evidence of a signed engraving by him now at Munich which is dated 1726, but, of course, it is possible that he did no more than provide the designs for the decorator to copy. Some have been attributed to von Löwenfinck, who painted partly in the Japanese style, but attributions need to be made cautiously.

Chinoiseries in gold silhouette were an early factory style also repeated by the *Hausmaler*, Seuter of Augsburg, on white Böttger porcelain which he purchased from the factory about 1730. The suggestion that Seuter alone was responsible for this kind of decoration, however, does not appear to be well-founded.

Landscapes and harbour-scenes, usually superbly drawn and painted, were introduced a year or two after Höroldt's arrival at Meissen. The first essays in this direction were in polychrome, but a type of painting in black monochrome – known as *Schwarzlot* – followed speedily. *Schwarzlot* was much used at Vienna, and by the *Hausmaler*, Preussler. Some early river-scenes by an unknown artist, perhaps J. G. Heintze, are exceptionally fine.

Christian Friedrich Herold became an enameller in 1725, and was responsible for *chinoiseries* and harbour scenes. His style has been identified from a number of signed pieces in existence. Heintze was responsible for many of the harbour scenes, as well as some small landscapes. Honey refers in his *Dictionary* to a signed plaque at Stuttgart, and I have seen a cup and saucer characteristically decorated bearing the initials, *JGH*.

The period under review was remarkable for the discovery of a number of coloured grounds – yellow, deep-green, sea-green, lilac, and a reddish-purple which resembles a raspberry in shade. These were used in conjunction with reserved panels characteristically decorated.

From surviving examples it would seem that the work of Fritzsche was confined to the earlier part of the period. Kirchner was appointed to take charge of modelling in 1727, but pieces which can be assigned to his hand are few. Among them is a large figure of St Paul, superbly modelled in a dramatic pose which, in some ways, recalls the later work of Bustelli at Nymphenburg, and a Pietà derived from Michelangelo's representation of this subject in St Peter's, Rome, which was later copied fairly closely at Chelsea, probably by Joseph Willems, and at Tournai.[1] A rhinoceros with a curious volute horn between his shoulder-blades is obviously derived from an engraving by Albrecht Dürer of 1515. The well-known group of St John Nepomuk poised on top of a pedestal has also been attributed to Kirchner, and it is obvious that he was a modeller of more than ordinary skill. Nothing has been identified with certainty of the work of von Lücke, although there are a number of things in existence which are likely to have been made by him.

Certain incised marks which appear mostly on the bases of porcelain of this period have been regarded as signifying the type of body used, but from their great diversity I consider it more likely that they are the identifying marks of workmen.

Kändler as Modellmeister

The advent of Johann Joachim Kändler in 1731 was an event of first importance in European ceramic history.

His first assignment was to model large figures of animals, some over four feet in height, for the Japanese Palace. A Paduan Cock, frequently illustrated, is one of the most spirited of his works at this time.

But these oversized things were too expensive and troublesome to make, and young Kändler turned his attention to the smaller figures which have caused him to be recognized as certainly the most prolific, and, with one exception, the greatest of all modellers for porcelain. Whether or not we agree as to Kändler's position – and there are some (myself among them)

1. This subject was also rendered by Rubens in a version inspired by Michelangelo's group.

who would award first place to Franz Anton Bustelli of Nymphenburg[1] – it is undoubted that Kändler created the art of the porcelain figure in Europe.

The actual number of different models created by Kändler during his long and successful career can only be guessed, but the total has been estimated by Robert Schmidt as in excess of one thousand. When we add to this the work of his assistants, Eberlein and Reinicke, who worked more or less in his style, we can estimate the astonishingly large number of models issued by the factory during the period. Of course, all these models were moulded for reproduction, although it is not possible to say how many of each were cast. The number would vary with their popularity and purpose.

Kändler's earlier work was largely in the *baroque* manner, and although his later figures are in the *rococo* style, he was not at home in it, nor did he catch its spirit.

Kändler's subjects are legion. He portrays the manners and customs of the Court and Society in his crinoline figures, groups of lovers, figures of gallants and ladies, and in many other ways. At the other end of the social scale, artisans, such as miners, carpenters, and so forth, were frequently modelled. The Italian Comedy (*Commedia dell'Arte*), performed by troupes of strolling players, attracted his attention, and his Harlequins in a myriad poses are lively, but with less sense of the theatre than can be seen in Bustelli's figures drawn from the same source. The fashion for *chinoiseries* is revealed in figures and groups, some of which are derived from engravings of these subjects by J. J. Bachelier after Boucher.

Figures of Turks, and others in national costume, some figures after Bouchardon's *Cris de Paris*, Musicians, Streetsellers, Animals, Birds, Freemasons, Huntsmen, Shepherds with their paramours, Apollo and the Muses and other inhabitants of Olympus, sets of figures emblematic of the Seasons, Continents, Elements, Senses, the Arts, the Sciences, the Months, and anything lending itself to similar treatment, poured from the factory

---

1. As this view is controversial, it is encouraging to notice that W. B. Honey in his *Dictionary* refers to him as 'perhaps the most gifted and individual genius of all modellers'.

in increasing numbers, and were copied by other European factories more or less exactly

Well known is a set of Monkeys playing musical instruments (the *Affenkapelle*) said to have been modelled as a satire on the Dresden Court Orchestra, although this is somewhat doubtful. The same set was copied by the English Chelsea factory, and an entry in the Auction Sale Catalogue of 1756 reads: *Lot 57. A set of five monkies in different attitudes playing on music.*

Apart from his figure work, Kändler brought a new style to table-wares, and his first important work of this kind was the *Swan* service for Count Brühl. This, made about 1740, is one of the early essays in the *rococo* style. The tureens are highly modelled with swans, dolphins, nereids,[1] and little *putti*, to an extent which left no room for painted decoration apart from enamelled embellishments to the modelling. The surface of the plates to services of this kind was also covered with moulded ornament.

A number of vases with modelled ornament, usually with some symbolic significance, were designed by Kändler. The commonest, although not the finest, are a set modelled with *putti*, and flowers and fruits, representing the Seasons.

The *rococo* style had its beginning about 1740, and it was plainly in evidence by 1750. By 1763 styles had undergone a distinct change, making the years from then until 1774 a transitional period, during which the style of Louis Seize slowly gained in influence. During this period Kändler shared his position of *Modellmeister* with Michel-Victor Acier. Kändler, however, continued work until his death in 1775 – the year of Marcolini's appointment as factory director. His latest things still have many of the elements of his old *baroque* style, although the rather more formal bases show some concession to the ideas then current.

Friedrich Elias Meyer, a sculptor, was at Meissen from 1746 to 1761, and worked to some extent in the style of Kändler. He later became *Modellmeister* at Berlin.

1. Sea-nymphs. Daughters of Nereus who attended Neptune; often associated with dolphins.

The Period of Expansion (1733–1763)

Between these years the Meissen factory was, for the most part, prosperous, and the leader of fashion in Europe. A large export trade was developed with almost every other European country, and trade with Turkey – started in the 1720s – continued to expand. The rare mark of the *caduceus* (or kite-tail) was used on porcelain destined for that country, the famous mark of the crossed swords, introduced about 1724, being regarded as a Christian symbol and therefore likely to offend Islamic susceptibilities.

It is impossible in the space available to do more than refer briefly to the principal kinds of decoration. *Chinoiseries*, previously discussed, continued to be popular, and some have curious and fantastic animals, usually said to be the work of von Löwenfinck, although other *chinoiseries* with equally fantastic animals may be properly attributable to Höroldt, or to someone working in his style.[1] The work of the Kakiemons continued to be popular, and the formal Oriental flowers – variously known as *indianische Blumen* or 'India Flowers' – were still common. The latter name was awarded to them because much Oriental porcelain was brought to Europe in the ships of the East India Companies.

About 1740 *indianische Blumen* began to give place to the *deutsche Blumen* – naturalistically-painted German flowers, either separately or in loosely-tied bouquets. These were introduced by Höroldt, and most were derived from engravings illustrating the works of Johann Wilhelm Weinmann. The addition of shadows to flowers and insects came somewhat later.[2] Small insects and flower-heads were used particularly to cover faults in the glaze, both at Meissen and elsewhere.

From about 1740 we find a series of subjects after the French painters, Watteau and Lancret, mostly of sophisticated pastoral scenes framed with elaborate gilding. Consignments of French engravings were sent to the factory in 1741 to provide the artists

1. Höroldt's style may be deduced from a number of signed engravings in existence.
2. This peculiarity is also to be seen on some early Chelsea porcelain.

with inspiration. Mythological subjects in the manner of Boucher are to be seen from about 1755 onwards.

Coloured grounds (*Fond-porzellan*) continued to be employed, but were rarely accorded the importance with which they were regarded at Sèvres. In the following period they largely fell into disuse, being replaced by the *Mosaik* border. The *bleu de Roi* of Sèvres was much envied, but not copied successfully until 1782.

Whilst very little underglaze blue was used, and the factory was rarely particularly successful with it, the well-known 'onion' pattern of Oriental flowers in underglaze blue was first used about 1730, and with some differences has continued in use until the present day.

Moulded details on services commenced with simple basket-work patterns (*Ozier*), to be seen, for example, on the ledges of plates. These moulded details became more elaborate with the passing years and the growing influence of *rococo*. At a later date moulded flowers were added, and the erstwhile border pattern spread over the surface, which, particularly with dinner-plates, was impractical, regarded from the functional aspect at least. The addition of modelled details to other items of the services has been mentioned in the preceding section. Scrolls in relief can be seen around the lips of jugs and coffee pots, and handles and teapot spouts blossom forth with little scrolls and flourishes.

Elaborate decorations for the banqueting table were undertaken, the most frequently quoted being the vast 'Temple of Honour' which was over four feet in height and surrounded by large numbers of separate figures scattered among the table appointments.[1]

During the 1740s we have the vogue for services with tureens in the form of animals and vegetables – a fashion closely copied at the English Chelsea factory at a somewhat later date.

The occupation of Dresden by Frederick the Great during the Seven Years War caused many changes. From this time dates the *Mosaik* border, a ground colour overlaid with

[1]. Before the discovery of porcelain in Europe, these table appointments were frequently modelled in sugar.

diapers which are usually meticulously drawn. The scale-patterns, later copied at Worcester, were probably derived from Chinese sources, although they may owe something both to Isnik pottery and Italian *maiolica*. Incidentally, it is possible that the popularity of portraits of Frederick the Great as decoration with the English factories may owe something to his action in putting a formidable competitor *hors de combat*.

Frederick's intervention put an end to the leadership of Meissen in European porcelain manufacture. Somewhat naturally it reverted to Berlin until the position eventually passed to the royal factory of Sèvres.

Mention must be made of a very rare model of an elephant covered with a light green celadon glaze which belongs to the end of the period. An example is in the British Museum (Franks Collection). This is the only instance of an eighteenth-century European factory using a celadon glaze.

The Academic Period (1763–74)

From 1763 onwards the factory strove to regain the leadership it had lost. The style of Louis Seize – the neo-classical – was making a beginning elsewhere, but it was one to which the particular genius of the factory's artists was ill-adapted. C. W. E. Dietrich, who introduced a stiff academic style, founded an Academy at Dresden for the purpose of 'improving' the quality of the painting. Höroldt relinquished his position in 1765.

The painted decoration made considerable use of the *Mosaik* border in several colours. Fantastic birds in panels, now painted in a more natural style, little *putti*, and the subjects popular in the previous decade, were used. Flower painting becomes less a matter of bouquets and more of exact botanical specimens, a tendency which culminated later in the century in the *Flora Danica* service from Copenhagen, each piece of which bears the Latin name of the flower on the underside.

The *rococo* moulding and scroll-work are gradually replaced throughout these years by symmetricality. Handles and spouts become plain, simple, and severe, and even, in extreme cases, rectangular. The little rosebuds, which had been used for the knops to the covers of teapots and such things, are gradually

139

replaced by formal pine-cones. Festoons of laurel are used as painted ornament, and occasionally in relief. Saucers become straight-sided instead of curved, whilst vases begin to acquire the severity of outline associated with classical Greek and Roman urns. In short, the current fashions at Sèvres were fairly closely copied.

Lace-work was a novelty first introduced shortly before 1770 and is to be seen on figures by Acier. Lace was dipped into porcelain slip and applied to the figure. The cotton thread burned away during firing, leaving a replica of its mesh in porcelain. This fussy decoration was confined at first to small additions to the dress. During the nineteenth century figures were made with elaborately flounced lace-skirts.

Count Camillo Marcolini (1774–1814)

The period of Marcolini's directorate at first saw some improvement in the factory's fortunes, but such factors as the rise of the Thuringian factories, and the growing popularity of Wedgwood's blue jasper and cheap cream-coloured earthenware made progress difficult. The Napoleonic wars brought about a virtual collapse.

The neo-classical forms had entirely replaced the *rococo* by 1780, and were accompanied by a strongly naturalistic manner in decoration. Precise topographical paintings became popular, usually framed with a narrow band of plain ornament. Subjects derived from such artists as Angelica Kauffmann, Canaletto, and Berchem, portraits in miniature, or (more frequently) black silhouettes, enamels in thick drops to represent jewels in the manner of Sèvres, striped grounds, and many another device for capturing trade was tried, but all of them were of little merit. About 1782 a ground colour copying the *bleu de roi* of Sèvres was devised, and often used in conjunction with figures in the manner of Angelica Kauffmann.

Marcolini, in an endeavour to raise money, sold by auction a great deal of defective white porcelain which had been accumulating over the years. Much of it was bought by 'outside decorators', of which more will be said in the section devoted to their work.

Kändler died in 1775, and Acier retired in 1781. Of Acier, it may be said that he was responsible for the prototypes of the simpering, sentimental, pastoral figures beloved of the Victorians. Whilst Kändler could not adapt his style to the changing fashion, his work was on an altogether higher plane than that of his colleague.

The bases of these later figures show considerable differences from those of the *baroque* and *rococo* periods. The *baroque* bases are mostly either plain or in the form of symmetrical pedestals, the *rococo* bases have the characteristic scroll-work of the style, but, from about 1770 onwards, bases became flat, and sometimes circular or oval in form, usually with a moulded border of key-fret or some similar pseudo-classical ornament, or else entirely plain and square-cut.

The fashion for *biscuit* porcelain was copied from Sèvres shortly after 1780, but the body in use was ill-adapted to this kind of work. Most things in the medium are close copies of the style of antique marble sculpture which it was intended to resemble.

The old clay deposits were exhausted about this time, and the body of most Marcolini wares is no longer of the earlier quality.

Meissen in the Nineteenth Century

The work of the Meissen factory after the Marcolini period was very uneven in quality.

A certain amount in the manner of Wedgwood was undertaken, and a heavy classical style was well to the fore until about 1833. Portrait busts of good quality and well-modelled were quite frequently made, and are restrained in taste, although they are sometimes a little pretentious.

About 1828 a novelty was introduced in the form of 'lithophanies'. These are elaborate and sentimental pictures on extremely thin porcelain intended to be viewed by transmitted light.

Between 1833 and 1870 – known as the Kühn period, after Heinrich Gottlob Kühn, director of the factory – the *rococo* style was revived in a debased form, although some things in the classical style, in the form of mythological figures, were also made. To this period belong many of the pierced dessert baskets on high stands, often in conjunction with figures and groups of figures. Elaborate candelabra, too, belong to the same period, and were made with three or four branches and decorated with figures. Many of the little cupids playing musical instruments, and in a hundred other poses, were manufactured at this time, and all these things were freely exported, and are not uncommon either in England or the United States. They are not at all difficult to recognize, because the colouring is completely different from that of the earlier pieces.

After about 1870 – referred to as *die Neuzeit*, the New Period – the factory made a few contemporary figures and groups illustrating such subjects as bathing-girls in nineteenth-century costume, groups of lovers, dancers, sportswomen, and so forth, which are not particularly important artistically, but throw amusing sidelights on the costumes and manners of the time. Many eighteenth-century subjects were translated into the nineteenth-century idiom, and some quite spirited animals and birds belong to the period. The Franco-Prussian War was the inspiration for a series of idealized models of soldiers, mostly with the familiar spiked helmet, and often with moustaches reminiscent of Kaiser Wilhelm II. These are not often seen outside Germany.

Less happy are grossly over-decorated mirror-frames, clock-cases, and things of this kind, in an unpleasant revived *rococo*, but dinner and dessert services frequently exceed in quality those which were made in England, and the painted floral decoration is often pleasant, if somewhat pedestrian. Massive electroliers belong to the end of the nineteenth century and the beginning of the twentieth. Vases and tureens were often elaborately modelled, but are seldom of much importance artistically, although they are sought after as interior decoration.

The factory had retained many of its old moulds, and it has often been said that they were willing to make casts of these to order. Certainly they issued a large catalogue towards the end of the century which included hundreds of plates of models they were able and willing to supply. This included many Kändler figures, as well as those of the Academic and Marcolini periods. The catalogue is now extremely scarce.

A little less scarce, but still seen only rarely, is an illustrated history of Meissen by Berling, which was issued in 1910 to mark the factory's bicentenary. This is entitled *Festschrift zur 200-jährigen Jubelfeier der ältesten Europäischen Porzellan-manufaktur Meissen*. An edition in somewhat curious English was also published, but is not often seen. This history is not particularly detailed in its treatment of early wares, although it contains a quite adequate pictorial survey of the factory's achievements.

The period from about 1890 to 1910 is referred to as the *Jugendstil* – the Youth style – which corresponds to the style better known, perhaps, as *l'art nouveau*.

The amount of porcelain exported to England and America in the latter part of the nineteenth century was prodigious, and most extant 'Dresden' porcelain belongs to this period, eighteenth-century examples being rarely seen outside private or public collections.

The Decoration of Figures

Most of the figures of the early period were intended to be painted in enamel colours, although in the case of the large figure of St Paul previously mentioned, this was impracticable, and lacquer colours were used. White figures which were in some way defective were sold off cheaply, and many have been decorated subsequently by fakers. The practice of scoring a cut across the mark to indicate that it was of inferior quality and not decorated at the factory started about 1760, but much earlier things which had been kept in stock can be found treated in this way.

It is often upon the painting that we have to rely in order to be sure of the period at which the figure was made, since, as may be deduced from the Introduction, the true porcelain of the German factories does not help either to establish age or provenance, except within certain limits. In the absence of enamel colouring it would be virtually impossible to detect whether or not a figure had been made in modern times from an eighteenth-century mould, and since the Meissen factory kept many of their moulds, and used them during the nineteenth century, any method of establishing the date of manufacture is highly important.

From the general unity to be observed, it seems obvious that the modeller usually dictated the kind of decoration to be applied. Naturally each style needed different treatment, and if a series of figures of all periods be arranged in order of chronology, the changes can most easily be seen.

The *baroque* style was accompanied by washes of unbroken colour, with large flowered designs on appropriate fabrics. Rich colours were used, but the white porcelain was also respected as decorative in its own right.

During the *rococo* period the colours lost their strength and became somewhat delicate and subdued. Extensive passages of black, commoner at an earlier date, disappeared entirely, and the colour was used only for small and appropriate articles of dress. The white surface is somewhat more in evidence. Costumes are decorated with small flower sprigs. The patterns become more elaborate towards the end of the period.

The *Louis Seize* style shows quiet pastel shades, with an increasing use of striped patterns on fabrics. The exposed flesh is coloured completely instead of in touches on cheeks, lips, and so forth to be seen in the earlier period.

Towards the end of the century the palette again tends to become darker and stronger, with colours inferior in quality.

Painting by 'outside decorators' may show some small variations from these colour styles, and nineteenth-century repetitions from the factory are usually obvious from the differences in colouring. An acquaintance with attested factory-decorated examples is essential to differentiate between the various possibilities.

These notes are intended to summarize general tendencies, and have a much wider application than to the Meissen factory only. More detailed information on this subject is given under various headings.

Table-ware and Miscellaneous Items

Some notes on eighteenth-century table-wares may be helpful at this point, and can be taken, with a few exceptions, to refer to European porcelain as a whole.

Dinner and tea services need little comment. Dinner services, of course, included the usual meat plates (the principal size being made in twelves or in multiples of twelve), large meat dishes oval in shape, and tureens and sauceboats for various purposes. Additionally, there were dishes for *hors d'œuvres*, deep soup plates, butter dishes and small butter boats, condiment sets with spoons, and knife and fork handles. Also included with some services were salad bowls, finger bowls, sweetmeat dishes, soup bowls (often with covers), etc. etc. Salts were often large and elaborate.

Tea-services were composed of a teapot, cream jug (often with cover), tea jar and cover, hot-water jug and cover (sometimes), sugar bowl (often with cover),[1] slop bowl, and tea cups and saucers. Frequently the tea set was combined with a coffee set which involved the addition of a coffee pot and coffee cups and saucers. At some factories it was the practice to make a combined set with twelve tea cups, twelve coffee cups, and *twelve* saucers. These services usually had one or two bread-and-butter or cake plates, but the small individual plates were not added until well into the nineteenth century.

There is little difference between the early tea and coffee cups. Later, the tea cups were shallow, and made either with handles, or without in the Chinese manner. The coffee cups were taller, and provided with handles, except for those made at Meissen for the Turkish market.

Chocolate pots are said to be those with the handle at right angles to the spout, but there is no certainty that this is so. Chocolate cups were made with two handles, a cover, and a large deep saucer. The saucers often had an interior ring into which the cup fitted. These are known as *trembleuse* saucers, which suggests that they were originally intended for a trembling

1. Also called a sugar-box.

hand, although, as anyone who has tried will appreciate, they may equally have been made for use in bed.

Cabaret sets are those for one or two people which are provided with a porcelain tray. Often the cups were stood directly on to the tray without saucers. A German *déjeuner* set included a large porcelain tray, a teapot, a cream jug, a sugar basin, one or two cups, and a porcelain spoon. Services for one person were *solitaires*; for two people they were listed as *tête à tête*.

The dessert service was often most elaborate, and no definite information as to its composition can be given. It included various sweetmeat dishes, often in leaf forms, with comports, sauceboats and tureens, wine and oil bottles, large refrigerators (which contained ice-water for cooling glasses and bottles), butter dishes with stands and covers, and centre pieces, either purely decorative or functional. In the latter case, it usually supported condiment containers. Many figures, of course, can be regarded as table decoration, and candlesticks were often made in the form of figures for table illumination. Occasionally figures were made holding containers for salt or sweetmeats. Warming dishes with a hot water compartment are sometimes seen.

'Confinement tureens' are Continental, and consist of a round tureen, cover, and stand, intended to be filled with sweetmeats and presented to the invalid.

There are many items difficult to classify. The *veilleuse* is a food-warmer with a covered bowl at the top, and a space for a lamp – the *godet* – below it. After 1800 these may be seen with a teapot replacing the food warmer. Tea kettles with a spirit lamp belong to this class.

Ink stands were commonly made, replete with ink and sand pots. Clock cases and watch holders were not unusual. Mirror frames are usually comparatively late. Wash basins, ewers, and chamber pots were often well decorated, although the latter are scarce. Spirit flasks, spittoons, night lights, eye baths – the list is almost endless.

Mention should be made of toys and miniature pieces. These comprise scent-bottles, seals, cane heads, bell pulls, patch-boxes, snuff-boxes, toothpick cases, tobacco boxes, pipe-bowls and tobacco stoppers, mounted in gold, silver, silver-gilt, or base metal where appropriate. The *Jungfernbeichen* (maiden's legs) with stocking and shoe are amusing and were popular at Meissen, although not often seen in these days. They are hollow, with a cover mounted at the top of the thigh. Porcelain flowers intended to be mounted on ormolu sprays were made in quantity.

Among the items rarely seen in English and American collections may be included buttons, small pieces of jewellery such as ear pendants, thimbles, needle and scissors cases, beads for rosaries and adornment, chessmen, table-bells, etc. etc.

Some of these things, such as the scent flasks, were highly modelled and of the finest possible quality. Boxes were skilfully painted with miniature landscapes and portraits, and form a very desirable group of wares.

(ii) VIENNA (1719–1864)

Vienna was the second European manufactory of hard porcelain to be established. Experiments were being made here by a Dutchman, Claudius Innocentius du Paquier, as early as 1716, and, in 1718, Charles VI, Emperor of the Holy Roman Empire,[1] granted a monopoly of the manufacture and sale of porcelain throughout his territories for a term of twenty-five years. Christoph Konrad Hunger arrived from Meissen in 1717, and Samuel Stölzel in 1719. Hunger was primarily an enameller, whose knowledge of the secret of porcelain-making was more than a little dubious. We shall meet him again hereafter. Samuel Stölzel was probably much more useful. He had been Böttger's kiln-master, and Vienna was making porcelain of good quality soon after he joined the factory. Legend has it that du Paquier went to Meissen and struck up an acquaintance with Stölzel at an inn, tempting him with an offer of a thousand thalers to bring the Meissen secret to Vienna. Porcelain history is full of such incidents. Stölzel remained until 1720 when, having made his peace with his erstwhile employers, he returned to Meissen, taking with him Johann Gregor Höroldt, who had been a

1. Of which it has been truly said that it was neither Holy, nor Roman, nor an Empire.

Vienna enameller. He is said to have left because du Paquier was unable to pay the promised salary.

Du Paquier continued the enterprise on a small scale, but could not make it a financial success. He was bankrupt in 1727 and, despite several loans from the State, was obliged to relinquish the factory to them in 1744, the year his original patent expired. He died in 1751, his last few years being spent in a managerial capacity.

The factory was then placed under Karl Mayerhofer, and, in 1747, Johann Joseph Niedermayer took over the position of *Modellmeister*, which he retained until 1784. From 1778 the leading modeller was Anton Grassi, a pupil of Wilhelm Beyer. For the most part he worked in the Louis Seize style.

From 1750 onwards the factory was progressively enlarged, and became continually more influential. After a period of bad trade it was offered for sale in 1784, but as no buyers appeared, Konrad von Sorgenthal was appointed to take charge. In 1805 control passed to Matthias Niedermayer, and it closed finally in 1864.

Under von Sorgenthal the factory enjoyed a certain amount of that commercial prosperity which had been denied it in the earlier period. To describe the ware produced at this time, we might well paraphrase a familiar quotation: *C'est magnifique, mais ce n'est pas la porcelaine.* A colour-chemist, Joseph Leithner, perfected a number of coloured grounds, and was probably responsible for the introduction of a method of gilding in relief. The result of these discoveries was that the white surface disappeared under a spate of coloured grounds, heavy gilding, and painstakingly painted decoration. The nineteenth-century work in the *Biedermeier* idiom is also over-decorated, and noted chiefly for pretentious and meticulous painting.

After the closure of the factory, much remaining white ware was bought by former employees and decorated at home. Ludwig Riedl decorated Vienna porcelain in the Sorgenthal styles. At a later date, white porcelain was procured from other sources and decorated in the same manner, but quality progressively declined until only tawdry rubbish was being produced.

Many of these later pieces (large plates in particular) were elaborately decorated with mythological scenes of a type calculated to sell freely to nineteenth-century middle-class buyers, the slightly draped and voluptuous female figure being much in evidence, these usually disguised suitably as such elevating subjects as *Perseus and Andromeda*.[1] There was, of course, a considerable school of enamelling of all kinds in Vienna during the nineteenth century, much work being done for less than honest reasons.

The du Paquier Period

The first known example of Vienna porcelain is in the Hamburg Museum. It is a chocolate cup inscribed with the year 1719, and the words: *Gott allein die Ehr' und sonst Keinem mehr*.[2] The early porcelain, as might be expected, much resembles that of Böttger. Primarily, decoration of the period is *baroque* – a style in which the factory excelled. *Laub- und Bandelwerk* – leafy scrolls and diapers – are to be seen on much of it, and these themes recur more frequently than at Meissen, principally in purple and iron-red with some gilding. Oriental flowers, both in Chinese and Japanese taste, are commonly to be seen in the first decade, as well as *chinoiseries* and figures in landscapes, reminiscent of Meissen decoration of the same period.

An unusual colour scheme included black, gold, and red – a kind of *Schwarzlot*. This class is mentioned in connexion with Preussler and Aufenwerth, the outside decorators, under the heading of *Hausmalerei*. It can be seen occasionally from Meissen on factory-decorated ware, and similar things have been attributed to Seuter and Bottengruber. Some Vienna porcelain with this kind of decoration was painted by Jakob Helkis, from Trieste, whose work is sometimes confused with that of Bottengruber. Helkis also worked in purple monochrome.

Deutsche Blumen appeared at Vienna somewhat earlier than at Meissen, between 1725 and 1730 to be precise.

The forms used are also reminiscent of the Böttger period, and owe much to contemporary silver and metal-work. A handle

1. This was, perhaps, one of the most frequently delineated subjects in nineteenth-century art. The reason is not far to seek.
2. To God alone and to none other be the honour.

in the form of a panther, the hind-quarters emerging from a foliate scroll, is a typically *baroque* conception to be seen in the earlier period. Applied masks are used decoratively, occasionally below the pouring lip of such things as coffee-jugs, which are both reminiscent of the earlier *bellarmine*,[1] or later mask-jugs from Berlin and Worcester.

Figures were certainly not made in any quantity. They were used as part of plastic decoration on vessels, but less frequently and with more restraint than at Meissen. In recent years some small figures have been attributed to the period, but these are exceedingly rare and highly valued.

The du Paquier period is of great interest, but until recently the literature of the subject in English was extremely small. This has now been rectified by the publication of a standard work which is noted in the Bibliography.

Generally, the influence of Meissen is not so much in evidence as might be inferred from the presence of Meissen artists.

Johann Jakob Ringler was at Vienna in 1744 where he learned the secret of porcelain manufacture. He is of considerable importance by reason of his association with other German factories in company with Johann Benckgraff, also a Vienna workman.

Porcelain of this period was rarely, or never, marked, except for the few pieces known signed by individual workmen, such as Helkis. A specimen signed by Bottengruber (page 168) and dated 1730 has been recorded.

The State Period (1744–84)

The productions of the first part of this period are, of course, in the *rococo* style. Figures were modelled by Joseph Niedermayer and Leopold Dannhauser. The latter's crinoline groups are his best known work. Niedermayer's figures have been identified by a signed group of *Hercules and Antaeus*, and he had considerable influence on the style of the earlier figure modelling. Apart from mythological figures, Callot dwarfs, hunting subjects, musicians, and the like, were all produced, but Vienna figures of the period are relatively scarce. The bases are

1. Rheinish stoneware jugs (*Bartmannkrüge*) which have a bearded mask as decoration.

usually plain, and the slight *rococo* scrolls were more often painted than modelled.

Subjects of decoration more or less follow those popular at Meissen, and landscapes, battle-scenes, and pastoral subjects somewhat in the manner of Watteau were popular. Many were painted by Philipp Ernst Schindler, later to become chief painter. Imari patterns can be seen in the early part of the period.

Rococo decoration of leaves in relief was used, and tureens and service-ware occasionally have the addition of small figures as knops, or for other purposes. A form of *ozier* moulding was employed between 1750 and 1760, and natural flowers, and, less often, fruit, were well painted.

Shortly after 1760 a blue ground with a kind of *caillouté* gilding in the manner of Sèvres (see page 195) was employed occasionally for some of the more important services. The influence of Sèvres can especially be noted in wares made towards 1780, and includes some ambitious painting in reserves.

The Sorgenthal Period (1784–1805)

The work of this period is far more widely known than that of the other two described.

The neo-classical style was, at this time, firmly established and well-marked. Leithner introduced some new colours, including a fine dark blue ground, and a red-brown which is peculiar to the factory. These colours were employed in conjunction with relief gilding. Often the complete surface was decorated with scroll-work and medallions, and sometimes with meticulously painted subjects derived from Angelica Kauffmann and others. The style at this time was more or less confined to Vienna.

Towards the end of the century, and after, we find such typically neo-classical things as *biscuit* figures, principally of subjects after 'the antique', and later, the winged sphinxes of the Empire style make their appearance. Relief decoration of classical figures was, perhaps, inspired by Wedgwood's jasper-ware to be described later. Topographical paintings can be placed to the first few years after the turn of the century. Cabinet cups and saucers, often straight-sided, sometimes the cups on paw-feet, are comparatively common.

Anton Grassi worked mostly in the Sorgenthal period. His figures show a neo-classical bias from the beginning. They are occasionally distinguished, but deteriorated in quality with the passing of the years. He was responsible for some extremely good work, but in a sentimental vein. In 1797 he was commissioned to design a large table-set for the Archduchess Clementina on the occasion of her marriage. Busts of historical personages come from his pupils, Schaller and Hütter.

Not much work of merit was done after 1805 under the managership of Matthias Niedermayer. Some of the figures are of good quality, but generally the years between this and 1864 show a continual decline.

(iii) HÖCHST-AM-MAIN (?1746–?1796)

A factory for the manufacture of *faïence* was founded here shortly before 1750 by Adam Friedrich von Löwenfinck, the Meissen enameller, with the help of two Frankfurt merchants, Johann Christoph Göltz and Johann Felician Clarus, who financed the undertaking. It was given a monopoly for the term of fifty years by the Elector of Mainz.

Von Löwenfinck left before the manufacture of porcelain was undertaken, and Ringler and Benckgraff, already mentioned in the section on Vienna, arrived in 1750. The first manufacture of porcelain took place either in this year or in the one immediately following. Benckgraff left for Fürstenberg in 1753.[1] Although there appears to be no definite information on the point, it seems likely that the factory was taken over in some measure by the State in 1757. It was completely acquired in 1778, and closed finally a year or two before the end of the century.

As we are concerned only with porcelain, the Höchst production of *faïence* must be passed over.

A number of artists worked here who later migrated to other factories : Johann Zeschinger, the painter, and Simon Feilner, a modeller, are examples. The latter was probably responsible for some models derived from the Italian Comedy. He was followed,

1. Benckgraff appears to have assisted in the establishment of the Berlin factory whilst still employed at Höchst.

in 1758, by Laurentius Russinger, whose style in many ways influenced the work of the following period. The most important modeller was Johann Peter Melchior who became *Modellmeister* at Höchst in 1767. His work was mainly in the *Louis Seize* style. Melchior numbered Goethe among his friends, and modelled an excellent portrait of the great German poet. His work was very considerable in quantity, but inclined to sentimentality. Pastoral scenes were a favourite subject, and many have a rocky and grassy base peculiar to Höchst at the time, but later copied to some extent elsewhere. Figures are inclined to be over-decorated, with striped and flowered fabrics well in evidence, and Melchior frequently used a light rose-pink not to be seen elsewhere, which helps to identify them. He left the factory in 1779 for Frankenthal.

Most of the painted decoration is in keeping with the taste of the period and follows the lines already discussed. *Chinoiseries*, Indian and German flowers, figure subjects, and the *Mosaik* border, are all to be seen. Landscapes in purple-carmine monochrome are more or less peculiar to this factory.

Höchst porcelain is not uncommon in England and America, and is usually pleasant, if somewhat pedestrian artistically.

(iv) BERLIN (1752 ONWARDS)

Berlin has already been mentioned in connexion with Frederick the Great and his descent upon Meissen.

With Frederick's encouragement, the Berlin factory was started in 1752 by Wilhelm Kaspar Wegely, a merchant, who had the assistance of Johann Benckgraff from Vienna. Frederick withdrew his patronage in 1757, and the factory was then closed.

Specimens, as may be imagined, are scarce. One is illustrated on Plate 28B, and much of the production resembles this, inasmuch as it was left unpainted. The example illustrated bears an incised mark, thus $\frac{1}{4}$. The upper figure is believed to refer to the body, the lower being the serial number of the model.

A number of models are in existence, including some Italian Comedy figures. Copying from Meissen was comparatively common.

Another factory was started by Johann Ernst Gotzkowsky in 1761 with the assistance of Ernst Reichard, Wegely's *Modellmeister*, who acted as art-director until his death in 1764. His place was then taken by Theodor Gotthilf Manitius. This factory was, in 1763, purchased by Frederick for the sum of 225,000 thalers. After Frederick's acquisition it became the *Königliche Porzellanmanufaktur*, which was necessarily altered to the *Staatliche Porzellanmanufaktur* after the First World War.

It is almost impossible to identify Gotzkowsky's porcelain with complete certainty. A few pieces are known marked with a 'G' overglaze, but much white ware made during this period was decorated later.

Much table-ware of fine quality was made, the best being for the personal use of the King and his friends. The King was in a position to assist the prosperity of his factory in no uncertain manner. For example, lottery clubs were compelled to take 6,000 thalers' worth of porcelain anually, and Jews who wished to get married or to purchase real property had, by a decree of 1769, to purchase and export at least 300 thalers' worth of royal porcelain. It is estimated that daily production at this time was about 3,000 pieces.

Flower decoration was extremely popular, as well as birds, landscapes, and Watteau, Boucher, and Teniers figures. The *rococo* style was handled with competence, and *Mosaik* borders were commonly used. Three of the principal painters, K. W. Böhme, Balthasar Bormann, and Karl Jakob Christian Klipfel, were brought from Meissen.

Figure-modelling was in the hands of Friedrich Elias Meyer and Wilhelm Christian Meyer. The former was *Modellmeister*, and had worked at Meissen from 1746 until 1761. As might be expected, his work resembles that of Kändler to some extent, but the smallness of his heads is a notable idiosyncrasy.

Meyer died in 1785 and was succeeded by Johann Georg Müller, of whom little need be said. He is best known for a series of allegorical models, but his work was generally unimportant. His place was taken in 1789 by J. C. F. Riese, who worked in association with the architect Hans Christian Genelli, and the sculptor Gottfried Schadow. Table-decorations in the form of large centre-pieces were produced at this time, some to the designs of Genelli. A table service and decoration was made for the Duke of Wellington at the instigation of Frederick William III at a cost of 28,542 thalers, and presented in 1819.[1] This is probably the last to be produced on a large scale. Parts of it were modelled by Schadow.

(v) NYMPHENBURG (1753 ONWARDS)

This factory is situated near Munich in Bavaria, and was first at Neudeck. For this reason the early work is occasionally referred to as 'Neudeck-Nymphenburg'. Some unsuccessful attempts to produce porcelain were made prior to the appearance of Joseph Jakob Ringler of Vienna in 1753. His work appears to have enabled the factory to establish itself on a firm basis. It was, for the great part of its existence during the eighteenth century, under the directorship of Count Sigismund von Haimhausen, and his portrait bust, superbly modelled by Bustelli, is in the Bayerische National Museum at Munich.

It enjoyed a somewhat uneven prosperity, the years from 1767 onwards being particularly difficult, and for some time the factory was in very low water.

Of the artists, Franz Anton Bustelli is infinitely the most important. Dominicus Auliczek was a competent modeller who mostly worked in the *Louis Seize* style, and Melchior was at the factory from about 1799 onwards.

It was leased to a private company in 1862, and has frequently copied its earlier work.

Franz Anton Bustelli (1723–63)

Before proceeding to a consideration of the productions of the factory, it is essential to say something of Bustelli. He was born in Locarno in 1723, and may have received his early training in Italy. His work has many affinities with the Bavarian school of woodcarving of the *rococo* period, and, at his best, he quite easily outstrips any other porcelain modeller of his time.

His art is sensitive, elegant, full of life, and of a movement

1. It is on view at Apsley House, now open to the public.

which has been forever crystallized at its most significant point. He had a strong sense of the theatre, and his theatrical subjects are usually his finest work. All his figures have the exaggerated gesture of the actor, to which the folds of the dresses often contribute.

His bases are flat and thin – unusually so; but the *rococo* scroll-work took on a new elegance and meaning in his hands, contributing in no small measure to the sense of movement evident in most of his figures. The scrolls are an integral part of the composition of the figure, not a mere decorative appendage. The Bavarian expression of the *rococo* is, in many ways, both unusual and important, and it is impossible entirely to escape the conclusion that Bustelli strongly influenced it. It remains only to say that, if the art of European porcelain finds its most perfect expression in the *rococo* style, so the style finds its own most perfect expression in the work of Bustelli. It is not too much to say that the fame of Nymphenburg rests almost entirely on the work of this artist, who overshadows all others of the period, including Kändler himself.

He was *Modellmeister* from 1754 until his death in 1763 at the early age of forty-one. Perhaps his death came at an opportune time, since it is impossible to imagine his particular genius happily married to the neo-classical style, and, at the time, the *rococo* period was already drawing to a close.

His name is occasionally spelled Bastelli and – erroneously – Pustelli.

Whilst he was not so prolific a modeller as Kändler, Bustelli's known works are fairly numerous. Models derived from the Italian Comedy (*italienische Komödie*) are undoubtedly the finest, and are as brilliant in conception as in execution. His Cavaliers and Ladies, either separately or on a common base, are distinguished by fine modelling. *Chinoiserie* figures are amusing, and appear in a variety of forms. Little *putti* were a favourite subject, and a series of the gods derived from the works of Ovid appear in this form. A group of a *Turkish Man and Woman taking Coffee* have a background of *rococo* scroll-work which is a characteristic Bustelli flourish. Singers and instrumentalists are brilliantly rendered.

A little unusual are some figures of hounds in varying poses, from quiescent to the most vigorous action. Some trifles, such as cane-holders, are rendered with Bustelli's inimitable genius.

*

Nymphenburg had nothing new to show in table-wares and vases. These were competently produced and painted but, *Hausmalerei* apart, they follow Meissen to a great extent in the early period. Natural flowers were extremely well painted by G. C. Lindemann, Joseph Zächenberger and Joseph Reiss, the last working until 1820. Landscapes and figure subjects are known signed by Lindemann. Birds and fruit were painted by Joseph Lerch. Some attractive landscapes belong to the years immediately after 1770, and, at the end of the century, a certain amount of work in the heavily gilded manner of Vienna was undertaken. The Nymphenburg mark, an impressed shield, slightly resembles that of this factory.

A factory specialty was the *réchaud* or *veilleuse*. These are of extremely fine quality, well-painted, and were made *en suite* with tea cups, sugar basins, and similar items.

After Bustella, the work of Auliczek is competent, but his subjects are, too often, no more than copies from Meissen. A figure of *Kronos*, for instance, is very closely copied from a model by J. F. Eberlein of about 1745, although the base is much more elaborate. In at least one case a copy was exact without even a perfunctory attempt at adaptation. Some well-modelled mythological figures, whilst still showing traces of the *rococo*, are also quite obviously under neo-classical influence.

Some unusual models of animals fighting can be attributed to Auliczek. These vary from the slightly gruesome subject of a horse attacked by a bear (in which the latter has succeeded in ripping the abdomen with a consequent protrusion of entrails), to a realistic group of hounds fighting.

Melchior's work was to some extent a continuation of his work at Höchst, but the neo-classical style is much more in evidence.

Apart from *réchauds* already mentioned, the table-services of

Nymphenburg show little that is important, and the fame of the factory rests principally on its plastic work.

Albert Bauml became factory director in 1888, and some repetitions of earlier things, as well as well-modelled animals and peasant figures, were made about this time.

There is very little information on this factory in English, but the comprehensive three-volume work of Professor Friedrich Hofmann should be consulted. It is listed in the Bibliography, but is extremely difficult to obtain.

(vi) FÜRSTENBERG (1753 ONWARDS)

The Fürstenberg factory in Brunswick was founded by Duke Karl I in 1747 and housed in a castle. No porcelain was made here until the advent of Johann Benckgraff in 1753. Benckgraff brought Johann Zeschinger and Simon Feilner from Höchst, and Feilner later helped to manage the factory. The Seven Years War, added to incompetent direction, made the early years extremely difficult, but after 1770 the factory enjoyed a considerable measure of success. It was transferred to private hands about 1860, and has latterly reproduced much of its older work.

The early porcelain was greyish in colour and of inferior quality. It suffered from minor defects which were not eliminated for some considerable time after production started, not, in fact, until about 1770. Many of the early plates and dishes are decorated with relief-work which helped to minimize the effect of the defective paste.

The earliest example of Fürstenberg porcelain which can be dated with exactness is a plate in the Victoria and Albert Museum bearing the year 1758. This is in the *rococo* style, and, of course, all these later German factories worked in this style from the beginning. They differed, somewhat, in their acceptance of the neo-classical style, some adopting it more quickly than others.

Feilner was responsible for an interesting series of figures based on the Italian Comedy. Most figures inspired by this source belong to sets which may contain as many as sixteen. Bustelli modelled one set of this size at Nymphenburg. Feilner also drew on Greek and Roman mythology for subjects, and modelled some miners and equestrian figures with a certain liveliness. Figures may have been abandoned for a few years after 1760, principally owing to difficulties with the body in use.

In the 1770s the modellers were Johann Christian Rombrich; Anton Karl Luplau; Desoches, a Frenchman; Karl Gottlieb Schubert; and Philipp Hendler. Luplau left for Copenhagen in 1776. A number of models of this period were little more than repetitions of Feilner's work, and of such things are Kändler's *Monkey Band*.

Luplau's best known work is the *Flohsucherin* – A Woman Looking for a Flea – an amusing and original subject. He also copied ivory-carvings by Balthasar Permoser. Desoches did *A Family at the Coffee Table*, possibly inspired by the work of Chardin. Neither Schubert nor Hendler did anything particularly original. Portrait reliefs in oval frames, sometimes blue and gilt, can be assigned to Schubert. A certain amount of work copying Wedgwood's blue jasper may be attributed to the influence of L. V. Gerverot, who was manager from 1795 until 1814. This man worked at a number of Continental factories, including Sèvres, and was at one time employed by Wedgwood.

Pastoral scenes were painted by Georg Heinrich Holtzmann, and much use was made of engravings as a source of inspiration. Some landscapes have been attributed to the Court Painter, Johann Friedrich Weitsch. The *Mosaik* borders were used, and the Berlin taste was followed very closely, including the use of relief moulding on the surface of table-wares. Of ground colours, blue and sea-green were the only two in use.

Vases were very commonly made here.

(vii) FRANKENTHAL (1755–99)

Frankenthal, near Mannheim in the Palatinate, is a little under seventy miles from the French border. It was started in 1755 by Paul-Antoine Hannong, an Alsatian of Strasbourg, with the help of J. J. Ringler of Vienna.

Hannong had already made porcelain in Strasbourg, but the effect of a monopoly granted to Vincennes was to compel him to close his factory, and he thereupon moved across the border.

This venture was not successful in the early years, and the Elector, Karl Theodor, bought it in 1762. Simon Feilner from Höchst and Fürstenberg was appointed director in 1775, remaining until 1797. During the last years it was involved in the wars with France, and closed finally in 1799.

The principal modeller in the early period was Johann Wilhelm Lanz, who had been at Strasbourg with Hannong. He was responsible for a number of interesting and well-modelled figures, mostly having bases with slight *rococo* scrolls which are sometimes a little reminiscent of Nymphenburg. His output was very considerable, and his range comprehensive. Sets of emblematic figures, such as Continents and Seasons, hunting figures and groups, *chinoiseries*, Italian Comedy figures, *genre* figures, musicians, and *putti*, are all to be seen. Perhaps the best-known is a large and finely-modelled *Toilette of Venus* with elaborate *rococo* scrolls.

Johann Friedrich Lück came from Meissen, and although he seems to have been responsible for a large number of models, his work is not always easy to recognize. Among the things attributed to him are some well-modelled Chinese figures, and an amusing Chinese House, as well as mythological figures and miniatures. A figure probably intended to represent the ballet dancer, Camargo, has been said to be by his hand, and resembles the general body of his work. This was derived from an engraving after Lancret.

Konrad Linck, the Court Sculptor who had studied at Vienna and Berlin, was *Modellmeister* until 1766, and retained his connexion with the factory for some years after relinquishing this position. His style is comparatively easy to recognize in most instances. He had a taste for the nude, and a fondness for exaggerated gesture and expression. Mythological figures were a favourite subject with this artist, and his influence was probably responsible for the introduction of the neo-classical style. Among his best-known groups can be placed the *Meleager and Atalanta*, which appears to have been derived from a seventeenth-century Italian bronze by an unknown artist that probably represented *Venus and Adonis*. His work included portrait busts of Karl Theodor and his Consort, Elisabeth Auguste. *Putti* in various guises, a set of the Nine Muses, such emblematic things as the Twelve Months and the Seasons, have all been attributed to Linck.

The work of Karl Gottlieb Lück has humorous touches. He was a cousin of J. F. Lück, and had been at the factory from the early period. He followed Linck as *Modellmeister*.

The work of K. G. Lück, is not infrequently to be found, and he modelled hunting groups, dancers, musicians, peasants, Chinese figures, and such things, with skill. One of his least successful groups, which is almost unique in porcelain figure modelling, is an elaborate and involved battle-piece.

Adam Bauer, who had been Court Sculptor at Württemberg, was *Modellmeister* about 1777. His work is competent, and chiefly of children. Elaborate allegorical and mythological subjects can be attributed to him. Simon Feilner has been awarded some allegorical figures and groups.

Johann Peter Melchior from Höchst became chief modeller in 1779, and his known work embraces allegorical figures and groups, and many portrait medallions whose subjects include Karl Theodor and Goethe. Small children and little *putti* – always a favourite subject with this artist – can be seen during his Frankenthal period, although they are much more common from Höchst.

In table-wares we find that Meissen was, once again, the chief source of inspiration in the earlier period, Sèvres taking its place from about 1765 onwards. The popular *œil de perdrix* of Sèvres – a gilded pattern of dotted circles often used over coloured grounds – was copied, and an unpleasant novelty in the form of an imitation of grained wood was sometimes employed. Service ware covered with brocade patterns, and *mit Goldstreifen* (gold stripes), is to be seen, and the neo-classical style becomes well marked by the end of the century. Feilner introduced *bleu de roi* and a light blue as ground colours, and is also said to have invented an underglaze black. Transfer-printing in underglaze blue was attempted here by Berthevin in 1769, of which – I believe – two examples are known to exist. The process does not appear to have passed beyond the experimental stage.

Vases were commonly made. Many are in an elaborate *rococo*

style, and decorated with painted landscapes, mythological scenes, and figures in the manner of Watteau.

Apart from the more usual things, clock cases, chandeliers, mirror-frames, chessmen, and figures supporting vases and clocks have all been recorded.

The work of this factory is both pleasing and competent, although it does not, at any time, assume the importance of that of the larger factories already discussed.

(viii) LUDWIGSBURG, 1756–1824

This Württemburg factory was started by Bonifacius Christoph Häckher in 1756. In 1758 it was taken over by Duke Charles Eugene. Ringler was director from 1759 until within a year or two of his death in 1804.

Figures are easily the most important of Ludwigsburg productions. Although the body was somewhat inferior to that in use at most of the other important factories, it lent itself to figure modelling by reason of a superior plastic quality.

The earlier figures are in the *rococo* style, and have been attributed to a collaboration between Gottlieb Friedrich Riedel, the chief of the painting department, and Johann Göz. Riedel was probably responsible for supplying subjects and engravings upon which the models were based. He is said to have worked at Meissen, Höchst, and Frankenthal, and ultimately became an engraver at Augsburg. These two may have been jointly responsible for an *Apollo* candlestick at Stuttgart, and a distinguished series of models in the same general style include a *Diana* candlestick, a *Toilet of Venus*, and a *Venus and Bacchus*. The influence of Frankenthal can be seen in some of the work of the period.

Johann Jakob Louis worked between 1762 and 1772, and his work has been identified by means of a conveniently incised 'L'. He modelled birds and animals. A *Turk with a Horse,* as well as a vigorous stag struggling with a hound, are by his hand. Chinese figures have been ascribed to him by Hannover, although Hans Christ (*Ludwigsburger Porzellanfiguren*) attributes them to Domenico Feretti, whose work is not easy to identify. Some vigorous boors carousing belong to about 1765.

Christian Wilhelm Beyer was *Modellmeister* from about 1764 to 1767, when he went to Vienna, ultimately to become Court Sculptor. Beyer, the finest of the Ludwigsburg modellers, worked largely in the neo-classical style in which the *rococo* base is replaced by a formal square or rectangular plinth.

The work of Pierre François Lejeune is difficult to identify, and has been the subject of some controversy. Johann Heinrich Schmidt worked from 1774 to 1821 as a 'repairer', and his known work includes some vases, and memorial columns with classical figures. Philipp Jacob Scheffauer and Johann Heinrich Dannecker worked in biscuit and supplied the factory with models during the later period.

Table-wares, vases, and so forth, follow the usual course of such things at other German factories. The *ozier* pattern was used, and decoration is often excessive. Some flower painting of distinction may have been executed by Friedrich Kirschner.

Many of the later figures are in dark colours of inferior quality.

(ix) GOTHA (THURINGIA), 1757 ONWARDS

The Thuringian factories were small and of minor importance. That of Gotha was founded about 1757 by Wilhelm von Rotberg. *Rococo* specimens are rare, and eighteenth-century wares are mostly in the neo-classical style.

After the earlier period, during which the wares had the primitive quality to be seen in most porcelain from this area, the quality was good, but nothing of outstanding merit has been produced, and no artists of note worked here.

The factory may still be working.

(x) ANSBACH (BAVARIA), 1758–1860

Porcelain was made here from about 1758 under the patronage of the Margrave Karl Alexander. Johann Friedrich Kändler, a cousin of the Meissen *Modellmeister*, was in charge of production. Ansbach porcelain is not well known outside Germany. They did some excellent work, but the quantity still existing is not great.

(xi) KLOSTER-VEILSDORF (THURINGIA), 1760 ONWARDS

Situated near Frankfort, this was the largest and most important of the Thuringian factories. The only name of importance is that of Nikolaus Paul, the arcanist,[1] who worked at a number of other factories.

Figures were competently modelled, but are rarely of much importance artistically. Classical subjects, particularly partially-draped figures of Venus, some Italian Comedy figures in the manner of Feilner, and numerous other things were made, some of which are confused occasionally with the products of Frankenthal and Fulda.

The factory may still be working.

(xii) VOLKSTEDT (THURINGIA), 1760 ONWARDS

The first porcelain to be made here was a type of soft-paste of which few examples now exist. The ordinary German paste was in use by 1767. Like Kloster-Veilsdorf, the factory had a reputation in the eighteenth century for forgeries of Meissen, a practice which led to much dispute. The hayfork mark used could be, and was, drawn carelessly to resemble the crossed swords. This manufacture of forgeries was also carried on during the nineteenth century.

Much of the work is in the Meissen manner, and apart from Franz Kotta, whose work has not been identified with certainty, no individual artists are worthy of note.

The moulded *ozier* patterns of Meissen and Berlin were freely copied, and some vases in a late *rococo* style with figures perched precariously on the handles seem peculiar to this factory.

From the fact that the factory had a monopoly granted to it by the Prince of Schwarzburg-Rudolstadt, it is occasionally termed Rudolstadt, and even Schwarzburg-Rudolstadt.

About 1800 it passed into the possession of one of the Greiner

1. The word 'arcanist' (literally 'one in possession of a secret or mystery') was first used by German writers to describe a man who knew the secret process of porcelain-manufacture.

family, who were extensively interested in Thuringian porcelain factories. It is still in existence.

(xiii) KELSTERBACH (HESSE-DARMSTADT), 1761–1802

This factory started in 1761 with the help of C. D. Busch of Meissen. There was a hiatus between 1768 and 1789, when the factory was in a state of suspended animation.

The early productions were of excellent quality, but the later work was inferior. Some figures were made in the manner of Bustelli, probably by Peter Antonius Seefried who had worked both at Nymphenburg and Ludwigsburg.

Generally, little original work was done.

(xiv) OTTWEILER (RHINELAND), 1764 ONWARDS

This factory was established under the patronage of Prince Wilhelm Heinrich of Nasaau-Saarbrücken with the assistance of Étienne-Dominique Pellevé in 1763.

Paul-Louis Cifflé, the French modeller, worked here for a short time about 1765, and French artists were commonly engaged by the factory. Specimens are rare, and it was even, at one time, suggested that no porcelain was made here.

(xv) FULDA (HESSE), 1765–90

The porcelain of this factory is rare, but of the finest possible quality, and has always been expensive. It was somewhat late in the field, and manufacture was under the patronage of the Prince-Bishop of Fulda. Nikolaus Paul from Berlin's Wegely factory was engaged as arcanist for a short time.

The premises were burned down in 1767 and re-established a year or two later.

Little definite information is available for the period after about 1768, but the style of Höchst and Frankenthal may be noticed in the figure modelling. The presence of Laurentius Russinger, the Höchst *Modellmeister*, has been inferred.

It has been suggested that a type of soft-paste porcelain was manufactured here in the early 1740s under the guidance of Adam Friedrich von Löwenfinck, who acquired his formula from Chantilly.

(xvi) LIMBACH (THURINGIA), 1772 ONWARDS

This factory was among those founded by Gotthelf Greiner, and started work in 1772. The wares made here were chiefly for the cheapest market, and are usually unimportant.

Greiner also acquired a factory at Grossbreitenbach in 1782. This made similar wares, and may be operating today. The same man leased a factory at Ilmenau which is also still in existence. Its productions were in line with those of the others mentioned. Imitations of Wedgwood's blue jasper plaques were freely made here. Gera was taken over by two members of this family about 1782. Nothing important was made, but Meissen was imitated and its marks forged. Rauenstein was founded in 1783 by the Greiner family, and mostly imitated the work of Meissen.

(xvii) HAUSMALEREI

Painting white porcelain at home, or in a studio distinct from the factory, was a common practice during the eighteenth century. For the most part decorators of this kind cannot be regarded as fakers. Indeed, in some cases, their painting is much sought after, and more valued than that done at the factory itself.

There were occasions on which these decorators proved formidable competitors to the factory, which stopped their supplies of white porcelain in consequence. They had, therefore, to resort to devious means to keep themselves supplied, even buying sparsely decorated factory ware and painting over it, or removing decoration with acid to provide a ground on which to work. Much work of this kind was done to special order from porcelain dealers and private individuals who required their own particular decoration, and replacements for broken parts of a factory-decorated service were sometimes handed to the 'outside studio'.

The word *Hausmaler* means, literally, *home painter*, and the names noted hereunder are of those who worked chiefly on Meissen and Vienna porcelain. Their work may be found on other German porcelain, however, although it rarely assumes the same importance.

In the first years of the Meissen factory's life, we find evidence that some of these 'outside decorators' were causing trouble by painting porcelain in cold colours which speedily rubbed off. This kind of work, of course, no longer exists, although one occasionally sees white pieces on which traces of colour remain. These are usually figures, where the processes of cleaning are neither so rigorous nor so frequently applied.

It is not possible here to do more than discuss briefly a few of the more important artists of this kind. It is disappointing to find that no serious attempt has been made to study the subject in England, but this is probably due to the fact that the essential literature is in German, and the principal work on the subject (by Gustav E. Pazaurek) has not been translated. It is included in the Bibliography to this book, but is very difficult to obtain.

The first *Hausmalerei* belongs to the seventeenth century, and is to be found on German *faïence*. The painting of many extant examples is extremely distinguished, and ranks with *faïence* painting from either France or Italy during their best period. A little later we find porcelain being decorated in this way at Augsburg. The first artist of note was Johann Aufenwerth – a goldsmith. His earliest work can confidently be assigned to about 1720, and occurs on Meissen porcelain of the Böttger period. Typical are figures in a landscape painted in iron-red and lilac with gilding. These are surrounded by a framework of *baroque* scrolls. This colour scheme was a favourite with Aufenwerth who used it frequently, principally on tea and coffee ware. Black alone (*Schwarzlot*) is more familiar from the hand of the Bohemian *Hausmaler*, Preussler, but it was also undoubtedly used by Aufenwerth, as well as a conjunction of black and iron-red.

There are some painted *chinoiseries* in the manner of Höroldt as early as 1725, and some in gold silhouette which can fairly confidently be placed to about 1720. Perhaps less likely is the date (1715) awarded by Pazaurek to some simple *chinoiseries* in gold silhouette, and it seems more probable that Aufenwerth purchased white porcelain of the Böttger period at a somewhat later date. Sabina Aufenwerth assisted her father.

Bartholomäus Seuter was an Augsburg painter and gilder who did some distinguished work at a slightly later date. Some Böttger porcelain in white was sold by the factory about 1730, and some of it appears to have been bought by Seuter. He worked in *Schwarzlot* (black with touches of red) and used Watteau subjects. Some *chinoiseries* in gilt silhouette are by his hand, and he is said to have added gilding to early Meissen blue-and-white ware, although most things over-decorated in this way are probably attributable to J. F. Ferner (later discussed).

The work of Christoph Konrad Hunger, already noted as working at Vienna, Venice, and elsewhere, can be identified by reason of a signed Meissen bowl of the Böttger period. He was originally a goldsmith whose earliest work included a kind of relief gilding in conjunction with enamel colours.

The work of Ignaz Bottengruber of Breslau can be found on both Vienna and Meissen porcelain, and is highly valued. He flourished between 1720 and 1736, and can be regarded as the most important of the outside decorators. He worked in a markedly *baroque* style, much of his work being framed with scroll-work and floral sprays. Some of his finest and most elaborate work is executed in a purple pigment, but he also used a more colourful palette. He specialized in battle and hunting scenes, but his classical subjects are often full of an unusual exuberance. Signed and dated pieces exist.

Daniel Preussler and his son Ignaz, were Bohemian decorators whose work was principally executed in black enamel – *Schwarzlot* – which was a characteristically Bohemian practice. This painting, principally confined to the period between 1720 and 1730, is of the highest quality. Their work may be found on both Vienna and Meissen porcelain, but whereas Daniel Preussler is regarded as having worked in black enamel, with perhaps some touches of iron-red, his son used a polychrome palette, as well as a purple monochrome.

Franz Ferdinand Mayer of Pressnitz is another Bohemian decorator, who worked at a slightly later date. Most of his surviving work seems to have been done between 1745 and 1770, and his choice of subjects was extremely wide – landscapes, figures, and mythological subjects being especially frequent. Much of his work survives. A somewhat curious painting of a Nymph and a Faun figured by Pazaurek (No. 318) is not without interest, as I have seen what was virtually a mirror-image of this subject engraved on a nautilus shell mounted in silver-gilt at Nürnberg about 1575. Whether it was then an original composition, or whether it is of even greater antiquity, I am unable to say.

Most of Mayer's work was on Meissen porcelain, and it has occasionally been confused with that of J. F. Ferner, which says little for the quality of the former.

J. F. Ferner worked about 1750. Little is known of him, and his work is often found on defective blue-and-white Meissen porcelain of a much earlier period. This he has over-decorated in gold or red. His paintings, often of pastoral scenes, are unsophisticated and inclined to crudeness in delineation and execution.

Several attempts to make porcelain at Bayreuth during the eighteenth century have been recorded. Johann Friedrich Metszch was a Bayreuth decorator, some of whose work has been said to be on Bayreuth porcelain. The origin of these pieces, however, is somewhat doubtful as to the porcelain, even though the hand of the painter may be inferred with greater certainty. His work can be found on *faïence*, as well as on porcelain made at Meissen, and in China. He appears to have worked between 1730 and 1751, and later was probably employed at Fürstenberg. Masks surrounded by *baroque cartouches* are regarded as being by his hand, and identification is helped by the existence of two signed and dated examples. Landscapes, figure paintings, and *chinoiseries* have all been attributed to him, and he had a number of associates, including Joseph Philipp Dannhofer, a painter from Vienna.

C. F. Herold was accused of decorating at home, and was undoubtedly in a favourable position to obtain supplies of porcelain. He urged in his defence that his work was such that the factory would not have undertaken it. J. G. Heintze caused much trouble in this way. After several warnings, he was actually imprisoned in 1749, thereafter breaking his connexion with the factory.

August Otto Ernst von dem Busch, Canon of Hildesheim, was an amateur decorator of porcelain who employed the unusual technique of engraving the decoration on to the glaze with a diamond, afterwards colouring the incised lines with black pigment which was unfired and will wash off. The remedy is to renew it with anything suitable, for example oil-paint or Indian ink (see Plate 34B). Another Canon of Hildesheim, J. G. Kratzberg, used the same technique. Anything done in this way it would be safe to attribute to one or other of these two, although a Worcester cup and saucer was reported with this kind of decoration a few years ago. It would seem likely, however, that this was an isolated example, since no more have come to light.[1]

The Dutch decorators already mentioned as overpainting Chinese porcelain (a process usually referred to as 'clobbering') also used Meissen porcelain from very early times. Their work was principally derived from Kakiemon or the Chinese *famille rose*, with some landscapes and Italian Comedy scenes.

Mention should be made of defective pieces sold off during the Academic and the Marcolini periods. The factory ordinarily divided all production into *gut, mittel, und Ausschuss* – good, middle, and rubbish – and most of the things thus auctioned were *Ausschüsse*. Pieces with a cut in the glaze scored across the middle of the mark were sold in white. One cut at the hilts or points usually denotes slight defects. Two or more cuts are used for wasters. The date on which this practice was started is a little difficult to determine. It is ascribed to the beginning of the Academic period. I have seen porcelain of 1725 cut across in this way, but it was probably old stock sold later. It is usually impossible to identify the decorators of this kind of ware, but the mark plainly indicates that it is not factory work. Its value must then depend on the quality of the painting which is usually very inferior.

1. The technique had been used for decorating glass since about 1580.

(xviii) FAKES, FORGERIES, AND REPRODUCTIONS

German porcelain of fine quality, and particularly early Meissen porcelain, has always been sought after throughout Europe, and, latterly, in America. We may expect to find, therefore, numerous forgeries and reproductions, more particularly of those things which ordinarily fetch high prices.

There are two kinds of reproductions. The first are imitations made at a price within reach of the less well-to-do purchaser and turned out in quantity. These are decorated by factory hands, and their detection is comparatively easy. The second kind are a more difficult proposition. They are made without much regard for cost, because the things they imitate are extremely costly. Much more care is taken to see that they follow the original as faithfully as the resources of the maker will permit. This applies to such things as the Meissen 'crinoline' figures, which can usually be relied upon to fetch several hundreds of pounds in the sale room. Obviously it is worth taking trouble with a forgery of this kind which can be sold at a price comparable with that of a genuine specimen.

The position is complicated by the fact that from time to time the important factories sold quantities of white ware to outside decorators, usually when they were in financial difficulties. If the decoration is of the eighteenth century and contemporary with the manufacture, or nearly so, the value depends largely on the quality of the work, and in some instances is higher than would be realized by factory examples. The work of Bottengruber is a case in point.

Some of the white ware was defective and second-grade, but a certain amount of good-quality porcelain was either sold openly or purloined by workmen and factory officials for resale to decorators. Moreover, stocks of slightly sub-standard ware were often kept for many years, and then offered in bulk, which leads to such curiosities as undoubtedly early porcelain with decoration of a later period. These cannot always be classed as fakes.

During the eighteenth century numbers of factories made close copies of Meissen porcelain for fraudulent purposes, quite apart from those who derived their inspiration from this factory and whose work, therefore, resembles it.

The position is made somewhat more difficult by the fact that all the German factories used a hard-paste (or true) porcelain. On the other hand, many forgeries of English porcelain, for example, are in the same hard paste, and since most English factories used a soft (or artificial) paste, these things are comparatively easily recognized for what they are.

Forgeries of Meissen, and later copies of early work from such factories as Nymphenburg, Frankenthal, Ludwigsburg, and so forth, can usually be detected by differences in the enamel colours and in the style of the painting, and this is the principal method used. The presence of such nineteenth-century colours as chrome green and a heavy rather unpleasant maroon will immediately condemn.

There is usually a certain 'slickness' about the forgery which is missing in the earlier examples, but it would be unwise to list some of the methods whereby these frauds can be detected, since there is always the possibility that a manufacturer with a more than usually close acquaintance with earlier things will find a way to avoid them.

For instance, it has been stated that all eighteenth-century figures have brown eyes, whereas blue-eyed figures were only made during the nineteenth century. Apart from the fact that brown eyes were undoubtedly given to some nineteenth-century figures, forgers quite frequently read books, and it is certain that so blatant an error would not long go uncorrected.

As a general statement, it can be said that eighteenth-century decorative painting exhibits a certain painstaking and meticulous quality which is absent from later reproductions. The early work will stand up to a reasonably powerful magnifier without noticeable deterioration; whereas the later work is usually slovenly, and carelessly carried out, with bad colouring and sketchy drawing. Moreover, it is difficult for a painter to keep out of his work the artistic idiom of his time, and whilst it was not always easy for the nineteenth-century *connoisseur* to detect a flavour which surrounded him continuously, it is mostly fairly obvious to twentieth-century eyes. Particularly, the sentimental approach of the nineteenth century, against which the last few decades have seen a strong reaction, can date a painting irrevocably.

Meissen copied its own eighteenth-century work in the nineteenth century, often using old moulds, but these later copies are usually accused by bad colouring. Such figures often have artificially induced damage and scratches to make them appear more plausible, but they are seldom entirely convincing. Unfortunately, chips to hard porcelain do not discolour in the same way as those to be seen in soft porcelain.

Some of the Ludwigsburg moulds were acquired by a factory at Amberg, and the firm of Dressel, Kister and Co. have copied Höchst figures, using the old moulds. These moulds have also been used for earthenware reproductions which are not, of course, in the least dangerous.

Karl Thieme of Potschappel was responsible for many copies of Meissen figures, a few of which are more than usually dangerous. Edmé Samson et Cie of Paris have made copies, some of which are quite close. Samsons say that all their copies are fully marked, with the addition of an 'S' to the factory mark. There is no reason to doubt their statement, but it raises a rather nice point in ethics, since they are certainly aware of the possibility of an unscrupulous dealer removing their mark with hydrofluoric acid in order to pass the figure off as genuine, and, more often than not, the acid would not leave any considerable traces. That this is done seems quite obvious from the number of figures by Samson one sees without the identifying mark. Fortunately, their copies are rarely good enough to deceive anyone except the novice, and the greater number of dealers have an extremely high standard of honesty. One known to me invariably removed gold anchor marks from Samson copies of Chelsea figures with acid to prevent them from being passed off as Chelsea by anyone less scrupulous. Apart from considerations of honesty, it is in everyone's interest, collector and dealer alike, that forgeries and reproductions should be known for what they are.

A large group of wares, very common in provincial salerooms, have the monogram of Augustus, 'AR', in underglaze blue. The monogram was used at the factory for royal gifts, and for things intended for royal use. It is extremely scarce on genuine specimens. The examples referred to, however, nearly always have floral panels alternating with panels of Watteau figures, the whole usually being gilded in a manner not at any time used by the factory. Cups, saucers, and such things, are often quatrefoil in shape. The decorator responsible for these was Madame Helena Wolfsohn of Dresden, and they are not in the least dangerous to anyone acquainted with early Meissen wares. The colouring is hopelessly inaccurate, and the type of ware quite impossible as a royal gift. It is, in fact, doubtful whether the lady intended her work to be deceptive. After a lawsuit with the factory, she was forced to change her mark to a crown, with 'Dresden' in script immediately under it. This class is sometimes known to the decorative china trade as 'Crown Dresden'.

The Voigt factory at Sitzendorf at one time made crude copies which are usually no more than sentimental derivations of a kind offered for prizes at fair-ground booths fifty years ago. Yet, even today, one finds them in the catalogues of the provincial auctioneer offered at 'Dresden'.

Not much serious faking of decoration was done on German porcelain. It is, of course, possible to remove slight enamel decoration with acid, although, so far as high-temperature glazes are concerned, it is usually difficult to disguise the fact that this has been done. The acid usually leaves a roughened area in place of the original enamel, and this can be seen under the superimposed painting.

This subject is further discussed in subsequent chapters, since it was a much more frequent practice on soft porcelain examples.

CHAPTER SIX

Italy and Spain

(i) FLORENCE

CHINESE porcelain was well known in Europe by the sixteenth century. In 1575 a type of artificial porcelain was made under the patronage of Francesco Maria de' Medici, the Grand Duke of Tuscany, and it has, consequently, been called 'Medici porcelain'. It is suggested that the first experiments in this direction were made by Orazio Fontana of Urbino with the help of an assistant of Levantine or Persian extraction. The connexion with Persia is in some measure confirmed by the appearance of decorative *motifs* drawn from the pottery of that country. I have, in the past, noticed specimens of Persian pottery of the sixteenth century which have been slightly translucent in places. Examination of the body from which they were made suggests that a certain amount of glaze material was included with the clay, and, therefore, these may have been experiments towards the manufacture of porcelain. If this is so, the 'Persian' assistant may have known of these attempts, and thus have been responsible for the direction of the Medici experiments.

From surviving documents it would appear that the Medici porcelain body included sand, glass, powdered rock crystal (silica), and white earth of Faenza, to which was added a proportion of Vicenza clay. The glass, and similar ingredients, were probably fused together, ground to powder, and mixed with the clay which was used to confer plasticity and cohesion on the mixture. The glaze is hazy, contains minute bubbles, and slightly resembles some early Chinese porcelain glazes in appearance, which may account for the fact that the two have sometimes been confused. It is probable that a proportion of tin oxide was added to the glaze – the *maiolica* technique.

Medici porcelain forms were inspired by Chinese porcelain, Persian pottery, and the native *maiolica*, and these styles were sometimes combined in one piece, although the mixture is rarely incongruous. Decoration was derived from the same sources, nearly always in blue, but occasionally in blue and manganese. One piece known in polychrome is of uncertain attribution.

About forty pieces are now known to exist, but as the last plate to be offered for sale fetched something more than one thousand pounds, the acquaintance of most of my readers with this early porcelain is not likely to be extensive. Specimens are in the large metropolitan museums. (See Plate 35.)

(ii) VENICE

There is record of an attempt at porcelain-making at Venice towards the end of the fifteenth century. Venice was a large centre for the manufacture of glass, and a white opaque glass to which tin oxide had been added was made at Murano. No pieces of porcelain survive which can be connected with Venice at this time, and it is possible that it was no more than a type of glass. A record in 1508 for seven bowls of *porcellana contrefacta* suggests that it was an imitation of some kind.

There is no further record of porcelain making at Venice until 1720, when a factory was started by Giuseppe and Francesco Vezzi, with the assistance of C. K. Hunger from Vienna. Unlike the earlier attempt mentioned, Vezzi porcelain is a true hard-paste of the same kind as the Austrian. It resembles that of Böttger, often fairly closely, and form and decoration usually owe something both to Vienna and to Meissen designs of the period.

Little is known of a short-lived factory started about 1758 by a native of Dresden named Hewelcke, but a few things are in existence which were probably made here.

Another factory was started by Geminiano Cozzi in 1765, and this lasted until 1812. The mark used, an anchor in red, is usually considerably larger than the Chelsea anchor and more conspicuously placed. The body is a type of soft-paste. Production was largely derivative, and in imitation of such factories as Meissen – a statement which applies both to figures and table-ware.

Jar of proto-porcelain. China. 3rd/5th century

Vase and cover. Yüeh ware. China. 10th century

(A) Jar and cover. China.
T'ang dynasty

(B) Vase and cover. Lung
Ch'üan celadon. China.
Sung dynasty

(C) Tea-bowl with 'hare's fur' glaze. China. Sung dynasty

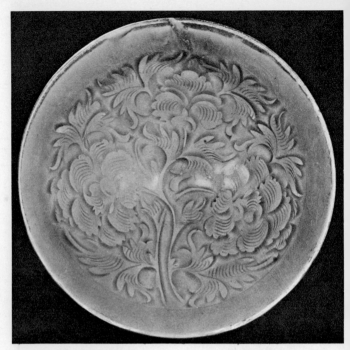

Bowl of Northern Celadon. China. Sung dynasty

Saucer-dish. Ting ware. China. Sung dynasty

(A) Bowl of Chün ware. China. Sung dynasty

(B) Vase with *ying ch'ing* glaze. China.
Sung dynasty

6

(A) Chün waster in sagger. China. Sung dynasty

(B) Vase of Tz'ŭ Chou ware. China. Sung dynasty

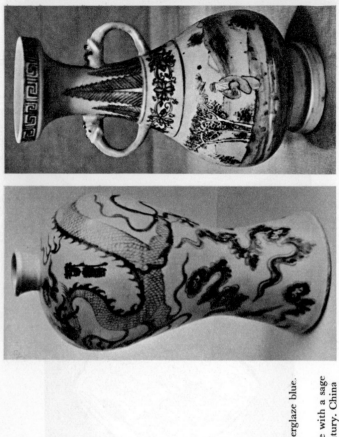

(A) Vase painted in underglaze blue.
14th century. China

(B) Vase painted in blue with a sage
in a landscape. 14th century. China

8

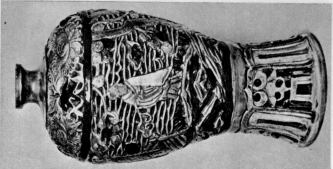

(A) Vase with reticulated
decoration. China. Ming
dynasty

(B) Ewer and cover. China.
Ming dynasty

9

Roof-tile in the form of a lion. China. Ming dynasty

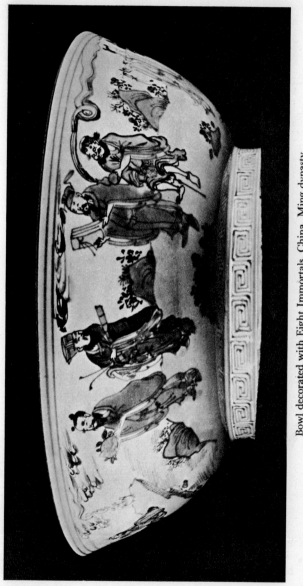

Bowl decorated with Eight Immortals. China. Ming dynasty

(A) Brush rest. China. Ming dynasty

(B) Vase and cover in underglaze blue. China. Ch'ing dynasty

(C) Bottle-shaped vase. China. Ch'ing dynasty

European figure from Tê Hua. China. 18th century

Supper set – enamel on biscuit. China. Ch'ing dynasty

(A) Brush holder. Yi Hsing ware.
China. Ch'ing dynasty

(B) Club-shaped vase. China.
Ch'ing dynasty

15

(A) *Rouleau* vase, powder-blue
ground. China. Ch'ing dynasty

(B) Pierced basket of silver pattern. China.
Ch'ing dynasty

16

(A) Bowl of grey-green celadon. Korea. Koryu dynasty

(B) Vase with pale grey celadon glaze. Siam. Sawankhalok

Pilgrim bottle. Böttger's stoneware. Meissen. *c.* 1715

Tea-jar made for the Archbishop-Elector of Cologne. Meissen. *c.* 1735

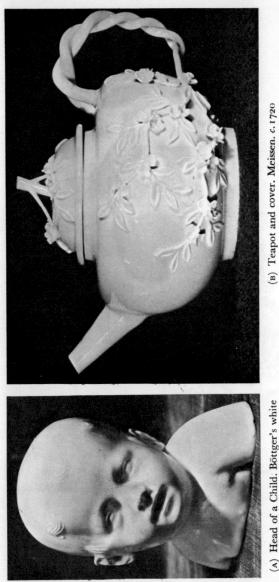

(A) Head of a Child. Böttger's white porcelain. Meissen. c. 1720

(B) Teapot and cover. Meissen. c. 1720

(A) Plate decorated by A. F. von Löwenfinck. Meissen. *c.* 1730

(B) Harlequin by J. J. Kändler. Meissen. *c.* 1738

21

(A) Triton by J. J. Kändler. Meissen. *c.* 1740

(B) Dish from the Swan Service. Meissen. *c.* 1740

Figure of a Magpie. Meissen. By Kändler. *c.* 1733

(A) Tureen, perhaps by Jakob Helchis. Vienna. *c.* 1735

(B) Dish painted in colour. Vienna. *c.* 1730

24

The Medicine Seller, by Simon Feilner. Höchst. *c.* 1753

A Chinese Emperor and attendants. Höchst. *c.* 1765

Lalage, by F. A. Bustelli. Nymphenburg. *c.* 1760

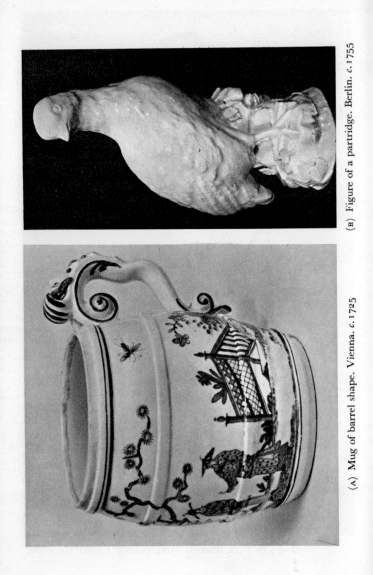

(A) Mug of barrel shape. Vienna. *c.* 1725

(B) Figure of a partridge. Berlin. *c.* 1755

(A) A Tartar Horseman, by F. A. Bustelli.
Nymphenburg. c. 1760

(B) A pastoral figure. Höchst. c. 1765

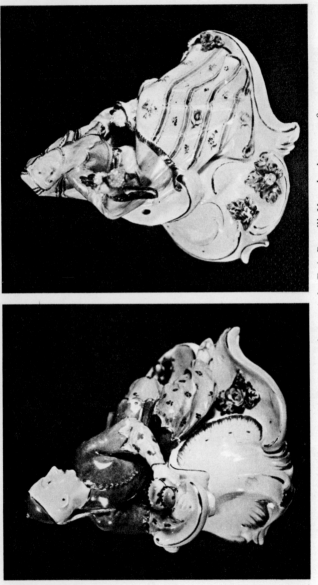

(A) and (B) Chinese man and woman, by F. A. Bustelli, Nymphenburg. c. 1760

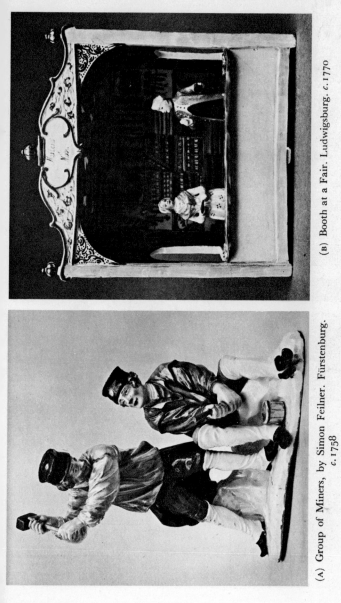

(A) Group of Miners, by Simon Feilner. Fürstenburg.
c. 1758

(B) Booth at a Fair. Ludwigsburg. c. 1770

31

(A) *The Three Fates*, by Konrad Linck.
Frankenthal. *c.* 1773

(B) Two soldiers agreeing on a truce.
Kelsterbach. *c.* 1761

(A) Vienna coffee pot decorated by Bottengruber. *c*. 1725

(B) Cream-pot and cover by Ignaz Preissler. Vienna porcelain. *c*. 1725

(A) Meissen teapot decorated by Bartholomäus Seuter. *c.* 1730

(B) Sucrier decorated by Canon Busch. *c.* 1750

Ewer painted in underglaze blue. Medici porcelain. *c.* 1580

(A) *Cachepot* decorated with figures.
Capo-di-Monte. *c.* 1750

(B) Dish painted in colours. Doccia. *c.* 1746

36

Dr Baloardo from the *Commedia dell'Arte*. Buen Retiro. *c.* 1765

FRANCE

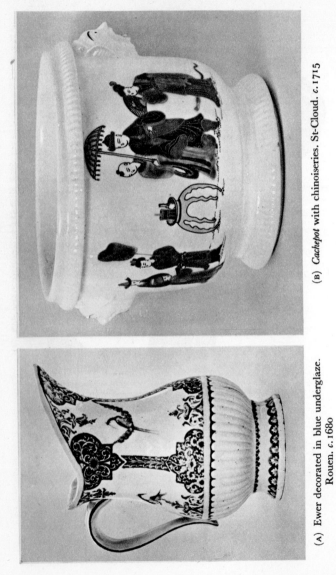

(A) Ewer decorated in blue underglaze. Rouen. *c.* 1680

(B) *Cachepot* with chinoiseries. St-Cloud. *c.* 1715

38

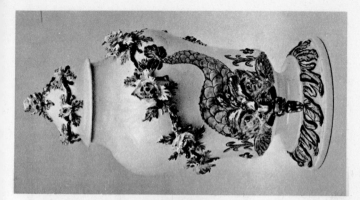

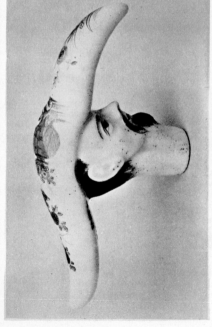

(A) Cane handle. St-Cloud. *c.*1740

(B) Fountain. Mennecy. *c.*1750

(A) Actor in a comic rôle. Mennecy. *c.* 1755

(B) Vase with Chinese figures. Chantilly. *c.* 1735

(A) Bowl with gold silhouette decoration. Vincennes. *c.* 1750   (B) Powder horn. Vincennes. *c.* 1753

41

Jardinière painted with Perseus and Andromeda. Vincennes.
c. 1753

42

(A) *Hercules and Omphale*. Vincennes. c.1750

(B) *The Bather*, by Falconet. Sèvres. 1758

43

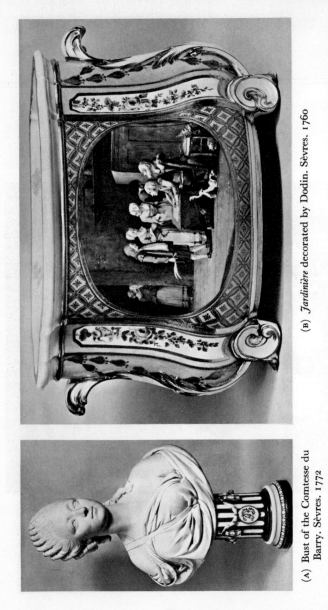

(A) Bust of the Comtesse du
Barry. Sèvres. 1772

(B) *Jardinière* decorated by Dodin. Sèvres. 1760

44

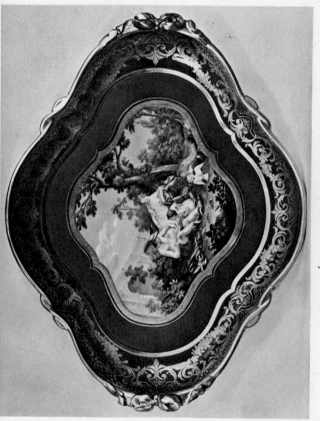

Tray, *L'Éducation de L'Amour.* Sèvres. 1760

One of a pair of vases in Louis Seize style, Sèvres. 1776

Le Baiser Donné. Biscuit group. Sèvres. 1765

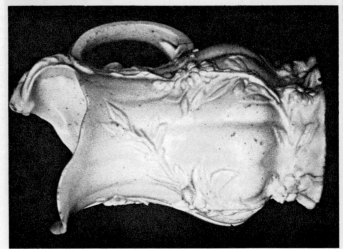

(A) Cream jug. Chelsea.
Triangle period. c. 1745

(B) A Beggar. Chelsea.
Raised anchor period.
c. 1752

48

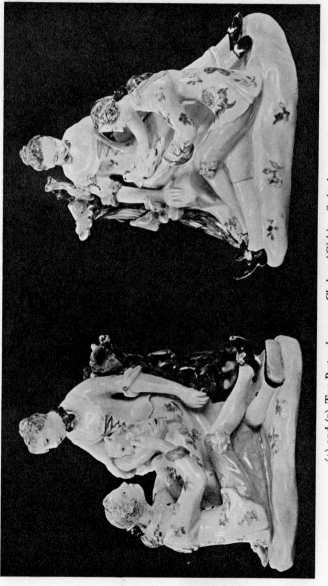

(A) and (B) Two Pastoral groups. Chelsea. 'Girl in a Swing' type. c. 1751

49

I

(A) *The Girl in a Swing*. Chelsea. *c.* 1751

(B) *The Fox, the Stork, and the Water Jar*. Chelsea. *c.* 1751

Chinese woman and small boy. Chelsea. Raised anchor period. *c.* 1750

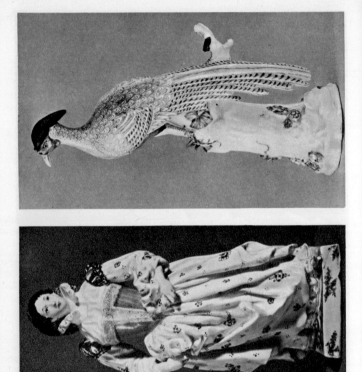

(A) *Isabella d'Andreini*. Chelsea.
Raised anchor period. *c.* 1750

(B) Peacock. Chelsea. Raised anchor
period. *c.* 1750

(A) *The Dancers*. Chelsea. Red anchor period. *c.* 1754

(B) Dish decorated with 'Hob in the Well'. Chelsea. Raised/red anchor period. *c.* 1752

(A) Tureen and cover in the form of a rabbit. Chelsea. Red anchor period. *c.* 1755

(B) *The Reaper*. Chelsea. Gold anchor period. *c.* 1763

Vase in the Sèvres style. Chelsea. Gold anchor period. *c.* 1763

Gardener and Companion. Bow. *c.* 1760

(A) Chamber candlestick painted in underglaze blue. Bow. *c.* 1755

(B) Sauceboat. Longton Hall. *c.* 1752

The Duke of Brunswick. Longton Hall. *c.* 1756

Chinese man and woman. Derby. *c.* 1750

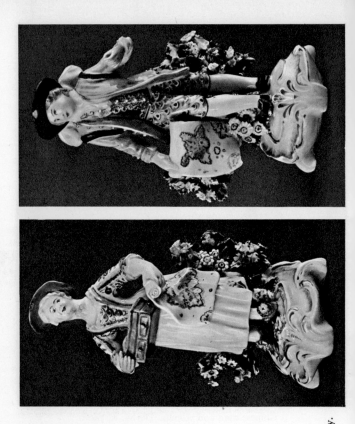

Map-seller and Companion. Derby.
c. 1765

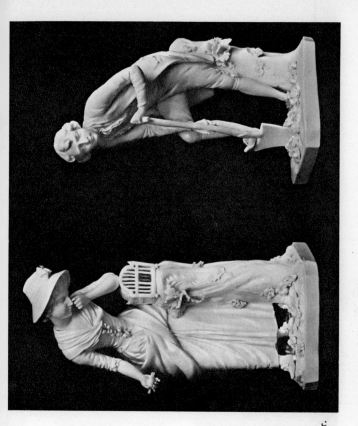

The Dead Bird, by J. J. Spängler.
Derby. *c.* 1795

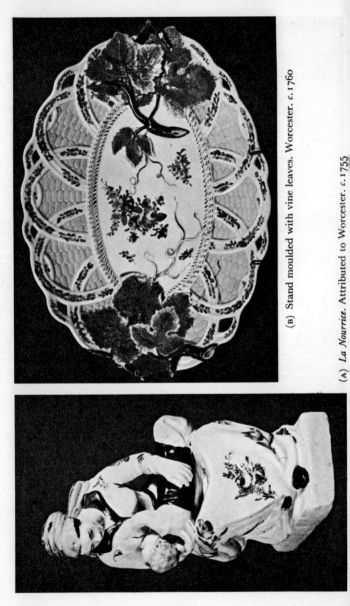

(B) Stand moulded with vine leaves. Worcester. *c.* 1760

(A) *La Nourrice.* Attributed to Worcester. *c.* 1755

62

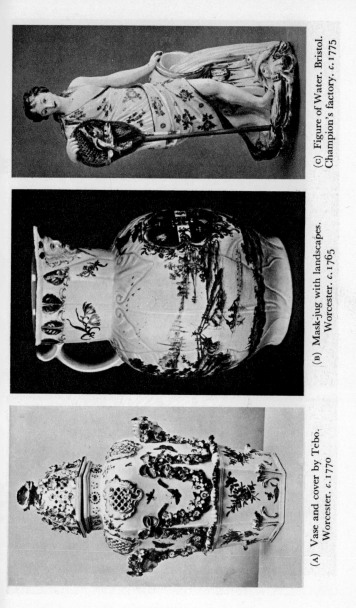

(A) Vase and cover by Tebo. Worcester. c. 1770

(B) Mask-jug with landscapes. Worcester. c. 1765

(C) Figure of Water. Bristol. Champion's factory. c. 1775

63

Vase and cover. Coalport. *c.* 1840

(iii) CAPO-DI-MONTE (NAPLES)

This factory was started in 1743 by Charles, King of Naples, who had married a daughter of Augustus III of Saxony.

Figures of superb quality were made, but are extremely scarce, and examples are seldom seen outside the large museum collections. It is also unusual to find table-wares which can convincingly be attributed to this source. Some excellent miniature painting is to be seen. Only a soft porcelain, with a yellowish-toned body, was used.

In 1759 Charles became King of Spain as well as of Naples, and the Capo-di-Monte factory was removed to Buen Retiro, near Madrid. The new premises were opened in 1760, but the Spanish wares do not generally resemble the Italian.

Buen Retiro porcelain is less scarce than that from Capo-di-Monte, but it is, nevertheless, far from common either in England or in America. The paste of the early period has been well compared with that of Saint-Cloud, which it much resembles. The quality of the wares was consistently very high, and most have a distinctively Spanish flavour in modelling, formation, and decoration. Little work in the *rococo* style was done, the main style being an Iberian variant of the neo-classical, but some examples decorated with scroll- and shell-work are known. *Biscuit* figures were made, but these are mostly late.

The factory closed in 1808, but porcelain was made at Florida, near Madrid, until 1850, where the styles of Sèvres were largely imitated, and some old stock from Buen Retiro was decorated. Another factory was started at Naples in 1771, which lasted until 1806, the stock of moulds then being acquired by the Doccia concern. The porcelain made here is scarce, and only of academic interest.

(iv) DOCCIA (FLORENCE), 1735 ONWARDS

This factory was founded by the Marchese Carlo Ginori about 1735, although it is uncertain whether porcelain was being made on anything more than an experimental scale until about 1745. The body was a type of hard porcelain, greyish white in colour, and most of the early work is in a well-marked *baroque* style. Some important work was done by Anton Anreiter, son of a painter from Vienna (see Plate 36B). Elements of the *rococo* style, already popular elsewhere, do not appear until the factory was taken over by Lorenzo Ginori, who directed it from 1757 to 1791. He made some improvements both to the body and the glaze, but a white hard porcelain body, similar to that in use elsewhere in Europe, was not introduced until about 1800. Soon after he assumed control, a decoration in low relief, usually based on Renaissance plaquettes in metal, began to be much used. These later became popular with collectors under the misnomer of Capo-di-Monte, and they have been the subject of numerous forgeries since. The later work of Doccia in this style, however, can no longer be regarded as forgeries, but as reproductions of their earlier work.

There has, too, been some confusion between the figures of Capo-di-Monte and those of Doccia. The former are in a soft porcelain, whilst the latter are in the characteristic greyish Doccia body which did not alter materially until the end of the century. Figure modelling at Doccia was extensively practised, and, from mid-century onwards, much of it is of excellent quality. Many were left in white, but decorated examples will often show a strong, bright iron-red which is characteristic. The factory is also noted for bright colours on its service ware.

Much of the earlier figure-work was extremely large, perhaps inspired by experiments in over-large figures at Meissen. The fountains of Rome by Bernini, too, were used as a source for models. Other subjects include the Italian Comedy, pastoral figures, peasants, and Oriental figures perhaps derived from Meissen.

(v) NOVE (VENICE), 1728–1835

A *faïence* factory was established here about 1728 by Giovanni Battista Antonibon. A type of soft-paste porcelain was made from about 1752 onwards. It is greyish in colour, and earlier painting particularly resembles that to be found on *faïence*. Flowers are the chief decoration to be noted.

Apparently the factory experimented with a hard-paste; at least we may assume so from a single example in this material which was possibly made at Nove. All other known examples, however, are in soft-paste, which is, nevertheless, somewhat harder than usual.

The manufacture of porcelain was discontinued about 1835.

(vi) VINOVO (TURIN), 1776–1820

This factory was started in 1776 by Giovanni Vittorio Brodel and Pierra-Antoine Hannong.

A type of soft-paste was used. Little of importance was made, and the productions are not well known outside Italy. The Turin Museum has an extensive collection.

(vii) FAKES, FORGERIES, AND REPRODUCTIONS

There is little to add to the remarks already made in the course of the discussion of the wares of Capo-di-Monte and Doccia.

The porcelains of both Capo-di-Monte and Buen Retiro have also been extensively copied by German factories, and these are replete with false marks.

The collector should consider carefully not only the scarcity of these early Italian porcelains, but the fact that they are seldom seen, either in England or in America.

I have not seen an attempt to forge Medici porcelain, despite its extremely high value. Attempts to copy this ware would almost certainly be foredoomed to failure because of the extreme care taken before making attributions to this source, as well as the fact that the whereabouts of all attested specimens discovered to date are well known. The Doccia factory attempted to reproduce it during the nineteenth century.

CHAPTER SEVEN

France and Belgium

HISTORICAL BACKGROUND

THE first successful European experiments in Florence towards the art of porcelain-making have already been described. Medici porcelain, however, was not made after about 1587, and we hear no more of European porcelain until 1664. In this year Louis Quatorze, himself a collector of Oriental wares, granted a monopoly of its manufacture to Claude Révérend of Paris for a period of fifty years. Révérend was an importer of *faïence* from Holland, and possibly manufactured it near Paris, but it has never been satisfactorily established whether or not he knew how to make porcelain, neither have we identified with certainty anything made by him.

We are on much safer ground in considering the porcelain of Rouen. In 1673, Louis Poterat – a manufacturer of *faïence* of Saint-Sever, near Rouen – applied for a monopoly of the making of porcelain, which was granted without reference to the earlier monopoly of Révérend.

Specimens which can be attributed to Rouen with even a reasonable degree of certainty are few in number. The most likely resemble, in form and decoration, the *faïence* made at that factory. There is evidence that the manufacture of porcelain was on the smallest scale, and it appears to have ceased by 1700 (Plate 38A).

At Saint-Cloud, not far from the Château of Versailles, there was, in the 1670s, a manufactory of *faïence* which had been established for many years. The *faïence* maker was Pierre Chicanneau, who has been credited with the discovery of a type of soft porcelain. His son, Pierre, was manager of the Saint-Cloud porcelain factory which seems to have been fairly well established by 1700. Examples are not infrequently to be found.

A small factory was established at Lille about 1711, and a much more important one at Chantilly in 1725.

By 1734, a *faïence* factory in the Rue de Charonne, Paris, which was under the patronage of Louis-François de Neufville, Duc de Villeroy, began to make porcelain, the arcanist being François Barbin. The factory was transferred to Mennecy in 1748, from which fact the porcelain made here is often referred to as 'Mennecy-Villeroy'. This enterprise was again transferred in 1773 to Bourg-la-Reine. The factory at Mennecy was in trouble with the authorities for manufacturing porcelain without permission, more particularly as their work competed with that of Vincennes, in which the King was interested.

The Vincennes factory was probably founded about 1738 by Gilles and Robert Dubois, who had previously worked at Chantilly. These two were not particularly successful, but, in 1745, a company was formed by Charles Adam with a twenty years' monopoly. In 1753 the factory was moved to Sèvres, about which more will be said in the section devoted to that factory. Sèvres was the royal factory, under the protection of Louis Quinze and the patronage of Madame de Pompadour, although some might hold that the rôles were reversed. The first practicable hard porcelain of the German type was made here about 1768.

This is a brief outline of the earlier development of French porcelain which will be discussed in more detail in the following pages. It must be emphasized, however, that before about 1768 all French porcelain, with the single exception of that made at Strasbourg, was of the soft, or artificial, variety (*pâte tendre*). The ingredients used were such things as sand, gypsum, and soda, which were fused together in blocks and ground to powder. To the powder was added a mixture of chalk and clay. This was not particularly plastic, and it was often necessary to add such things as soft soap so that it would retain its shape during the process of formation and firing.

Moulds were used very freely, the material being unsuited for formation on the wheel. It was far from easy to mould or to model *rococo* scroll-work of the partially-detached variety to be seen on German figures of the period. For this reason much of the finer French porcelain is mounted in *ormolu*, thus providing the fashionable flourishes to an otherwise plainly-formed specimen. For the same reason, too, accent was thrown on richness and quality of decoration. No doubt porcelain makers using these early soft-pastes greeted the more severe Louis Seize style and the advent of the hard-paste formula with enthusiasm as bringing some relief from earlier problems of formation. For obvious reasons, only a few of the smaller pieces are likely to have been wheel-thrown.

French hard-paste porcelain (*pâte dure*) probably owes its beginnings to Paul-Antoine Hannong, whom I have mentioned in the chapter on German porcelain. Hannong visited Vincennes, and exchanged information, in the hope of being granted licence to extend his Strasbourg factory, but in 1754 it was forcibly closed, and he transferred the undertaking, as I have recorded, to Frankenthal.

The next step on the road to the discovery of hard porcelain is to be found in 1765 when a chemist, one Guettard, discovered a bed of *kaolin* near Alençon, and from it succeeded in making some experimental pieces. The Comte de Brancas-Lauraguais, who is also reputed to have made hard porcelain in England, was experimenting in 1763 with a certain amount of success.

Paul-Antoine Hannong died in 1760, and his son, Pierre-Antoine, was sufficiently foolish to make over the secrets to the Royal Manufactory at Sèvres in 1761 in exchange for a lump sum, and an annuity of 3,000 livres. Since neither the lump sum nor the annuity were paid, on the ground that the materials described in the formula could not be found in France, no doubt he bitterly regretted his credulity.

At length, the requisite materials were discovered at Saint-Yrieix in Perigord by an apothecary, Villaris, and French hard-paste porcelain was settled in its successful career. The earlier production up to the date of the introduction of hard-paste porcelain, however, is infinitely the more important.

Two notable French innovations were the *biscuit* figure, probably introduced by J. J. Bachelier, art-director at Vincennes, and porcelain flowers, which were also first made at Vincennes.

From the time of Frederick's occupation of the factory at Meissen, Sèvres assumed the leadership of fashion in Europe which it retained for many years. There were a number of factories in Paris principally occupied with manufacturing decorative porcelain, mostly in the style of Sèvres.

(i) SAINT-CLOUD (SEINE-ET-OISE), c. 1675–1773

This factory, said to have been under the protection of the King's brother, was fairly well established by 1700. After the death of Chicanneau sometime before 1679, his widow – Berthe Coudray – seems to have been largely responsible for the development of porcelain manufacture. She married Henri-Charles Trou in 1679, and, at her death in 1722, the factory, together with an associated enterprise at the Rue de la Ville-l'Évêque in Paris, passed to the Trou family. Until this time Berthe seems to have kept control of the factory, and a record of September, 1700, discussing a visit of Madame la Duchesse de Bourgogne, refers to her as 'MM Chicanneau'. It is not possible to regard any existing specimens as having been made before 1700.

The earliest porcelain made here has a somewhat primitive body of fine grain and excellent quality. In colour it is yellowish, with a clear glaze which has few bubbles. Generally, pieces are somewhat heavily formed, and the larger number of surviving examples are in white. Many have a relief pattern of overlapping scales, probably the most frequently seen of early Saint-Cloud specimens.

The white porcelain of Tê Hua was often copied, particularly the sprays of prunus blossom in relief which can be seen on cups and saucers and such things. The fashion for *chinoiserie* may be noted in the extremely rare figures from this source. Grotesque figures, and candlesticks in the form of tree-trunks, were being made about 1731, although there appears to be no record that any of the latter have survived.

The Japanese taste is reflected in the use of decoration derived from the work of Kakiemon, in a palette which resembles the original fairly closely. Pieces were decorated both in an excellent underglaze blue and in enamel colours. The earliest styles owe something to *faïence*, but many specimens are in Oriental styles.

Silver patterns were used in forming many of the vessels, and in this the factory was doing no more than conform to the prevailing taste. Silver-mounted pieces are not uncommon, and leaf-forms are to be seen occasionally.

It has been suggested that the works were destroyed by fire in 1773, and that insufficient money was available to rebuild them. Another authority suggests that the factory went into liquidation in 1766. Later wares were often imperfect, and have a slightly smoky colour.

(ii) LILLE (NORD), c. 1711–30 AND 1783–c. 1800

This factory was started by Barthélémy Dorez and Pierre Pélissier in 1711, and continued until about 1730. The Municipal Council of Lille subsidized the undertaking, but the King refused to allow the establishment of a warehouse in Paris, which closed this market to them. It is probably for this reason that the enterprise was unsuccessful.

Few specimens are known, and these are of somewhat doubtful attribution, but the paste and glaze seem to have been similar to early Saint-Cloud porcelain, although not so competently produced.

A factory for the manufacture of hard-paste porcelain was established in 1783, with a privilege for fifteen years and permission to describe itself as *Manufacture Royale de Monseigneur le Dauphin*. It was subsidized by the Municipality. The founder, Leperre, was the first person in France to use coal for firing. There is, in the Sèvres Museum, a saucer inscribed, *Fait à Lille en Flandre, cuit au charbon de terre*, 1785.

Although little porcelain from this factory still survives, enough is in existence to say that it was of excellent quality, well-decorated, and usually gilded. Both table-services and figures were made. The factory was sold in 1790, and appears to have ceased operations soon afterwards. The mark used was a crowned dolphin (referring, of course, to its royal patron, the Dauphin).

(iii) CHANTILLY (OISE), 1725-1800

Among the more avid collectors of Arita porcelain in the early part of the eighteenth century must be numbered Louis-Henri de Bourbon, Prince de Condé. He provided money and protection for the porcelain experiments of Ciquaire (or Sicaire) Cirou, and the factory at Chantilly was founded about 1725.

Cirou, in an application for a patent in 1735, says that it had been his aim at Chantilly since its inception to produce porcelain similar to that of Arita, and that he intended to sell his products abroad to England, Holland, and Germany, as well as in France.

Cirou died in 1751, and the factory was thereafter in several hands. In 1792, after the Revolution, it passed to an Englishman named, appropriately, Potter, who relinquished it in 1800. This man had previously owned a small factory in Paris, and is reputed to have been the first to practise transfer-printing in that city.

Adam Friedrich von Löwenfinck, from Meissen, is reputed to have worked at this factory as a decorator between about 1738 and 1740.

The early Chantilly paste usually resembles that of Saint-Cloud, except that 'moons' can often be seen in plates, dishes, and such things, from the former, but do not, in my experience, appear in wares from the latter factory. Fortunately, however, to make attribution easier, Chantilly used tin oxide in the glaze during the period of Cirou's tenure. This is primarily a *faïence* technique which provided a smooth, opaque glaze well suited to painting in enamel colours, and easily distinguished from the ordinary transparent porcelain glaze. It is often said that this practice was given up about 1735, but some plates with the moulded *ozier* borders of Meissen, often in conjunction with blue sprig decoration, disprove the assertion by exhibiting a glaze of this kind. It is probable that it was used up to the time of Cirou's death, and even beyond.

It has also been said that the practice of adding tin oxide to a porcelain glaze was not used elsewhere than at Chantilly, but this statement needs some qualification. Tin oxide was, in fact, used by some of the early English factories for the same purpose, but only in small amounts, and the Chantilly glaze is always unmistakable. A normal lead glaze seems to have been brought into use about 1750.

Most early Chantilly porcelain is decorated in the Kakiemon style in a palette which is fairly close to the original. The 'quail', the 'wheatsheaf', and the 'squirrel and hedge' are well-known patterns also employed at a number of other factories, although I feel that the squirrel was originally a rat. Typical lobed Arita forms were used with this kind of decoration. Grotesque figures based on Chinese and Japanese originals were made but are rarely found today, probably because production was small.

At a later date we find Meissen styles freely copied, both the moulded *ozier* border and the *deutsche Blumen*. A type of decoration in black and green enamel was used after 1750 – a style which may be related to the fashion for landscapes in this manner popular at the English Chelsea factory a little later. Later still, the coloured grounds of Sèvres were occasionally imitated, a canary yellow being particularly successful.

Unlike the factories already discussed, Chantilly plates survive in some quantity. The greater number were made from 1750, and are simple both in design and decoration. Even porcelain anterior to this date is not so rare as that from some of the other early French factories mentioned.

The 'Chantilly sprig' – a pattern of small flower sprigs, usually in blue – was extremely popular, and was later copied at several English factories, notably that at Derby. It was also popular in Paris at the end of the century.

(iv) MENNECY (ILE-DE-FRANCE), c. 1735–85

François Barbin, who was first manager of this factory, had previously been a manufacturer of *faïence*. He continued at Mennecy from 1735 until his death in 1765. The undertaking then passed to Joseph Julien, a sculptor, and Charles-Symphorien Jacques, a painter, both of Sceaux (see page 202). The factory was transferred to Bourg-la-Reine in 1773 under the patronage of the Comte d'Eu. Little or no porcelain was made after about 1785.

In 1748 Barbin applied for permission to establish a factory in the City of Paris, but this was refused because a monopoly had already been granted to Charles Adam of Vincennes. Whilst Barbin was not absolutely prohibited from manufacturing porcelain, he had severe disabilities imposed upon him which barred him from copying Vincennes porcelain in any way. It says much for the influence of the Duc de Villeroy that the Mennecy factory was not closed altogether, and the jealous manner in which the interests of the royal factory were guarded largely accounts for the fact that this factory, and others, remained small in size, and, except sometimes in the realm of quality, relatively unimportant. The situation in France was somewhat different from that facing the German porcelain manufacturer. France was a unified kingdom, and the king had a long arm, the weight of which was felt as heavily at nearby Chantilly as in faraway Strasbourg. In Germany, the manufacturer who incurred the displeasure of one of the ruling princes could move his factory across the border into the next State, and continue without any great inconvenience, always provided, of course, that he was astute enough to get out of reach in time.

Probably the first Mennecy porcelain was, in essentials, made in the same way as that of Saint-Cloud. The paste of attested specimens ranges in colour from dark ivory to milky white. The glaze is usually of excellent quality.

Kakiemon patterns were used in the early period, and, at a somewhat later date, copying from Vincennes and Sèvres is fairly obvious. A purple-rose colour is characteristic, and as the factory had been prohibited the use of gold, this is often replaced with rose, blue, or yellow. Flowers were frequently used for decorative purposes.

Plates and dishes are extremely rare, but tea-ware, coffee pots, vases, flower-pots, and such things, seem to have been produced in fair quantity. Small fluted custard cups and covers are quite frequently seen.

Some sophisticated figures were made, although many were naïvely modelled. The modeller Nicolas-François Gauron worked here before going on to Tournai and Chelsea. Italian Comedy figures, whilst rare, are unusual and amusing in conception. Some obvious copies of Meissen models have been noted, and a few pieces in *biscuit* are known.

The mark 'D V' incised appears on some specimens of porcelain from Mennecy. This, presumably, refers to the duc de Villeroy.

The productions of Bourg-la-Reine, which continued to use a soft-paste porcelain, are often difficult to separate from those of Mennecy.

(v) VINCENNES-SÈVRES, c. 1738 ONWARDS

In 1738 two discharged workmen from Chantilly, Robert and Gilles Dubois, arranged to communicate the secrets of that factory to M. Orry de Fulvi, who was brother to the Comptroller-General. M. de Fulvi obtained, through his brother's influence, the use of some buildings attached to the Château de Vincennes, in which the brothers Dubois were installed and given the necessary financial assistance to continue their experiments. The first saleable porcelain was produced in 1740, and François Gravant became associated with the enterprise at the same time.

The production of these first years was very uneven in quality, and about five-sixths of the kiln firings emerged in the form of 'wasters'. De Fulvi, faced with heavy losses, discharged the brothers Dubois, whose reputation in the first place had been distinctly unsavoury. Gravant, however, was made of different stuff, and he procured fresh workmen from Chantilly. Recipes were deposited in his name with a Paris notary in exchange for a monetary consideration, and he supplied the pastes and glazes until 1765.

In 1745 a company of financiers was formed, with Charles Adam at the head. A privilege was obtained in July of that year from the King in the name of Charles Adam which ran for a period of thirty years, and the administrative affairs of the company were placed in the hands of a Civil Servant, Boileau. This man was an excellent administrator despite his somewhat less than honest treatment of Hannong already mentioned.

Jean-Baptiste de Machault was appointed general director

about 1746. He, in turn, was responsible for the appointment of Jean Hellot, a chemist and Director of the Academy of Sciences; Duplessis, the royal goldsmith and a sculptor; and Mathieu, an enameller. A gilding process was purchased from Frère Hippolyte, a Benedictine monk of the Abbey of Saint-Martin des Champs.

Jean-Jacques Bachelier came to the factory in 1748, and was appointed art director in 1751. He, it is said, introduced the *biscuit* figure in the latter year. His was one of the most important of the early appointments, and Bachelier exerted great influence on the factory's affairs until his death in 1791. Mention must also be made of one Hults or Hulst, who held an indeterminate position and probably advised on matters of style. The three most outstanding figures at this time, when the question of artistic development is considered, were undoubtedly Bachelier, Duplessis, and Hulst. Duplessis was responsible, no doubt, for the predominance of silver forms in the earlier wares.

By 1750 the factory appears to have been well established, employing about one hundred workmen. Auscher says there were three sculptor-modellers, two mould-makers, five throwers, two moulders (probably these men were mould-makers), twenty-seven 'repairers', two chemists, seventeen male and female painters, and two female burnishers of gilding. Another authority quotes ten throwers, eleven moulders, seven makers of handles and spouts, ten modellers, ten painters, and forty-six girls who were engaged in making porcelain flowers – a Vincennes speciality which were mounted on wire stems with metal leaves. Of the spread of this fashion to other European factories, more will be said in its place. These workpeople were forbidden under severe penalties either to divulge secrets of manufacture, or to seek employment elsewhere.

De Fulvi died in 1751, and the factory was reorganized under Éloi Bichard, Charles Adam retiring. The King was a shareholder in the new undertaking to the extent of 200,000 livres, and, as a consequence of the royal interest, we find, in 1753, a new set of prohibitions issued which forbade the manufacture of porcelain in France, and which even placed severe restrictions on the decoration of *faïence*.

At the same time the royal mark of the crossed 'L's', previously used occasionally, was confirmed to the factory, and the system of date-marking by letters of the alphabet was commenced. The date letter was placed in the space left in the centre of the monogram, A indicating 1753, B 1754, and so on until Z 1777. The letter 'K', which the French ordinarily use only in words of foreign origin, was included, but 'W', to which the same remarks apply, was omitted. In 1778 the letters were doubled, starting with 'AA'. The system was finally discarded on the 17th July, 1793, finishing with 'PP', after which marks applicable to the Republic were used.

In 1756 the factory was removed to Sèvres, and the letters A, B, and C refer, therefore, to the last three years of Vincennes production.

From 1753 the factory was officialy designated the *Manufacture royale de porcelaine*, and, in 1757, the sculptor Étienne-Maurice Falconet was appointed to supervise modelling, a position he held until 1766.

At this point it is desirable to mention a great advantage enjoyed by the Vincennes-Sèvres factory over its earlier competitors – the interest and patronage of the Marquise de Pompadour. Jeanne-Antoinette Poisson, Marquise de Pompadour, was born in Paris in 1721, and became the King's mistress about 1740 – a position which was probably an essential amelioration of the *mariage de convenance* that was the lot of European royalty of the period. Of the humblest origins, when she first caught the King's eye she was no more than Mme Le Normant d'Étoilles, wife of an official of the Mint. Her father was the son of a peasant, who made a fortune from Army contracts and then had to flee to Germany to escape being hanged for corrupt practices. Her mother was a butcher's daughter, pretty enough to have made some useful friends, particularly a certain M. de Tournehem whose influence gained M. Le Normant as a husband for Jeanne-Antoinette.

The interest of de Tournehem in her upbringing had provided her with an excellent education, and she moved in a circle of writers, artists, and philosophers. Admirers were many, but she avoided *affaires* by telling would-be lovers that she would be

unfaithful with no one but the King. These words were pro-
phetic, and by 1745 she had been installed at Versailles, and her
Royal lover had bought for her the estate of Pompadour.

She soon became patroness of learning and the arts, with an
entourage which included such figures as Voltaire, Quesnay,
Boucher, and Greuze. Her desire for luxurious living led her to
take great interest in the decorative arts, and her utmost influence
at Court was exerted first in favour of Vincennes, and later of
Sèvres. She had some financial interest in the factories, probably
given her for services rendered, and is reputed to have said that
'not to buy this china, as long as one has any money, is to prove
oneself a bad citizen'. As leader of fashion at Court, it is easy to
understand how great was her influence on the fortunes of the
factory and on its artistic development. Her enemy, the Marquis
d'Argenson, records that she once formed a mid-winter garden
for the King of spring and summer flowers at her Château of
Bellevue, all of which were of porcelain so arranged as to be
almost indistinguishable from natural flowers.

The Marquise died in 1764. Her influence is perpetuated in
the name of a rose-pink ground colour – the *rose Pompadour*,
invented, probably by the chemist, Hellot, in 1757. In England,
for some unknown reason, this colour has been given the
name of the Comtesse du Barry, who succeeded to the position
of king's mistress in 1769. The du Barry was, herself, a considerable patron of the factory, but her reign was too short for
her to be able to exert any notable influence.

In 1753 the buildings at Sèvres were begun. The site selected
was near to the Château of Bellevue, the residence of the
Marquise de Pompadour, and work was completed in 1756. By
1759, as the result of financial losses which were partly due to
the badly-planned nature of the buildings, the King took over
the factory, and from this time onwards subsidized it as became
necessary. This created an unfortunate situation for members of
the Court, since the more porcelain they bought, the less were
the King's losses, and both the King and his mistress were
assiduous in pressing porcelain on to frequently unwilling
purchasers.

As soon as the factory became royal property edicts against

other manufacturers multiplied, and were the more rigorously enforced. In 1766, however, the manufacture of porcelain was permitted, provided it was fully and clearly marked, and decorated either in blue or in one colour *en camaieu*.[1] Gilding was the prerogative of the royal factory, as was the making of statues and figures, glazed or unglazed.

Some account has already been given of the finding of the materials necessary for the manufacture of a hard paste (*pâte dure*), and its introduction took place in 1768. For some considerable time both pastes were used, with the hard paste gradually taking the lead. Although it was inferior artistically, it had many manufacturing advantages, and reduced the incidence of kiln-wastage – an important factor in the financial success of a factory.

In 1774 Louis Seize came to the throne, and stylistic changes were soon marked. The death of Boileau, perhaps, contributed, since this administrator had been a man of talent in his own sphere. His successor, Parent, was a failure as an administrator. He engaged workmen from Germany for the new hard-paste manufacture, but, after some years, he was accused of embezzling funds and imprisoned, his position being given to Regnier in 1778.

In the meantime, other factories had made headway, and were affecting the prosperity of Sèvres so seriously that, in 1784, attempts were made to revive previous edicts against them. It was noted that manufactories in the neighbourhood of Paris had increased to such an extent that the supply of wood fuel for the capital was seriously endangered. Nevertheless, for various reasons, the new prohibitions were not put into force with any degree of stringency. The Revolution of 1789 put an end to all these prohibitions, and nearly to the royal factory itself.

By 1786 Sèvres was in serious trouble, the demand for fine porcelain lessening daily as the condition of the country became worse. In 1789 the wages of the workpeople were greatly in arrears, and there was no means of paying them. Many fell away and obtained employment at other factories, and the King poured out money in an effort to save the situation.

1. *En camaieu* – in several tones of the same colour.

During the years of the Revolution the workpeople denounced Regnier frequently to the Committee of Public Safety. Eventually he was arrested, and one of his denouncers, J. B. Chanou, was given the position, which, no doubt, was the reward at which he had aimed. When the pot boils, the scum comes to the top, and Chanou was not content with theft and embezzlement, but tried to involve the cashier, Barreau, in order the better to enrich himself. I regret I have been unable to find that he eventually made the acquaintance of Madame la Guillotine, under whose knife so many better heads had fallen, but the Committee eventually reorganized the directorate, appointing, among others, Hettlinger – a Swiss chemist – who had been associated with Regnier.

The serious financial position was in evidence for several years more, so much so that, in 1795, the Government distributed sacks of putrid flour to the workpeople to keep them from starvation.

Eventually, in 1800, Alexandre Brongniart was appointed director, and in 1806 Bonaparte decided to take the factory under his protection.

Brongniart took over at a time when the most drastic measures were necessary to put the factory back on its feet. But the man and the hour were well matched, and despite the regret which we must feel for his decision to cease the manufacture of soft-paste entirely, it must be admitted that circumstances probably demanded it.

Bonaparte freed the industry from all restrictions, so that, henceforth, Sèvres had to meet uncontrolled competition. But times were now propitious, and there was no lack of orders, both public and private.

Sèvres had its share of enemy occupation, being taken over by the Prussians in 1815, but little damage was done, and they seem to have contented themselves with purloining a few services and raiding the petty cash.

Under Louis XVIII, Charles X, and Louis-Philippe, production continued to grow in quantity, and the quality was much improved. Many new colours were developed. Brongniart died in 1847, and his place was taken by his associate, Ebelmen, who died in 1851. Victor Regnault was then appointed, and he was responsible for considerable technical development, although, artistically, the factory began to decline rapidly.

A feature of the period was the introduction of the *pâte-sur-pâte* technique, that is to say, painting in a semi-fluid white slip – an innovation for which Robert, the head of the painting department, was responsible. It was brought to England by Marc Solon, who left the factory during the Franco-Prussian War of 1870 to work for the English firm of Minton.

After some delay caused by the War, the factory removed to new premises near Saint-Cloud which were opened in 1876. A committee of artists, potters, and critics was appointed in this year to consider ways of improving the artistic taste of the productions, and an annual subsidy was granted to the factory. Artists such as the sculptor, Carrier-Belleuse, were employed, and a certain amount of porcelain in the Yung Ch'êng and Ch'ien Lung styles was produced, principally celadons, *flambés*, and the *famille rose* types. Carrier-Belleuse held the position of art director from 1876, and Auguste Rodin did some work for the factory towards the end of the century.

At one time efforts were directed towards reproducing the old soft-paste body and styles, principally from 1887 to 1900. These wares are distinguishable from the earlier examples, not only by differences in paste and glaze, but by the characteristic nineteenth-century style in painting. A turquoise ground was commonly used with pastoral figures in reserves. *Biscuit* figures were repeated about the same time.

The factory is still working, and its museum is well worth a visit.

*

The porcelain of the brothers Dubois has not been certainly identified, but there is good reason to think that it was made and decorated principally in the Japanese taste, probably derived at second-hand from Meissen Kakiemon patterns. It is thought that the wares of this period were made from a somewhat greyish paste, coarsely potted, and with a clear glaze. The few likely examples surviving appear to bear out the supposition, but there is a large measure of uncertainty in discussing this phase of the factory's existence.

In 1748, porcelain flowers formed five-sixths of the production. These were either mounted on wire stems, or applied to such things as vases, where they are distributed over the surface or cluster around the handles. A good deal of the more ordinary wares were produced – such things as cups and saucers, jugs, bowls, butter-dishes, candlesticks, and the like – but there was small hint of the magnificence to come.

Hitherto, ground colours had, for technical reasons, been little used. Meissen used them occasionally, but they do not appear to have regarded them with the adulation accorded by the French. *Gros bleu* is a dark blue ground used underglaze which was introduced in 1749. Mazarin blue was an English version of this particular colour. In 1752, the *bleu turquin* was introduced. This brilliant turquoise enamel ground is, even today, difficult to reproduce in its original brilliance. The rare *jaune jonquille* dates from 1753 – a yellow different in intensity from the much paler shade commonly used at Meissen. Pea-green was invented in 1756, and in 1757 either Xhrouet or Hellot introduced the *rose Pompadour*. In support of the latter's claim it has been advanced that the colour seems to disappear in its original form after 1766, the year of Hellot's death. A rich enamel blue ground – the *bleu de roi* – was introduced about 1757. Violet, apple-green, and other colours were also in use, but are seldom seen.

The ware at this period was first fired to *biscuit*, the glaze then being sprayed on. Several successive firings were necessary to fix enamel colours and gilding, and the colours sank deeply into the soft glaze – a distinct and important feature of Vincennes-Sèvres decoration.

The expanse of ground colour was often broken up and relieved with elaborate gilding. This was sometimes used in patterns, of which the best known are the *œil de perdrix* – the 'partridge eye' – and the *caillouté* or 'pebble' pattern. The former consists of dotted rings, which was also used on a white ground in enamel colours; the latter is of ovals connected into a network, occasionally copied at Worcester on some of its finer services, as well as at Derby.

Panels of white porcelain were reserved in the coloured grounds, which it was the custom to decorate with various subjects, the meeting of white and colour being covered with gilding which was usually thickly applied and chased.

At this period, flower painting far exceeded in quantity all other decorations; landscapes, figures, and birds being distinctly less in favour. The rarer figure subjects were inspired by such painters as Boucher, and mythological and pastoral scenes, and elaborate battle subjects, have all been recorded. Some examples of these may be seen in the Wallace Collection, which is especially rich in the finest Sèvres porcelain.

The decorative styles changed considerably with the advent of hard-paste, which presented the decorator with many new problems. Although, for some years, a slightly softer glaze than the ordinary feldspathic type was in use, the colours would no longer blend with the glaze in the same way as with that of the soft-paste, neither were ground colours so effective. Some deterioration in the quality of the decoration is, therefore, to be noticed at this time.

Furniture decorated with porcelain became popular about 1760, and plaques painted with a variety of subjects were inset. There is recorded at least one example of a coach decorated with panels in this way, which belonged to a prominent courtesan.

In 1781 we find an innovation in the form of 'jewels' made from drops of thick translucent enamel. This somewhat vulgar effect is rarely to be seen, and may actually have been developed at Saint-Cloud at a much earlier date.

Some attempts were made to imitate Wedgwood's coloured jaspers, and a few large blue-ground *biscuit* vases and plaques of this kind are in existence.

Naturally the Revolution was not without its effect on the factory. Phrygian caps and the tricolour make their appearance, together with an increasing tendency to adopt a more severe neo-classical style. Much soft-paste white porcelain already in stock, and for the most part more or less defective, was decorated and put on to the market, or else sold to decorators in an endeavour to raise money quickly. More will be said of this in its place.

The campaigns of Bonaparte provided inspiration, and the 'Egyptian' style emerged and, fortunately, ran its course speedily. This was part of the 'Empire' style, popular during the First Empire, and such Egyptian *motifs* as sphinxes were freely used.

Brongniart introduced new colours, including the chrome green, which is not seen on any porcelain before 1802, and gold was used lavishly, probably inspired by the *Biedermeier* style of Vienna. An excess of decoration became the rule, and the white porcelain disappeared under a spate of colour.

By 1832, porcelain plaques with meticulous copies of famous pictures were being produced with more technical skill than good taste. By mid-century the *pâte-sur-pâte* process had been devised, and elaborate paintings of all the usual subjects in great variety were being offered for sale.

A principal feature of Sèvres production from the earliest times was the production of vases, sometimes of large size and considerable elaboration. These often took the form of such things as vases fitted as candelabra, whilst some have clocks inset. Vases with elephant heads are a peculiarly ugly design made to flank the *vaisseau à mat* – a vase in the form of a ship.

The porcelain of Sèvres was intended to be a luxury product, and there was no intention to appeal to a wide market, at least, until the Revolution. Usually the finest workmanship was lavished upon its manufactures, regardless of cost. The *ormolu* mounts were of the finest quality, all carefully chased and chiselled after casting. They were extremely popular for porcelain and other materials.

Cabarets, elaborate services, toilet things, inkstands, and the like, are obvious show-pieces, and production for everyday use is entirely lacking.

The *baroque* style is never in evidence. The earlier things are entirely *rococo* in conception and execution, the neo-classical style first becoming noticeable before the accession of Louis Seize.

The nineteenth century is, for the most part, a mere repetition of past glories – a judgement which holds good for almost every country, and in relation to the arts generally. The decorative arts were, of course, mainly in the hands of a conservative section of society, and therefore tended to lag a long way behind the *avant-garde*. For this reason the art of porcelain remained completely untouched by such vital influences as those of the Impressionists and the Post-Impressionists, and, although Rodin did some work for the factory, he does not appear to have left any lasting impression of his presence.

The *biscuit* porcelains fall naturally into two groups – those made from the soft-paste, and those from the hard. The latter came into use in 1769, and, being much easier to use for figure modelling, was widely adopted immediately. The soft-paste figures are much the rarer, and infinitely the more desirable. Glazed and painted figures were made at Sèvres during the early period, but only about twenty examples are known, and all are very highly valued.

A *biscuit* figure, to be saleable, must be perfect, and each one was worked on by the modeller before firing to ensure that it was of the highest possible quality. The soft-paste examples are inclined to have a creamy tone, the hard-paste being chalk-white in colour.

Artists of importance were commonly engaged. Falconet has already been mentioned in passing, and his *Bather* is especially well known. Sculptors of the stature of Pigalle, Houdon, and Clodion supplied the factory with many models for reproduction. A few large pieces are known, and attempts were made to fire very large figures without success. Portraits of the royal family and such notables as Voltaire, Rousseau, Mme du Barry, and others of the time were made, and portraiture was, in fact, quite common. The theatre was a frequent source of inspiration, and we have actors and dancers in variety. Literature was not left unillustrated, as witness a series of figures taken from *Don Quixote*.

Table-decorations were undertaken, some of which were extremely elaborate, and the fashion for decorating clocks with *biscuit* figures was one which was adopted in England at Derby, which also supplied *biscuit* figures for this purpose.

Much glazed porcelain from this factory bears a sign or

workman's mark indicating the artist who decorated the particular specimen. A more or less complete list is given in such volumes of marks as Chaffers's *Marks and Monograms*, and in W. B. Honey's monumental *Dictionary of European Ceramic Art*. It is much too long to reprint here, but close attention should be paid to these marks, since forgers sometimes supply their work with the mark of an artist who either was not working at the time indicated by the date letter, or who did not do the kind of work appearing on the porcelain. The list gives details of the dates of entry and of leaving, and of the kind of work done.

One authority has given it as his opinion that more than one half of what purports to be early Sèvres in private hands, and in some Museum collections, was not *made and decorated* at the period indicated. This question is examined in some detail in the section devoted to forgeries, and, owing to the high prices which old Sèvres porcelain has always commanded, it has been a fruitful field for the faker and the forger. The utmost caution is necessary in acquiring this kind of porcelain which, unless the purchaser has had considerable experience with it, should only be purchased from reputable and knowledgeable sources. Actually, it is very much a rich man's hobby, although prices are much lower than they were fifty years ago.

(vi) STRASBOURG (ALSACE-LORRAINE), ?1751–81

Charles-François Hannong established a successful factory here for the manufacture of *faience* in the early part of the eighteenth century.

In 1721 a workman named Wackenfeld, an Ansbach *faience* maker who may have been at Meissen, became acquainted with Hannong, and it has been claimed that porcelain was first made in 1726. There is, however, no proof of this contention, and the oft-cited service, said to have been of porcelain, presented to the Strasbourg City Council was probably of *faience*, perhaps decorated in the manner of porcelain. In 1732 the factory passed to Paul-Antoine Hannong, and the arcanist, J. J. Ringler, arrived from Vienna about 1750, Adam von Löwenfinck having come from Höchst in the previous year. By 1752 the production of hard porcelain was firmly established and had attracted the attention of the Vincennes administration. Despite the efforts of Hannong to obtain a privilege for his undertaking, the influence of the royal factory in Court circles was amply sufficient to prevent it. In 1755, therefore, Hannong was compelled to transfer his porcelain interests to Frankenthal.

He died in 1760, and his place was taken by his son, Joseph-Adam. Pierre-Antoine, a younger son, negotiated with Sèvres for the sale of the hard-paste secret, with disastrous results to himself. Joseph-Adam Hannong manufactured a hard-paste porcelain at Strasbourg from about 1766 onwards.

Little can be said of the first Strasbourg porcelain of Paul-Antoine Hannong, and it is difficult to separate the few existing specimens from those of Frankenthal. It has been suggested that figures with a grassy mound base may be correctly attributable to Strasbourg, those with *rococo* moulding to Frankenthal, but this is uncertain.

The work of Joseph-Adam Hannong shows some considerable differences from these, the *Louis Seize* style being noticeably in evidence as might be deduced from the time which had elapsed.

Some *chinoiseries*, and flowers reminiscent of those used on *faïence*, have been noted, and there was some use of *biscuit* porcelain for figures. Some tureens have a very curious tapering leg with flutings which ends in an almost globular foot, reminiscent of the leg of a grand pianoforte.

Generally, the later work of this factory cannot be regarded as important artistically.

(vii) NIDERVILLER (MOSELLE), 1754 ONWARDS

A factory for the manufacture of *faïence* was established here in 1754 by Baron Jean-Louis de Beyerlé, Director of the Strasbourg Mint, with the assistance of a chemist, François-Antoine Anstett.

The production of porcelain was first undertaken in 1765, but it was not until 1768 that it was put on a commercial footing.

In 1770 the factory passed to Adam Philibert, Comte de Custine, and the management was assigned to Claude-François Lanfrey. Despite statements to the contrary, it is probable that the sculptor, Charles-Gabriel Sauvage, called Lemire, was employed as early at 1759. He was associated with the modeller, Paul-Louis Cyfflé, and they may have been at Lunéville together.

Cyfflé had, at one time, a factory of his own at Lunéville at which he made, among other things, small figures in a *biscuit* ware known as *Terre de Lorraine*. He was also at one time at Ottweiler in Germany, as I have already recorded.

Niderviller passed into the hands of L. W. Dryander early in the nineteenth century, and has continued working up to the present day, often copying its older wares.

Niderviller was the only factory seriously to compete with Sèvres in the quality of its figure work. Lemire was responsible for allegorical figures with a classical bias, whereas Cyfflé usually preferred such *genre* subjects as the *Chimney Sweep* and the *Pastry Cooks*. Some *Cries of Paris* have been attributed to Lemire. Porcelain flowers were made at Niderviller, as were some large and elaborately ornamented *biscuit* vases.

The decoration of table-wares commonly followed current fashions elsewhere, although especial mention must be made of some well-painted subjects derived from La Fontaine's *Fables*.

There is no reliable evidence that porcelain was ever made at Lunéville.

(viii) LAURAGUAIS, *c.* 1763

A small quantity of an inferior greyish porcelain was made by Louis-Léon-Felicité Brancas, Comte de Lauraguais, some time shortly after 1763 from *kaolin* found near Alençon. Surviving specimens are few and doubtfully attributed.

In 1766 he took out an English patent for the manufacture of hard porcelain. Sir Arthur Church, in his South Kensington handbook on English Porcelain, mentions the Count's *known* acquaintance with Cornish *kaolin*, although he adduces no evidence to support his statement. There are a number of contemporary English references to the Count's discovery. Whilst his patent antedates that of William Cookworthy (see p. 211) by two years, there is no reason to suppose that, even if he had found *kaolin* in Cornwall, his discovery was made before that of Cookworthy, which probably took place about 1755.

Some possible specimens, one decorated in the Chelsea style, were lost in a fire which destroyed an important loan collection at the Alexandra Palace in 1873. Present opinion is inclined to doubt whether the Count made porcelain in England at all, and no extant specimens are regarded as authentic.

(ix) LIMOGES (HAUTE VIENNE), 1771 ONWARDS

The finding of *kaolin* at Saint-Yrieix led to the establishment of a porcelain manufactory by the brothers Grellet, in association with André Massié and a chemist named Fourniera. This was in 1771, but Massié had been a *faïence*-maker since 1736.

The factory was acquired by the king in 1784 and produced white porcelain for decoration at Sèvres. This speculation proved to be unsuccessful, and the factory was resold.

A number of other factories were started in the district during the nineteenth century, attracted by the proximity of their principal raw material.

Porcelain made in the eighteenth century has a yellowish cast, and is usually slightly decorated with flowers and flowersprigs.

Later productions are purely commercial, and consist mostly of services with competent but undistinguished decoration.

(x) SCEAUX (SEINE), c. 1748–94

This factory was founded about 1748 by an architect named de Bey, and was managed by Jacques Chapelle, described by one authority as a 'universal genius', who had some skill as a sculptor, painter, chemist, and physicist.

The edicts were at that time so strictly enforced that it is very doubtful whether more than token amounts of porcelain were made until 1763, in which year Jullien and Jacques took over the factory (see p. 186).

It was not until 1775, when the works secured as a patron the Duc de Penthièvre, High Admiral of France, that porcelain could be made freely and without fear of reprisal. In 1784 permission was given for painting in colours with gilding to be used.

The earlier Sceaux porcelain is rare, and, as may be expected, resembles the later work of Mennecy. The later wares – the 'Sceaux-Penthièvre' period – are in the Louis Seize style.

Flower paintings, and exotic bird paintings, are often of fine quality. Some rare landscapes are in the style of Sèvres.

The factory closed in 1794.

(xi) ORLEANS (LOIRET), c. 1753–c. 1811

A factory was established here in 1753 for the manufacture of *faïence*. It may also have made a soft porcelain at this period, although such specimens as have been attributed are doubtful. About 1760 the factory was taken over by Claude-Charles Gérault d'Areaubert and came under the protection of the Duc de Penthièvre. Nothing of importance was made at Orleans, but a class of unmarked *biscuit* figures may properly belong here.

(xii) PARIS AND ENVIRONS

There were a large number of factories situated in Paris and in the country round about. Apart from the production of those already discussed in detail, not much of outstanding importance was made. The City is the home of Messieurs Edmé Samson et Cie, of the Rue de Béranger, who specialize in reproductions of old porcelain of almost every conceivable kind. There are few collectors who, at some time or another, have not been deceived by some of Samson's work, although the reproductions of Continental wares are usually more dangerous than those of English porcelain.

Paris porcelain, generally, is hard-paste, and, in the absence of a mark, it is often almost impossible to differentiate between factories with any pretensions to accuracy. The older specimens belong to the late eighteenth and early nineteenth centuries, and are either in the Louis Seize or the Empire styles. Sèvres designs were plagiarized freely.

A few of the more important factories are noted below.

La Courtille, 1771–1840

This was established about 1771, and was managed for some time by Laurentius Russinger, the Höchst *Modellmeister*. As might be expected, German porcelain was freely imitated. Well-made *biscuit* figures were produced in some quantity, and this factory was said (by Auscher) to have been the first to 'cast' hard-paste porcelain in moulds, about 1794. This process has been fully discussed in the first chapter, and the claim is, of course, incorrect.

Rue Popincourt, 1782 onwards

Founded by Johann Nepomuc Hermann Nast in 1782, this factory reached a large size and continued to manufacture porcelain of all kinds well into the nineteenth century. It made such curiosities as porcelain clock cases, often freely ornamented with applied flowers, as well as the more usual table-services competently painted with flowers. Copies of Wedgwood's blue jasper are to be seen occasionally, and the influence of Sèvres is fairly well marked.

Biscuit figures were made in some quantity. Its productions have only commercial importance.

Clignancourt, 1775–c. 1800

This factory was founded in 1775 by Pierre Deruelle under the patronage of Monsieur, the King's eldest brother, who afterwards became Louis XVIII.

Productions were of good quality, somewhat in the style of Sèvres. Figures were made, but are rarely seen.

Rue Thiroux, 1778 onwards

Founded in 1778 by André-Marie Lebœuf, this factory was under the protection of the Queen, Marie-Antoinette, and was known as the *Fabrique de la Reine*.

Productions were principally close copies of Sèvres.

Fontainebleau (Seine-et-Marne), 1795 onwards

A factory was established here in 1795 which was bought by Jacob and Mardochée Petit about 1830. Much decorative china of a purely commercial kind has been made, including imitations of Meissen. The initials 'JP' – for Jacob Petit – have commonly been used as a mark. The *veilleuse* – already described – was here made in the form of a figure. These are known as *personnages*. They have been reproduced extensively in recent years.[1]

The other Paris factories are not of sufficient importance to mention in any kind of detail. Their wares have no special value to the collector, and when offered for sale, must be judged on their merits, which are usually slight.

(xiii) TOURNAI (BELGIUM), 1751 ONWARDS

There was a *faïence* factory at Tournai from very early times, but there is no record of porcelain having been made here before its acquisition by François-Joseph Peterinck in 1751. Peterinck received financial assistance from the Municipal Council, and the Empress, Maria Theresa, granted a monopoly for the term of thirty years.

It is known that Robert Dubois was a director in 1753, and it is probably to him that Peterinck owed the formula on which the factory started working. The fact that they had a formula needing little experiment is suggested by the fact that, in 1751, an important order was received from Charles de Lorraine, Governor of the Low Countries.

The factory also manufactured a salt-glazed stoneware in the English manner, and *brun de Rouen* (coarse brown-glazed ware), as well as continuing the manufacture of *faïence*.

In 1752, Charles de Lorraine awarded the factory the title of *Manufacture Impériale et Royale*, and its porcelain rapidly improved in both quality and quantity. Artists were recruited in

1. I am indebted to Mr Harold Newman for much information on these unusual types of ware, most of which has had to be omitted for reasons of space.

Belgium, France, and Germany, and a more or less close connexion was maintained with the English Chelsea factory, whose proprietor, Nicholas Sprimont, came originally from Liège. A number of artists who worked at Chelsea and Derby also worked at Tournai. Prominent amongst them are Joseph Willems, Henri-Joseph Duvivier, Nicolas-François Gauron (who had also been at Mennecy and Vincennes), and perhaps Nicolas Lecreux.

During the eighteenth century the works at Tournai were of considerable size, some hundreds of workpeople being employed, and a considerable and thriving export trade to most of the countries of Europe was carried on.

Tournai was a considerable rival to Sèvres, being sufficiently far removed from Paris, and with protectors powerful enough to render the French king's displeasure a matter of little moment. Many of their copies of Sèvres porcelain are extremely close. There are many points of resemblance between certain kinds of Chelsea and Tournai porcelain, and during the nineteenth century Chelsea wares were copied deceptively.

For the most part Tournai decoration was derivative, but usually with a certain amount of individuality which makes it fairly easy to identify.

A considerable amount of figure work was done, some of which was copied at Chelsea during the tenure of William Duesbury of Derby, probably under the influence of Gauron. I have seen Derby *biscuit* figures which were faithful copies of Tournai models.

Painting *en camaieu* in various colours was a Tournai speciality, and much work was done in polychrome. Coloured grounds with chased gilding are well known, and birds – some exotic, and some taken from illustrations to the work of Buffon, the naturalist – are extremely effective, many of the exotic specimens being painted by Henri-Joseph Duvivier.

After 1796 the son of Peterinck – Charles Peterinck-Gérard – took over for a short time, and the factory eventually passed to Henri de Bettignies who operated it until 1850. It was then purchased by Boch *frères*, under whose direction the earlier porcelain of Sèvres, Chelsea, and Worcester was freely copied, both here and at Saint-Amand-les-Eaux which was under the same direction. The older wares of Tournai were also repeated.

A certain amount of Tournai porcelain was decorated at The Hague at a small factory in that city. When The Hague mark is painted overglaze, the inference that the porcelain was made at Tournai can be drawn with reasonable safety.

(xiv) FAKES, FORGERIES, AND REPRODUCTIONS

Forgeries of early French porcelain are especially numerous, and the subject has not been examined or studied in such detail as with German and English porcelain.

The wares of Sèvres, being especially valuable, have always been the prime target of the forger, and when it is realized that two or three thousand pounds is a not uncommon price to be paid for a really fine specimen it can easily be seen that it offers a strong temptation.

Forgeries of this factory's wares can be divided into two main classes; those which are entirely and completely fraudulent, and those which have a 'faked' decoration on a genuine porcelain foundation. I have already recorded that Sèvres was compelled to sell its stock of white porcelain during the Revolution. Much of this was used for nefarious purposes, and it is certain that none of it escaped the attentions of the decorator, since it was bought for this purpose.

A certain amount of ware with slight decoration was also made by the factory, and the enamel colours have sometimes been removed with hydrofluoric acid to provide a base suitable for redecoration. The same thing has been done by grinding off the decoration with abrasives.

It is usually possible to detect when porcelain has been re-decorated at a later date, and since these hints are equally applicable to all types of soft porcelain, they are set out in some detail under the appropriate heading in the chapter on English porcelain. Sèvres *biscuit* figures which have been glazed and painted show similar defects to those to be seen on redecorated service ware.

Sèvres porcelain which has been maltreated in this way will show some distinct differences in colouring, and in the quality of the painting, from attested pieces, and an acquaintance with the best work of the period is the safest way of differentiating between true and false. The finest collection of Sèvres porcelain in England is in the Wallace Collection, and will repay careful study.

The factories of Paris were extensively engaged in forging the early wares of Chantilly, Saint-Cloud, and Mennecy, of which those of Chantilly are the most dangerous, principally because the opaque tin oxide glaze covers what would otherwise be obvious faults of colour and quality in the body.

The reproductions from Tournai and Saint-Amand already mentioned are often extremely dangerous. These are in a type of soft-paste, whereas those of Paris are in hard-paste. Herend of Hungary made similar hard-paste reproductions. A decorator, Baldock of London, did some redecoration, and painted suitable English porcelain in the Sèvres style. The Welsh factory of Nantgarw especially addressed its endeavours to copying the Sèvres soft-paste body.[1] Thomas Martin Randall made a soft-paste imitation of Sèvres porcelain at Madeley in Shropshire, and the decorating establishment of Robins and Randall, in London, did much painting in the Sèvres style. More or less close copies were made by Coalport, nearly always unmarked, and by Mintons, usually properly marked. All these are apart from work in the earlier style which was done in the late nineteenth century at Sèvres itself, and Sèvres styles were freely copied at many contemporary European factories.

I have already mentioned the Sèvres marks and what may be learned from them. In examining a suspected piece, therefore, due weight must be given to any marks it may have. If, for example, the mark of an artist known to have painted flowers can be seen on a piece decorated with figures, the inference is obvious. Likewise, the date mark should be carefully compared with the style of decoration to see that the two are in reasonable accord. Naturally a date letter prior to 1770 will not be seen on hard-paste porcelain. The soft-paste examples will be coloured

1. Nantgarw porcelain is usually properly marked.

in soft washes which sink into the glaze. Later painting is 'lighter' lying on the glaze surface.

Since soft-paste French porcelain has always been the most highly valued, most forgeries are of this type, and few forgeries of the hard-paste varieties are to be seen which are really dangerous.

Overglaze marks of other factories have been removed from hard-paste specimens with acid, and Sèvres marks substituted without alteration to the decoration. The remedy is not to use marks for diagnostic purposes, and although I include a brief list of marks at the end of this volume, I am, in fact, entirely against using them for this purpose at any time, and for any reason.

A mark can safely be regarded as confirmatory evidence *only if everything else is seen to be right*, but it is certainly the least useful indication of any. Overglaze marks can be fired on with comparative ease, and Hannover, who was probably the greatest Continental authority on porcelain, very truly said that the surest way to get together a bad collection is to rely on marks.

Always suspect the elaborate and the over-decorated, no matter how well it may have been done. It may be genuine, but it is safer to take a hint from the French legal code and assume a specimen to be guilty until it has proved its innocence.

CHAPTER EIGHT

England and Wales

HISTORICAL BACKGROUND

THE early English factories, except for small and short-lived ventures at Plymouth, Bristol, and New Hall,[1] used a soft-paste exclusively, although there were at least three major variations in the manner in which it was employed. The honour of being the first in the field, can, most probably, be awarded to the Chelsea factory. Chelsea is a Thames-side borough to the west of the City of London. The contender for the position is a factory at Bow, in the east, and at one time Bow was given first place, a supposition which subsequent investigation has not supported.

Chelsea began production about 1743, and suggestions that it was operating as early at 1730 have no factual confirmation. In 1744 a patent was registered in the joint names of a Bow glass-maker, Edward Heylyn, and Thomas Frye, a painter, for a type of porcelain made from a clay called *unaker* which had been discovered in the American colonies. Unfortunately, no certain evidence has come to light that porcelain was made to this specification, and the Bow porcelain later to be discussed was made to a formula patented by Frye alone in 1749. At first it was assumed that these two patents had little or nothing in common, but recent research suggests that the difference may not be as great as has hitherto been supposed.

The beginning of the Chelsea factory is equally obscure, and were it not for a mere handful of pieces which bear the year 1745, and the word *Chelsea*, incised into the base, we might well be at a loss to know when it was founded.

The position of *unaker* in English porcelain history demands very careful examination. The clay used by the Chelsea factory was obviously of exceptional quality, and a number of suggestions have been put forward as to its source. Old and some-

1. The New Hall factory adopted a bone-china body early in the nineteenth century. It closed a few years ago.

what unreliable records to the effect that it was imported from China directly remain unproven, but the possibility can be indirectly inferred from an interpretation of some of the scanty evidence available. The Heylyn and Frye patent of 1744 speaks of *unaker* as follows:

The material is an earth, the produce of the Cherokee nation in America, called by the natives, *unaker*.

Within recent years, researches in America have brought to light the fact that porcelain was being made experimentally by Andrew Duché of Savannah, Georgia, possibly as early as 1738.

In 1745, William Cookworthy of Plymouth, who first discovered *kaolin* and *petuntse* and manufactured true porcelain in England, wrote to a friend:

I have lately had with me the person who has discovered the Chinese earth. He had with him several samples of the China ware, which I think were equal to the Asiatic. It was found on the back of Virginia, where he was in quest of mines; and having read du Halde, he discovered both the petuntse and the kaolin. It is this latter earth which he says is essential to the manufacture. He has gone for a cargo of it, having bought from the Indians the whole country where it rises. They can import it for £13 per ton, and by that means afford their china as cheap as common stoneware, *but they intend only to go about 30 per cent under the Company*.

I have emphasized that part of the letter which is obviously the most important for our purpose. Chaffers [1] quotes this, and adds that the Company here mentioned was evidently the Bow Porcelain Company, which (says he) was the only one at that time known to be in existence in England. In this conclusion, other writers have somewhat incautiously followed him. At the time, however, the Bow factory was experimental and little known, and the fact that the person who was with Cookworthy went for a cargo of *unaker*, makes the conclusion that he had brought only samples with him a reasonable one. In fact, I suggest that the Company referred to *was the East India Company which was certainly importing Chinese porcelain in large quantities*. Whether we can go on to infer that they were also im-

1. *Marks and Monograms.*

porting Chinese *kaolin* is another matter, but the extract quoted certainly does not preclude it. The letter does not state clearly whether the porcelain was to be manufactured in England or in America, but documentary evidence is in existence of the importation into England of quantities of *unaker*. Later research may confirm or deny that Chinese *kaolin* was brought to this country in the ships of the East India Company, but if it was so brought, then there is a strong possibility that the Chelsea factory was using it.

At a much later date, in 1765, we find a small quantity of *unaker* arriving in Bristol from Virginia, and samples were sent to Worcester for testing. After this date, no further attempt seems to have been made to sell it in this country, and it could hardly have competed in the matter of price with *kaolin* from Cornwall. Small quantities were imported by Wedgwood.

The body first to be used in England was similar to that developed at Saint-Cloud and Mennecy, and was, fundamentally, a kind of ground glass mixed with clay. In 1749, however, Thomas Frye patented a body which called for the addition of what must have been, after due allowances are made for the purposely obscure language of the specification, a substance known as bone-ash which was obtained by burning animal bones. Bones freed from gelatinous matter contain both lime and phosphates, as every gardener knows who uses bone-meal as a fertilizer. Whilst the use of calcined bone was a new departure in the manufacture of porcelain, it had been used almost centuries before in the manufacture of glass. In small quantities, up to about five per cent, it acts as a flux, that is to say, a substance which assists the fusion of the other ingredients, but it was added to Bow porcelain in massive quantities of up to forty-five per cent. The presence of phosphates can be detected in porcelain by a comparatively simple chemical test, and the application of this test has led to the much more certain attribution of a large amount of early English porcelain. The value of bone-ash to the manufacturer was principally in providing a more stable body which was not so much inclined to warp and collapse during firing as the earlier French body – a considerable asset to the commercial producer of porcelain. With the exception of Chelsea, which appears to have been under the patronage of the Duke of Cumberland, the early English factories had to make their own way, and a substance which provided advantages of this kind was obviously of the utmost value.

It is not surprising to find that the use of bone-ash was rapidly and widely adopted at a number of English factories, and about 1800 the hard-paste body, discovered independently some years previously by William Cookworthy at Plymouth, was modified by the addition of bone-ash to provide the standard English bone-china body. This is now universally employed in England, although it has not, as yet, met with much favour on the Continent, where the principal factories still use the hard-paste formula.

Another type of body was elaborated in the West of England, and first makes its appearance at a small factory at Bristol about 1748. The main ingredient was soap-rock, of which there are extensive deposits in Cornwall. This acted in the kiln in much the same manner as the Chinese *petuntse*. It formed a similar natural glass, but at a much lower temperature. Porcelain made in this way is a true soft-paste, exhibiting few of the hard-paste qualities. Opinions on the origin of its use are apt to vary somewhat, but my own opinion is that we probably owe it to William Cookworthy who was well versed in the letters of Père d'Entrecolles and others, and who was searching for the Chinese ingredients at the time. It is extremely likely that he experimented with soap-rock as a possible substitute for *petuntse*.

Soap-rock was not an entirely satisfactory material, but porcelain of extremely high quality was made from it for many years, and it was not finally abandoned until about 1823. After this date the superior advantages of the bone-china body led to soap-rock being discarded in favour of the new formula.

There are a number of references in contemporary literature to factories operating in and around London between 1745 and 1760.

Vauxhall, Greenwich, and Stepney have all been cited, but their porcelain is unknown, neither is any definite information forthcoming on such matters as location, ownership, and so forth.

A factory at Limehouse, in the East End, is known from an advertisement discovered by A. J. B. Kiddell, in the *Daily Advertiser* for 1 January 1747. The actual locality is still undetermined, although a number of suggestions have been put forward. Its productions are unknown, but, as it would now seem likely that all Bow porcelain contained phosphates, a primitive non-phosphatic bowl decorated in underglaze blue, now in the collection of Mr and Mrs Sigmund J. Katz, may properly be regarded as having come from Limehouse. It accords with what little we know of this porcelain, and cannot be placed to any other factory of the period.

There were a number of factories making porcelain, and porcellanous ware, in Staffordshire towards the end of the eighteenth century, but little is known of them. Ralph Wood, a member of the noted family of Staffordshire potters, made some figures which resemble his work in earthenware.

Viewing English porcelain over the largest possible field, it is fair to say that it was, during the eighteenth and nineteenth centuries, largely derivative so far as decorative styles are concerned.

From about 1750 to 1760 the influence of Meissen undoubtedly predominates. All the principal Meissen decorative innovations were freely copied, including such things as *chinoiseries*, harbour scenes, *indianische Blumen*, and *deutsche Blumen*. The Kakiemon patterns, much used in the earliest years, may have come at second hand from Meissen rather than directly from imported Arita porcelain. The Imari style, discussed in more detail on page 111, was immensely popular with some English factories, lingering on throughout the nineteenth century in the form of the so-called 'Japan' patterns, and many Chinese styles, mostly of the Ch'ing period, were copied directly.

We find that Japanese porcelain, particularly that with the Kakiemon designs, was the more popular as a source of inspiration at Chelsea, not only the decoration but the octagonal and fluted forms being used in the early period, whereas the Worcester factory distinctly favoured Chinese porcelain, which they no doubt copied from imported specimens.

Sèvres *rococo* styles began to gain a foothold after about 1758, rapidly increasing in popularity. These were much favoured at Worcester, lingering on long after the neo-classical advance had ousted them elsewhere.

The neo-classical style acquired considerable momentum soon after 1770, led by William Duesbury among porcelain-makers, and by the pottery-manufacturer, Josiah Wedgwood. One of the predisposing factors was the publication of details of the collection of antiquities from Pompeii belonging to Sir William Hamilton, Ambassador to Naples and husband of Nelson's mistress.

Neither the *Biedermeier* nor the French Empire styles ever became very popular in England, although Spode made some vases obviously inspired by the latter, and other factories occasionally ventured into this field.

For the most part we find, when we come to consider nineteenth-century wares, that technical virtuosity outruns artistic discretion. Much of the work during the first half of the century was a repetition of earlier, eighteenth-century, styles, principally a debased form of *rococo*. Japan patterns were extremely popular at Derby, and the modern Crown Derby Porcelain Factory has continued to use this style on a good deal of its production. Applied flowers, used with discretion on many eighteenth-century pieces, become at this time the flower-encrusted vases and baskets of Coalport and Derby, and it is hardly an exaggeration to say that the fashion came to an end only when the workmen could find no more vacant spaces on which to put a flower.

Gilding was often lavish, but of the brassy mercuric variety, whereas, for much of the eighteenth century, honey gold was sparingly and tastefully applied. Honey gold is somewhat duller than the brassy mercuric gold, but it is infinitely richer in appearance.

The early nineteenth century saw a fashion for well-painted landscapes, which often continued around vases and such things without any kind of formal frame or border. The 'named view' was particularly popular on the better quality porcelain, often in conjunction with coloured grounds. Views of this kind provided a more or less romantic interpretation of the appearance of English, Irish, and Continental beauty spots, with the name written on the reverse in the case of plates and dishes, and on the base of vases.

Feathers and shells, meticulously painted, had a short life soon after 1800, and naturally painted flowers were popular at a number of factories. Fruit is less often seen, but decorative plaques were sometimes painted with this subject.

Factories, of which Davenport is an example, produced plaques copied from such artists as Birkett Foster. James Rouse, who also worked for Derby, was particularly adept at this kind of work.

Designs derived from export *famille rose* patterns of the Ch'ien Lung period were frequently used on porcelain, on ironstone semi-china, and, somewhat surprisingly, on black basaltes made by Wedgwood and others. Chinese figure-subjects in the 'Mandarin' style were especially used on ironstone semi-china by Masons and others.

The *Indian Tree*, a pattern of Chinese derivation in the *rose* palette, was first introduced at Coalport in the early years of the century, and became extremely popular, being extensively copied by other factories on both pottery and porcelain. It is, in fact, occasionally used today.

Transfer-printing in underglaze blue was much used, principally on pottery and the cheaper kinds of porcelain, and, later, printing in overglaze colours became popular.

The porcelain of Nantgarw and Swansea is a somewhat different case, being made to a formula which was purely eighteenth-century in derivation, and was of much finer quality than most porcelain of the period. It did, in fact, approach very closely to the Sèvres soft-paste body, and much of it was decorated in London in Sèvres styles. I have noticed one specimen which faithfully copied an early Meissen design in the *baroque* style, even to the *Laub- und Bandelwerk*, but this was probably painted as a replacement for a broken piece of a Meissen service.

By mid nineteenth century we find Worcester producing a god deal of ornate and over-decorated porcelain with various ground colours which included royal blue, pink, turquoise, scarlet, and green – some with imitation jewels. A service 'jewelled' in this way was presented to the Countess of Dudley in 1865 by the City of Worcester as a marriage gift. The influence of Japanese export pottery is noticeable, particularly in some pilgrim bottles richly gilt and chased. Gilding was in several shades, and the factory prided itself on an imitation bronze lacquer with which these Japanese-inspired specimens were decorated. There was, in fact, considerable interest in Japanese art, which may have stemmed from the introduction of the Japanese colour print into England. The influence of Japanese art is obvious in the work of painters such as Whistler and Van Gogh.

A somewhat unusual derivation from early German work in another medium is provided by an imitation nautilus shell cup on a high 'Renaissance' foot, decorated in gold and colours. This was the work of James Hadley. Hadley was the factory's chief modeller, and later founded a factory of his own which was incorporated into the Worcester Royal Porcelain Company in 1905. His independent work is usually decorated in the *art nouveau* style, mostly on a biscuit-coloured ground.

A somewhat unusual Worcester innovation was enamel painting in white on a dark blue ground, inspired by a type of Limoges enamel. This was executed by Thomas Bott, who sometimes favoured slightly over-plump nudes reminiscent of the work of Etty. These were at one time valued extremely highly and favourably attracted the notice of the Prince-Consort.

Worcester drew on the work of such artists as Landseer, Watteau, and Sir Joshua Reynolds. Even Holbein was laid under contribution. They introduced an ivory porcelain body that had considerable success at the time. It was used for figures of the Venus de Milo, and of the nymph Iris, principally, one assumes, because these subjects provided excuse for rendering the undraped female figure in a manner which could be exhibited in the Victorian middle-class china-cabinet without offending the more delicate susceptibilities.

Parian, the nineteenth-century equivalent of the Derby *biscuit* body, was discovered by Copeland about 1846 and extensively employed in the production of figures.

Mention must also be made of an innovation from the small

Irish Belleek factory. This was an extremely thin porcelain covered by a thick glaze which reflected light somewhat in the manner of mother-of-pearl. This factory did much work shaped as shells which plumbs the depths in an age not at any time noted for good taste. Some delicately modelled baskets with much fragile applied ornament from the same factory are more acceptable.

A curious fashion for Moorish and Persian styles possibly stemmed from the admiration accorded (not at all unworthily) to some kinds of Near Eastern pottery, principally Turkish pottery from Isnik in Anatolia, which was, at the time, quite erroneously called 'Rhodian' because fragments were found at Lindos, in the island of Rhodes. This style was used at Worcester and elsewhere.

At Minton's, Marc Solon introduced *pâte-sur-pâte* from Sèvres, and Worcester made much porcelain carefully pierced with holes in elaborate patterns, probably inspired by the 'devil's work' of the late Ming period.

Towards the end of the century we find the beginnings of the *art nouveau* style which, in the case of some of my middle-aged readers, probably formed the background of their childhood so far as interior decoration is concerned.

Latterly Wedgwood have achieved considerable distinction with some excellently formed ware having clean, severe lines. This may ultimately emerge as the principal style of the twentieth century. Decorations by Eric Ravilious and figures by John Skeaping are examples of an enlightened attitude at variance with that of some of the more conservative manufacturers who are still wedded to repetitions of eighteenth- and nineteenth-century styles.

Studio potters suffer badly from an adulation of Sung porcelain. This belongs to eleventh- and twelfth-century China, not to Europe in the atomic age. No doubt it was originally a healthy reaction from the bad taste of the nineteenth century, but, personally, I must confess to gaining more satisfaction from some modern laboratory ceramics than from derivations of this kind.

No doubt all works of art must, to some extent, be based on

the productions of the past, but these should only be used as a source of inspiration upon which to build.

(i) CHELSEA (S.W. LONDON), 1743–85

The year 1743 as the possible date at which this factory was established is not certain, but it can be inferred from the existence of a number of small jugs of extremely fine quality which occasionally bear the year 1745 incised into the base. Obviously such accomplished work would not be done in the first year or so of the factory's life, but argues a certain experience. It seems probable that the formula was given to the founders of the factory, Nicholas Sprimont and Charles Gouyn, by a chemist, Thomas Briand, who demonstrated a fine white porcelain to the Royal Society in 1742. We have very little information about Briand, but it is at least possible that he was a migratory workman from one of the French factories – perhaps Saint-Cloud. The jugs themselves are moulded in the form of goats with a modelled bee applied, and are referred to as 'Goat and Bee' jugs. They are based on a silver pattern, and a few silver jugs in this form are in existence.

Like most of the early English factories, the history of Chelsea is very badly documented, and we are usually in the position of having to make inferences from old rate-books, newspaper advertisements, letters, and things of this sort when we attempt to reconstruct the course of events. This work is far from complete, and the skeleton structure is constantly receiving additions from new research. On the other hand, it seems unlikely that anything will now be discovered which will upset present attributions, except in a small minority of instances.

The founders of the Chelsea factory appear to have been Nicholas Sprimont, a silversmith, who came originally from Liège, Charles Gouyn, a jeweller who probably provided the capital, and Thomas Briand, already mentioned. The factory was situated at Lawrence Street, Chelsea, and the Chelsea rate-books show Sprimont to have been in residence in 1748. Unfortunately, the rate-books before this date are missing, so the exact date of the commencement of his tenancy cannot be fixed with certainty.

Fragments have been excavated on the old kiln-sites which show continuity between the earliest productions and those of the later period, and, from a number of advertisements in existence, it is obvious that Gouyn severed his connexion with the factory about 1750. Briand seceded some years before this date, and some remarks on his later career will be found elsewhere in this chapter. About 1750 Sprimont found a patron in the Duke of Cumberland, the subject of a very distinguished small portrait bust made at this time, and the Duke appears to have acted through the agency of his secretary, Sir Everard Fawkener.

We have an important letter dated June 1751, from Sir Charles Hanbury Williams, Ambassador to the Saxon Court at Dresden, who wrote as follows:

I received a letter about ten days ago from Sir Everard Fawkener who is, I believe, concerned in the manufacture of china at Chelsea. He desired me to send over models for different pieces from hence in order to furnish the undertakers with good designs, and would have me send over fifty or three score pounds worth. But I thought it better and cheaper for the manufacturers to give them leave to take any of my china from Holland House and to copy what they like.

This letter should be remembered when we later consider the influence of Meissen porcelain on that of Chelsea.

In 1757 Sprimont contracted an illness, possibly some form of gout, and was forced to travel extensively to various spas in search of relief. It is at least possible that he visited Tournai during this period, and became infected with the Tournai predilection for Sèvres styles, since we find the factory once more at work in 1758 and producing porcelain which is much more in the manner of Sèvres.

In 1763 Sprimont fell ill once more, and it would seem that the factory was at this time partially closed. It was certainly offered for sale, as contemporary advertisements prove, and these are worded in such a manner as to imply that little work was being done. In 1770 it was finally purchased by William Duesbury of Derby, and henceforward the porcelain produced is generally termed 'Chelsea-Derby'. It is extremely difficult, and in some cases impossible, to be certain whether any given model was, at this period, made at Chelsea or in Derby, but, for the most part, no importance need be attached to exactness in the matter after about 1770 .

During the earliest period the Chelsea factory used the mark of an incised triangle, although this mark is also known in blue underglaze. Care is needed in identifying specimens with the incised mark. Some of the triangles have been scratched in during modern times, for the reason that marked examples are apt to be somewhat more valuable than unmarked. Since the genuine mark was incised into the raw clay *before* firing, and the 'faked' mark has been incised *after* firing, the difference is usually apparent under a magnifying glass. Provided a specimen marked later has not been damaged in any way by the operation, and the price is no higher than would normally be asked for an unmarked example, there is no need to reject it, since all porcelain of this period is extremely scarce. This mark was discontinued about 1750.

From 1750 to about 1752 the factory employed the mark of an anchor raised on a small medallion – the so-called 'raised anchor' mark. This was probably introduced to prevent 'outside decorators' from marking porcelain from other factories in order to pass it off as coming from Chelsea.

About 1750 the factory used a crown intersected by a trident in underglaze blue. So far only about ten pieces have been identified bearing this mark.

The mark from about 1752 was a small anchor painted in red. On figures particularly this was often placed in an inconspicuous position, whereas anchors on forgeries are usually large and prominent. About 1755, the gold anchor made its appearance, was used until 1770, and occasionally appears in the Chelsea-Derby period.[1] Some marks attributable to this period appear in the index of marks.

1. Gold anchor marked pieces in the neo-classical style may be regarded as 'Chelsea-Derby'.

We are fortunate in having a number of surviving auction sale catalogues of Chelsea porcelain, since it was the practice to sell at least some of the manufacture in this way. The two most useful belong to the years 1755 and 1756, and help us to date a large number of models with accuracy.

Of the artists who worked at Chelsea, William Duvivier came to England about 1743. It is possible that he had worked at Tournai as a *faïence* painter. He died in 1755. When he came to England he brought with him his son, Henri-Joseph Duvivier, who was born in 1740, and who learned the art of painting on porcelain at Chelsea. He went to Tournai in 1763, when the Chelsea factory was offered for sale, and became chief painter there. Zachariah Boreman learned the art of painting on porcelain at Chelsea, and went on to Derby when the London establishment closed. Jeffryes Hamet O'Neale, the Irish miniature painter and 'outside decorator', first learned his art at Chelsea, possibly under William Duvivier, and he may have taken young Henri-Joseph under his tutelage at the death of the father. Richard Askew, painter of cupids, worked at Chelsea, and went on to Derby in 1772.

Joseph Willems, a sculptor of note who came originally from Belgium, modelled a number of fine things for Chelsea, returned to Tournai in 1766, and died in the same year. Several Chelsea models for which he had been responsible were found among his effects.

The sculptor, Louis-François Roubiliac, was one of Sprimont's intimates, and he has been credited with modelling for the factory. Attributions are not, however, very certain, although a few pieces are similar to his work in other mediums. A group of figures marked with an impressed 'R' were formerly ascribed to this artist, but they bear no relation to his other work, and the attribution is quite definitely erroneous. Nicolas Gauron, from Tournai, worked at Chelsea for a time about 1773, and Nicolas Lecreux may have done the same. This last suggestion rests principally on the close similarity of some later Chelsea-Derby or Derby models to his known work at Tournai.

The names of other artists are known, but little can be said of their work since documentary evidence is not available. Of the two catalogues previously mentioned, that for 1755 has been reprinted by William King (*Chelsea Porcelain*) and that for 1756 by myself (*Eighteenth-Century English Porcelain*). Another, for 1761, is reprinted by Dr F. Severne Mackenna (*Chelsea Porcelain: The Gold Anchor Wares*).

Chelsea productions up to 1750 were, for the most part, copied from contemporary silver, or, less often, from the white porcelain of Tê Hua. Silver forms vary considerably, an acanthus-leaf type being especially fine and desirable. The Tê Hua-inspired examples are mostly cups and the like, with prunus and tea-plant *motifs* raised in relief. These were made at the end of the period, and many belong to the first part of the raised anchor period. Most triangle wares are in white, but a few specimens decorated in enamel colours may properly be attributed to the extreme end of the period. Few figures are known to have been made, and these, likewise, are relatively late.

The raised anchor period – 1750–2 – shows a widening range of interests, and Kakiemon designs in colours were freely used. Arita fluted and octagonal shapes were adopted, and sometimes employed in conjunction with European decorations. Decorative *motifs* which appear far more frequently on red anchor porcelain can be seen occasionally at this time. Many of the decorations were derived from early Meissen originals. Few figures were made, but some, such as the Italian Comedy figure of Isabella d'Andreini, are of the highest possible quality.

The early part of the following red anchor period shows considerable invention as well as many close imitations of Meissen styles. Harbour scenes in the manner of Herold were probably painted by William Duvivier. Some fables, taken from Aesop and sketched with a humorous brush, were done by the young O'Neale in panels on a service at one time in the possession of Warren Hastings. Other rather more serious and elaborate 'Fable' paintings have been attributed to Jean Lefebre, about whom little is known. At a slightly later date, *deutsche Blumen* from Meissen were freely used, and the small insects added at the German factory to hide faults in the glaze were employed at Chelsea for the same reason. About 1755 paintings of natural flowers and plants were popular, and are much prized today.

These were inspired by plates in the *Gardener's Dictionary* of Philip Miller, who was gardener to the Worshipful Company of Apothecaries at their Botanick Garden in Chelsea. This garden was under the patronage of Sir Hans Sloane, who has given his name to Sloane Square.

The figures made at this time, whilst quite often derived from Kändler models, are frequently superior to the originals in quality, and they are undoubtedly the finest to be produced by any European factory. There is little to be gained by listing them *in extenso*, but such subjects as the gods and goddesses of Greece and Rome, Italian Comedy characters, emblematic figures in great variety, figures based on the contemporary theatre and things of this sort, were freely made. These form the cream of old English porcelain figures for which extremely high prices are paid, several hundreds of pounds for a single example being quite common.

Mention must be made of tureens in the form of fruit, vegetables, and, less often, of animals and birds. These were popular at Meissen in the late 1740s, and most Chelsea examples belong to the years between 1753 and 1755. Leaf-forms, too, were frequently used for plates, dishes, sauceboats, and such things.

About 1755 we find styles undergoing a distinct change, and Mazarin blue as a ground colour, as well as more elaborate gilding, was first used in that year. By 1758, when the factory reopened, we find that a claret ground had been added, and further colours of the kind already in use at Sèvres were speedily developed. These included turquoise, green, and yellow, used as ground colours in conjunction with flowers and exotic birds. Decoration at this period became generally more elaborate, with painting of unusually fine quality. The *rococo* style, not particularly obtrusive in the preceding period, was by now extremely marked, vases especially being provided with wildly contorted handles. These vases were decorated with elaborate figure paintings after such artists as Rubens and Boucher, and one large figure group of 1760 was based on a painting by Rubens in the Rijksmuseum. This – *The Roman Charity* – was modelled by Joseph Willems.

This period of full-blown *rococo* ended for all practical purposes in 1763, and I know of nothing before 1770 which can be said to show signs of the impact of the neo-classical style. During the Chelsea-Derby period, however, most of the important things were in this style which was used side by side with repetitions of models in the late *rococo* fashion.

Figures marked with a gold anchor are of fine quality, but lack the vitality and the superb artistry of the earlier things. The flowering maybush, sometimes called the *bocage*, was frequently used with considerably more taste than elsewhere. *Biscuit* figures were not made until 1770, although I have had the opportunity to examine an unglazed group which appeared to have been made about 1763. This was incomplete, and it proved impossible to decide whether it had been intended as an attempt at *biscuit*, or whether it was a 'waster' which had not been glazed. In either case, it was of more than usual interest to the student.

The Chelsea-Derby period is noted for the obvious influence both of Tournai and Sèvres. Vases begin to show such ground patterns as gold stripes, either on white or blue, with landscapes and figure subjects in panels. Towards the end of the period Chelsea may have been little more than a decorating establishment for Derby wares, and on its closure the best artists were taken to Derby.

The production of small 'toys' – scent-bottles, seals, *étuis*, watch-boxes, and so forth – was extensively undertaken at Chelsea, and they form a very desirable class of wares.

The Kakiemon patterns of the raised anchor period are mostly in a palette resembling that of Arita, whilst harbour scenes and such things approximate closely to the Meissen originals. At a later date, the palette becomes less obviously an attempt to imitate the colours in use at the German factory. The earliest figures are sparsely decorated with washes of solid colour, but by 1755 sprigged flower designs are used to suggest fabrics. The much more sumptuous colouring of the gold anchor types is immediately evident. Gilding was used from shortly after 1750, and is, at first, sparsely employed. Its use is much more generous in the gold anchor period; it is often chased on the finest examples. Elaborately flowered fabrics are much in evidence at

this date. The Chelsea-Derby period, on the other hand, shov
a preference for the pale pastel shades which went hand in har
with the neo-classical style.

The earliest body is a glassy type which somewhat resembl
that of some of the earlier French factories. It has, in fact, bee
mistaken for white glass. About 1750 a somewhat different ty
of body was introduced. This contains the 'moons', the natu
of which has led to a certain amount of controversy. Rece
examination has shown them to be flattened disc-shaped caviti
in the body, and they appear as brilliant circular patches whe
the porcelain is viewed by transmitted light. They are general
to be seen in flat wares such as plates and dishes. About 1755
bone-ash body, similar to that in use at Bow, was introduce
and the 'moons' are no longer to be seen, possibly owing to t
fact that the new body had superior plastic qualities.

The gold anchor period is notable for a thick, rich, gla:
which is sometimes crazed, and which was especially suitab
for fine painting and ground-laying. Both enamels and grour
sank into this glaze in a way somewhat similar to that found
Sèvres specimens. The earlier glazes were not so suitable f
this kind of work.

Chelsea plates, dishes, and such things have three or fou
defects in the glaze at the base inside the foot-ring which mar
the place where the piece stood in the kiln on three or fou
cone-shaped stilts.

Ultra-violet radiation has been much used in dating specime
of Chelsea porcelain made prior to about 1754, inasmuch as the
fluoresce with a noticeable peach colour. After 1754, the gla:
usually shows a deep violet reflection, the alteration perha
being due to the addition of bone-ash.

The body of the Chelsea-Derby period is of good qualit
although it differs in some respects from that of the gol
anchor period. The glaze, too, is thinner and less rich, and muc
resembles that of other Derby porcelain of the period.

The quality of the porcelain and its decoration during t
raised and red anchor periods ranks with any in Europe. Th
gold anchor style is less happy. The *rococo* scroll-work is a litt
too wild, the decoration a trifle too consciously luxurious. Th

work of the last period, under the guidance of Duesbury, hardly compares with earlier specimens, although it is always competent and of excellent quality.

'Girl in a Swing' Porcelain

The superbly modelled figure shown on Plate 50A is represented both in the Victoria and Albert Museum in London and in the Boston Museum of Fine Arts in the United States. Whilst this book was in preparation two hitherto unknown groups belonging to this class were unexpectedly discovered in London, and I am able to record these on Plate 49.

There are approximately three dozen different models known which can be dated to some extent by the existence of one representing Britannia mourning the death of Frederick, Prince of Wales. This event took place in 1752.

Opinion at present is somewhat divided on the question of their origin. A substantial section would regard them as having been made in Chelsea at the Lawrence Street factory some time between 1748 and 1752. Others, myself among them, consider that they may have been made at a small factory believed to have been started by a group of workmen who seceded from Chelsea, probably under the guidance of one of the earliest proprietors, Charles Gouyn.

At the time of writing there is insufficient evidence to warrant any definite statement of opinion, although there can be little doubt as to the date of manufacture.

(ii) BOW (E. LONDON), ?1744–76

Like most English factories, the history of the Bow enterprise has been pieced together from a few records which are, for the most part, incomplete.

In 1744 a patent was taken out by Thomas Frye, an Irish painter, and Edward Heylyn, a glass merchant, for a porcelain body, the specification of which referred to *unaker*. Edward Heylyn had a glass-kiln in an indeterminate area which may have been either Stratford or Bow, and this, no doubt, was used for experimental firings of porcelain.

In 1749 another patent was taken out by Frye alone which, although it does not refer to bone-ash specifically, leaves no doubt that this was intended. I have already mentioned the use of bone-ash as a flux in the manufacture of glass, and it is possible that he first discovered the possibility of bone-ash as a material in porcelain manufacture from a consideration of its effect upon certain types of glass.

Nothing has, apparently, survived of the experimental pieces made before 1749, although from time to time various specimens are put forward as being likely. Unfortunately, none of them have, so far, possessed any factors of a determining nature. The tentative attribution is usually made either because the piece is an obvious primitive which it is impossible to place elsewhere, or because it bears a close resemblance to a known early Bow model, but is made in a body which does not include bone-ash.[1]

In 1750 two London merchants, Weatherby and Crowther, became interested in Frye's patent, and a factory was established and given the name of 'New Canton'. We are fortunate, inasmuch as a few circular inkwells have been preserved with the inscription: *Made at New Canton*, and with a date which can be either 1750 or 1751. These were probably made as samples of the new manufacture.

Other records which have survived include some newspaper advertisements, and the note-books of John Bowcocke, clerk to the factory, from which we can get some idea of the scale on which it operated. We know that by 1755 the prodigious amount of eighteen thousand pounds' worth of porcelain was being sold annually. The figure quoted must, of course, be considered in relation to the value of money at that time.

From about 1750 to 1753, William Duesbury, later proprietor of the Derby factory, was operating an outside decorating establishment in London in a manner somewhat analogous to the

1. Since this was written Dr John A. Ainslie has drawn my attention to the fact that fern-ash, which was included as an ingredient in the body described in the 1744 patent, contains phosphates. This means that it would react chemically in much the same way as the later porcelain. We may, in fact, be able to re-date certain primitive Bow specimens to the 1744–8 period in consequence.

larger German studios, except that he was willingly supplied by most of the existing factories because they found it difficult to do their own enamelling. He decorated a considerable amount of Bow porcelain, although we have not yet been able to separate his work from that of the factory with complete certainty, in spite of a number of suggestions which have been put forward for so doing.

The dating of Bow porcelain is a somewhat easier task since, in common with other English factories, it drew on Meissen extensively for inspiration. Unlike that of the English factories, the history of the Meissen enterprise is fairly well documented, and it is, therefore, a comparatively simple matter to give an approximate sequence to Bow porcelain, partly by considering the progression from early primitives to more sophisticated work, and partly by assuming that the adoption of Meissen styles took place in the same chronological order as at the German factory. Unlike Chelsea, which only rarely used the colour, Bow began to use underglaze blue extensively from the early period, and a large number of surviving specimens are decorated in this way. Mostly they are copies of Chinese blue-and-white, or the patterns are based on Chinese originals.

Transfer-printing, too, came into use at a comparatively early date. This process was discovered by an Irishman, John Brooks, who was an intimate of Thomas Frye. It was first used on enamels made at Battersea between about 1753 and 1755. The majority of the Bow examples can reasonably be attributed to the most notable practitioner of this kind of work, the engraver, Robert Hancock, who left London for Worcester in 1757. Bow prints are in red, lilac, or sepia. Printing in underglaze blue may have been used, but most known specimens have some element of doubt. Bow seems to have initiated the practice of printing in outline for colouring, which enabled a far greater number of semi-skilled workpeople to be used.

Thomas Frye remained as manager until 1759, in which year failing health caused him to retire. Weatherby died in 1762. Crowther became bankrupt in the following year, but seems to have avoided the worst effects since the factory continued working on a much reduced scale.

It seems probable that it closed finally about 1778,[1] and what remained of the machinery, moulds, and such things, may have been bought by Duesbury. There is no definite information on the point, but there are a few pieces in existence which make it likely. There are not many specimens which can reasonably be awarded a date as late as 1770, and these are usually of inferior workmanship.

Little profit could come from a discussion of the possible appearance of the earlier Bow porcelain. I propose, therefore, to begin with the year 1750, and specimens which can be given this date with reasonable certainty are not excessively rare. These are usually copies of the white porcelain of Tê Hua decorated with applied sprays of prunus blossom. Occasionally the sprays have been touched with enamel colour. The great majority of surviving specimens are cups and saucers, plates, bowls, and the like. Other items of service ware, and small vases, are known, but are definitely scarce.

The Kakiemon patterns were in use shortly after 1750, the most popular being the 'Quail'. These are not at all rare, and are carried out in the Arita palette, but the colours are somewhat inferior in quality to those of Chelsea. Copies of Chinese *famille rose* flower-paintings belong approximately to the same period, and are much rarer. These things, together with blue-and-white and the occasional transfer-printed pieces, were probably the most popular at the time. Chelsea artists came to Bow during Sprimont's illness, when the West London factory was closed, and they were responsible for some rare plates decorated with the so-called 'Hans Sloane' flowers taken from the work of Philip Miller already mentioned. Porcelain decorated with armorial bearings is uncommon. Chinese figure subjects can be seen occasionally, and much the same applies to the *deutsche Blumen*. A comparatively common type was decorated with a powder-blue ground, in conjunction with small reserved panels containing slight Chinese landscapes in blue. This type was repeated at Lowestoft, Worcester, and Caughley. There are other kinds of

1. The date usually given is 1776, but Dr Ainslie has since discovered a basket with what appears to be the date, 1778, disguised as a pseudo-Chinese mark.

decoration which defy classification, but they can usually be traced to German, Chinese, or Japanese originals in essentials, and are not often seen.

Mention must be made of a group of wares decorated at the outside decorating establishment of James Giles of Kentish Town. Giles fulfilled much the same function as Duesbury, but at a later date, the earliest items which can be attributed to him being painted around 1760. His work on Worcester porcelain was extensive. He will be discussed in more detail later, but when the same style of painting is to be seen on Bow, Worcester, and Chelsea porcelain, it is reasonably safe to assume that the artist in question was employed by Giles. At Bow a group of wares, particularly figures, marked with an anchor and dagger have now been awarded to Giles's workshop, although this was at one time regarded as a factory mark.

Figures were very commonly made at Bow, and the subjects are mostly derived from Meissen directly or by way of Chelsea. This is not invariably so, however, and mention should be made of the striking portraits of Henry Woodward, the actor, and Kitty Clive, the actress, which may have originated at Chelsea. Another model, which has caused some speculation, is that of Peg Woffington as a Sphinx. A similar model of Kitty Clive was made at Chelsea.[1]

An amusing and primitive series of models all by the same hand are best represented by some original figures of the Muses. The name of the artist is unknown, but he has been called the 'Muses Modeller'. These all appear to have been made between 1748 and 1752, and they can be distinguished by an oval face and a distinctly receding chin.

An impressed mark, T^o, has been linked with a Mr Tebo. A modeller of this name was employed by Josiah Wedgwood in 1774, and there are reasons for thinking that he was at work at Bow from about 1750 or shortly afterwards. These reasons are lengthy and somewhat controversial, and I have examined the question at some length in an article on this man in *Apollo* (July 1953). If I am correct, he was probably the most prolific of the Bow modellers, although his style is unsophisticated.

1. A similar subject was used at Fulda about 25 years later.

Some extremely fine-quality figures were made, of which a pair of Cooks are notable. These are often attributed to John Bacon, the sculptor, but the ascription is not well-founded.

Most of the early Bow figures are in white, but from a few surviving specimens bearing traces of cold painting, they appear to have been painted with oil-colour originally.

The *bocage* was much used at Bow, but took a cruder form than at Chelsea, and, usually, these form the least desirable class of Bow figures.

Many figures from here have a square hole at the back. This was used to carry an ormolu mount, either for flowers in the Vincennes style, or for a porcelain candle-holder and drip-pan.

Bow figures, generally, exhibit considerable diversity in subject matter. Many are emblematic of such things as the Seasons, the Elements,[1] the Continents, the Senses, and the like, and are in sets, although a complete set is very rare today. Animals and birds are often well-modelled. Monks, nuns, and Church dignitaries were represented in some variety.

The earliest figures have plain bases, but the *rococo* scrollwork makes its appearance at a comparatively early date. The mid years show a certain amount of variety in the type of base, but by about 1760 a comparatively typical four-footed base had been evolved, and was much used. At a slightly later date, a variation of this type, more heavily constructed with a central shell-like *motif*, became the rule.

Since the mark of the anchor and dagger is now recognized to be that of Giles, it is fair to say that the factory had no especial mark. It certainly copied the Worcester crescent on figures which are characteristically Bow in appearance. It used a number of workmen's marks, as well as some crude and almost meaningless pseudo-Chinese marks which, with some difficulty, can usually be seen to have come from a late Ming reign-mark. Capital letters were sometimes used, but have no discernible meaning in the present state of our knowledge. 'F' has been assumed to refer to Thomas Frye, but there is no very definite proof of the assumption.

The body of Bow porcelain is generally heavy for its size,

1. Earth, Fire, Air, and Water.

and breaks with a sugary fracture. It is not always particularly translucent by transmitted light, and will usually reveal a brownish-orange colour when examined in this way. When tested chemically it reveals the presence of a considerable quantity of bone-ash.

Care is needed in attributing porcelain decorated in under-glaze blue to this factory. Lowestoft used an almost exactly similar body and glaze, and separation is often difficult. Lowes-toft examples which may be confused with Bow were made some five or ten years later.

(iii) DERBY (DERBYSHIRE), ?1745 ONWARDS

The first mention of the Derby factory in the history of English porcelain refers to about 1745. The late Frank Hurlbutt sug-gested that a group of reclining lambs marked with an incised pentagon (possibly imitated from Chelsea's incised triangle) might have been made by a certain André Planché about this date. There is also reason to think that Thomas Briand, almost certainly to be identified with the chemist who demonstrated before the Royal Society, endeavoured to start a porcelain factory in Derby about 1745 in company with James Marchand.

About 1750, William Duesbury, born at Longton in Stafford-shire in 1725, was operating a decorating establishment in London, and his surviving account books mention that he was painting porcelain from Chelsea, Bow, Derbyshire, and Stafford-shire. These early Derbyshire figures (that is, examples made prior to about 1756), have now been convincingly identified.

In 1753 Duesbury was finding it difficult to obtain supplies of porcelain in white, probably because, by this time, most factories had been able to provide their own enamelling shops. He evi-dently decided that the only safe way to secure regular supplies was to make his own, because we find that, by 1756, he had returned to the Midlands, and was actively negotiating with André Planché, china-maker, and John Heath, gentleman, for the establishment of a porcelain factory at Derby to replace the existing enterprise, in which, no doubt, the two others were actively interested. Duesbury is described as an enameller in a draft agreement drawn up but not subsequently ratified. In 1770, he purchased the Chelsea factory.

Planché must have been dropped within a year or two, but Heath remained until 1780, when he became bankrupt. In 1778 it is probable that Duesbury acquired what was left of Bow, and in 1777 we find Giles applying to him for a loan. Giles's own establishment was later taken over with the others.

All this demonstrates that Duesbury was a man of more than ordinary commercial astuteness, but he did not reap the expected reward of his manoeuvres, for Josiah Wedgwood had produced a cheap cream earthenware, as well as the jasper-ware later described. At this time both Duesbury and Wedgwood were exploiting the neo-classical style, although Derby porcelain made greater use of enamelled decoration.

The elder Duesbury died in 1786, and was followed by his son, William Duesbury the second. The son died, however, in 1796, shortly after he had taken Michael Kean into partnership. Kean seems to have been distinctly unpopular with the factory artists, since many changes were made about this time, some of the finest leaving to find employment elsewhere. Kean married the widow of his partner, but his disputes with the workmen caused him to withdraw after a short period.

William Duesbury the third entered the firm about 1808, and later was in partnership with William Sheffield whose daughter he had married. The firm was then styled 'Duesbury & Sheffield'.

The premises were leased to Robert Bloor in 1815. Bloor had been a clerk, who had taken considerable executive responsibility. He took over when the factory was going through a difficult period, and, in order to raise money, sold, by auction, the accumulated stock of second-class ware which the factory had hitherto refused to sell.

He continued production with a certain amount of success until 1828, although his wares were inferior to those of the eighteenth century. In 1828 he began to suffer from failing health, and the factory passsed into the managership of James Thomason. On Bloor's death in 1845, it passed to Bloor's relative, Thomas Clarke. Many of the moulds were sold to Samuel Boyle of Fenton about this time. He, in turn, sold them to

Copelands, and they were accidentally discovered in 1920. Something over ten thousand pieces were found, some of which belonged to the early Chelsea and Derby factories.

The original works were finally closed in 1848, but the firm of Locker and Company was established in Derby by some of the workmen. After 1859 this factory was continued under the style of Stevenson & Company, and later, as Stevenson & Hancock.

In 1877, the Crown Derby Porcelain Company was established at Osmaston Road, Derby, by Edward Phillips of the Worcester Royal Porcelain Company. Manufacture has been continued in Derby until the present day by this firm, and it is perhaps best known for its Japan patterns. Since the term 'Crown Derby' is often used loosely to refer to wares both of the early factory and to those of the enterprise mentioned above, it should be stated that the term can properly be applied only to the productions of the Crown Derby Porcelain Company. 'Duesbury Derby' or 'Bloor Derby' are reasonably descriptive of the earlier wares.

The Derby factory of Duesbury's time is comparatively well documented from about 1770 onwards, and we know a good deal about the artists who worked there. This aspect is examined in more detail in the following section.

*

The suggestion has been made that André Planché made porcelain in the neighbourhood of Derby as early as 1745, and the late Frank Hurlbutt assigned to him a pair of reclining lambs with an incised pentagon mark under the base. After careful examination of this model, however, I am inclined to regard the Planché attribution as not proven, but to accept a Staffordshire origin and a date of around 1750 as likely in all the circumstances. William Duesbury's acquaintance with William Littler of Longton Hall has been remarked in passing. Longton Hall is in Staffordshire, and from here, or from the neighbouring town of Newcastle-under-Lyme, came an interesting group of models, mostly with saltglazed stoneware affiliations, which have been dubbed 'Snowmen' from the appearance of the thick glaze with which they are covered. These, too, appear to have been made around 1750, and they strongly resemble the group of lambs.

The Victorian and Albert Museum has an interesting cream jug, decorated around the base with strawberries and leaves in relief, which is marked 'D. 1750'. One is known with the word 'Derby' incised, and it is therefore reasonable to suppose that the factory was in existence as early as 1750. At this time there was a factory at Cockpit Hill, Derby, in which John Heath was interested, and it is probable that we owe the earliest Derby models to them. These can be identified by a glaze retraction at the base, which leaves what has been aptly termed a 'dry edge'. Some of the bases have a curious funnel-shaped hole, and the service-ware so far identified contains 'moons', a peculiarity which I have also observed in an early figure.

The modelling of the 'dry-edged' Derby figures is often remarkably sophisticated and of fine quality. An interesting and important link between these and the later Derby wares is provided by a figure which is usually called 'King Lear', which also exists in an early version of this period, although the later examples are much the more common.

About 1756, which appears to be the date of Duesbury's intervention, the style changes. The paste and glaze also change, and there is some resemblance to late red anchor Chelsea figures. There is, however, the difference that the glaze often contains tin oxide, which opacifies it to some extent, and, in this particular, Derby porcelain more nearly resembles that of Longton Hall. Derby, however, had adopted the method of placing figures in the kiln on three or four clay pads, which leave a mark on the underside of the base that is usually termed a 'thumb' or 'patch' mark. Whilst these marks are not peculiar to Derby, they appear so rarely on porcelain from other factories that they can be regarded as fair presumptive evidence of a Derby origin when other things are in agreement. Moreover, Derby figures are somewhat lighter in weight than comparable Longton figures. The enamelling often resembles that of Longton, and it seems fair to suggest that Duesbury enamelled some Longton porcelain as well as his own manufacture.

By 1760 we find distinct changes. The glaze containing tin

oxide fell into disuse, and was replaced by a thick glassy glaze which has often crackled and pooled in hollows. It usually has a greenish tinge where it is thickest. Chelsea, during the gold anchor period, used a somewhat similar glaze, and it is likely that it was adopted at Derby in order the more nearly to copy Chelsea productions.

Reviewing Derby porcelain between 1750 and 1770 it becomes evident that, for the most part, production was intended to imitate Chelsea. This was almost certainly an extension of a practice indulged in by Duesbury during his days as an enameller in London. In a previous work I have suggested that the reason Duesbury eventually found it impossible to get supplies of white porcelain from Chelsea was because he was attempting to pass off inferior porcelain as coming from that factory. Rare Chelsea examples with the raised anchor overpainted in red have been attributed to the Duesbury workshop.

It is noteworthy that, with one or two minor exceptions, Derby porcelain between 1750 and 1770 does not bear a factory mark, although I have seen specimens as late as around 1760 bearing the Chelsea mark of the red anchor.

I have dealt with this point at somewhat greater length than it might, at first sight, seem to demand. But for many years Derby porcelain, particularly that made between 1760 and 1770, has been confused with Chelsea of the gold anchor period, and although the confusion is lessening as the subject is studied in greater detail, it is still not uncommon to find Derby porcelain wrongly attributed.

With the beginning of the Chelsea-Derby period we find that recognizable factory marks become usual, both on wares which can reasonably be assumed to have emanated from Chelsea, and those which were undoubtedly made at Derby. The reason is obvious – Duesbury no longer needed to pass off his porcelain as being of Chelsea manufacture.

Many Derby wares of the period between 1750 and 1770 are based on models popular at Meissen, and this raises the question of whether they were copied directly, or by way of Chelsea. Whilst it is frequently not possible to identify a Chelsea original of a Derby model, it seems likely that most of the early Derby wares had a Chelsea inspiration. Particularly, the *bocage* was very much favoured, although it is cruder than the occasional Chelsea excursions into this field, whereas the *bocage* was not at any time popular at Meissen. Essentially it seems to have been derived from the porcelain flowers of Meissen and Vincennes, but it probably owes something to contemporary stage scenery. More porcelain figures of the period were of actors and actresses in popular rôles, and the *bocage* was used in stage settings quite frequently.

Derby was responsible for many *biscuit* figures and groups of exceptionally fine quality. *Biscuit* seems to have been a Duesbury innovation in England, the first figures in this medium dating from about 1770. The earlier examples have a white, rather waxy-looking surface, which is in part due to the deposition of a glaze of volatilization during firing. The later specimens are apt to be chalk-white in appearance. There is in existence a factory catalogue (reprinted by John Haslem, *The Old Derby China Factory*) which gives a price-list of some three hundred and ninety models. These are listed as being made both in *biscuit* and in an enamelled version. *Biscuit* figures, to be saleable, had to be modelled with exceptional sharpness, and without flaw or blemish. Therefore, the second-quality figures were glazed and enamelled, only the finest being left in a *biscuit* state.

The neo-classical style was much used at Derby after the acquisition of the Chelsea factory. Painted decoration was an especial feature of Derby porcelain at this period, some artists of exceptional ability being employed. It is not possible to discuss these artists at length, but among the more important may be numbered Zachariah Boreman and 'Jockey' Hill who painted landscapes; Richard Askew, who painted cupids, mostly in *rose camaieu;* James Banford, who painted classical subjects; George Complin, who was responsible for fruit and birds; and, at a somewhat later date, 'Quaker' Pegg, who painted single flower sprays, which he mostly named on the reverse of the plate.

Edward Withers was a flower painter of skill who worked in the older style, and William Billingsley, who will be discussed at greater length under the heading of *Nantgarw & Swansea,* introduced the newer style of flower-painting in which the flower was painted in full colour, the highlights being wiped out. This was in direct contrast to the old style in which they were left unpainted. He was also fond of long sprays emerging from the centre floral grouping, and of white flowers. His painting is comparatively rare and sought after.

Among the modellers was John Bacon, R.A., to whom Duesbury paid the sum of £75 7s. 4d. in 1769 for models. He is reputed to have modelled figures of *Milton* and *Shakespeare*, which are more than usually distinguished. William Coffee did a number of important things, of which the most frequently quoted is a clothed version of an antique statue of Adonis. Little is known of John Rossi, but a pair of figures of *Aesculapius* and *Hygeia* are usually attributed to him. Pierre Stephan was relatively prolific, and was responsible for such things as a group of *Three Graces distressing Cupid*, inspired by the work of the painter, Angelica Kauffmann, and at one time attributed to Spängler. The subject mentioned, incidentally, was used as painted decoration at Vienna, where the kind of inspiration provided by the fair Angelica was also appreciated.

Jean-Jacques Spängler was a Swiss, a son of a director of the Zürich porcelain manufactory, and caused Duesbury a great deal of trouble. He possessed an artistic temperament with which the Midland manufacturer had scant sympathy. Spängler modelled a number of figures for ordinary purposes, as well as some special pieces for a London clock-maker named Vulliamy who used them for mounting on clock-cases.

Much of the painted decoration at this period was in conjunction with coloured grounds in the manner of Sèvres, and the forms are principally classical urn shapes, a particular favourite being based on the Greek *krater*. The straight-sided coffee-can was an especial favourite towards the end of the period. This was derived from Sèvres and Vienna, and the cans were made in pairs for cabinet display, much care being lavished on the decoration. Landscapes, classical figure subjects, and flowers, were the most often used, and Derby painting between 1770 and the end of the century is usually of the highest quality.

After the turn of the century we notice a certain falling-off in the quality of Derby productions.

Landscape painting remained a factory speciality, and Robert and John Brewer were responsible for some of the best. They probably replaced Boreman and Hill in 1795 when many of the older artists left the factory. John Brewer was a drawing-master who died in 1815, and painted landscapes, figures, and hunting scenes. Robert Brewer remained until 1817. The latter was a one-time pupil of Paul Sandby. Whilst this artist did not work for Derby, he exercised a distinct influence on its landscape painters, Boreman's technique being, in part, derived from the same source. But the differences between the work of the Brewers and that of Boreman are not difficult to distinguish. Of the two, the work of Robert is probably the most in evidence. 'Quaker' Pegg resumed flower painting for Derby for a short time after 1813, but had left finally by 1817.

After about 1815 fruit painting was in the hands of Thomas Steele, and birds were painted by Richard Dodson. Cuthbert Lawton did hunting scenes, and George Robertson was a landscape painter who also painted shipping. He was a contemporary of the Brewers, leaving about 1820.

Elaborate Japan patterns were much in evidence, and continued to be popular. The 'Chantilly' pattern of a central pink or carnation with some smaller sprigs scattered about was made in immense quantities.

The figures of the period, heavily coloured with thick, paint-like enamels and much gilding, were, in part, repetitions of eighteenth-century styles. Among the modellers we notice Edward Keys who left about 1826 to work for Mintons. He modelled a set of the Monkey Band after the earlier Meissen and Chelsea models, as well as portrait statuettes of George IV and Napoleon. His brother, Samuel Keys, turned to the theatre for inspiration, modelling such players as Liston, Madame Vestris, and Miss Foote in character. He made two figures of Hebe and Innocence which were twenty-eight inches in height, richly decorated with gilding and painted with flowers by Leonard Lead. Only one pair were finished, another being damaged in firing. We find, from time to time throughout the nineteenth century, essays in the manufacture of these overlarge figures at various European factories, but porcelain is hardly suited to things of this size, and such attempts are rarely successful artistically. Samuel Keys left in 1830. A number of amusing figures representing the adventures of Dr Syntax were by his hand.

The mark of Stevenson & Hancock is usually seen on somewhat crude repetitions of the earlier Derby wares. The mark adopted, that of the Duesbury factory, with the addition of the letters 'S' and 'H' on either side, is sufficient identification when it has not been tampered with, but specimens exist from which the letters have been removed with acid. The differences between these mid-nineteenth-century productions and those of the earlier period are such that no one acquainted with Duesbury's porcelain should be deceived.

The later Crown Derby porcelain is best known for its Japan patterns, which are usually based on those of the earlier period. This work is competent, but undistinguished artistically.

Bloor porcelain is markedly inferior to that of the eighteenth century, and many specimens have a glaze which is covered with a fine network of cracks. Discoloration of the glaze is not uncommon.

(iv) WORCESTER (WORCESTERSHIRE),
1748 ONWARDS

The only factory which has an unbroken line of continuity from the earliest years of English porcelain manufacture to the present day is the Worcester Royal Porcelain Company, which celebrated its bicentenary in London with an exhibition of early wares in 1951.

In fact, the factory from which it grew was established in Bristol about 1748, and the correct attribution of some of the earliest wares is so uncertain that we often use the term 'Bristol/Worcester' to signify that the specimen might have been made at either place.

The Bristol venture was established at Redcliffe Backs on a site which is now part of Bristol docks. The factory had been, originally, a glass-house in the possession of William Lowdin, and, according to the letters of Dr Richard Pococke who visited it at the time, it was established by one of the principals of the small factory at Limehouse in London which failed in 1748. The wares of Limehouse have not yet been identified.

The names of William Miller and Benjamin Lund are known, and Lund obtained a licence to dig and search for soap-rock in Cornwall in 1748. Soap-rock is the substance which has already been discussed in the introduction to this chapter, and was used for porcelain manufacture at Bristol, Worcester, Liverpool, and Caughley.

Bristol has received a number of names from different authorities. 'Lowdin's Bristol', 'Lowris China House', and 'Redcliffe Backs' may be found in the older works, 'Lowris' being an erroneous form of 'Lowdin's'. 'Lund's Bristol' is most in accord with the facts, and this has now received general assent.

Of the wares undoubtedly made here, we have the figure of a Chinese Immortal which bears, on the base, the inscription *Bristoll 1750*. There are also some sauceboats and butter-boats bearing the word *Bristoll* which are of certain attribution.

The glaze is often heavily blued, more particularly on blue-and-white examples, and has the appearance of having had an addition of tin oxide. When we remember that Bristol was the centre of a large and flourishing manufacture of *delft*, this addition is easily understood.

The painting of Chinese subjects, both in blue and in polychrome, is often extremely delicate and well-executed. European subjects are much rarer, and are more likely to have been done at Worcester. The separation is made the more difficult, however, by the fact that some of the artists went to Worcester about 1752 when the Bristol establishment was transferred to that city. The hand of the artist is not a certain guide to the date of manufacture, and, therefore, to the origin of the specimen.

There is in existence a partnership deed dated 4 June 1751. The most important signatories were Doctor John Wall, Richard and Josiah Holdship, Edward Cave, who edited the *Gentleman's Magazine*, and William Davis, although William Bayliss was the largest single shareholder.

Of these people, Wall and Davis were selected for special treatment, being awarded an additional amount equivalent to their share-holding in exchange for the secret of making soap-rock porcelain. It would appear most likely that Wall and Davis were entrusted by the newly-formed Company with the task of acquiring the necessary manufacturing process from the Bristol vendors, and of making certain that no untoward difficulties would be experienced in manufacturing porcelain to this formula after the transfer, and for this especial service they received the award mentioned. Payment was also made to Robert Podmore and John Lyes of Bristol, but they were not given shares in the Company. It is possible that Podmore was somewhat disgruntled by this treatment, because he later went to Liverpool and sold the soap-rock secret to Richard Chaffers.

It has long been the fashion to speak of Worcester porcelain made between 1752 and 1783 as belonging to the 'Wall' period. Actually Wall did not become effective head of the factory until 1772, and he died in 1776. The period has been extended for convenience until the purchase of the factory by Thomas Flight in 1783.

It has become increasingly apparent that, until 1772, the moving spirit was, in fact, Josiah Holdship, and that it would be more in accordance with the facts as we know them to split the old 'Wall' period into the 'Holdship' period, running from 1752 to 1772, and the 'Wall' period from 1772 to 1783. Richard Holdship sold his share in 1759, and retired to Derby to sell the soap-rock and transfer-printing secrets to Duesbury.

Duesbury made very little use of either, probably because he was producing a satisfactory porcelain of his own, and his background as a decorator did not make him particularly sympathetic to the mechanical printing process. It seems likely that he merely wished to stop Holdship from assisting in the establishment of a new factory elsewhere. Worcester, about this time, had in their possession the formula for a bone-ash paste, but it has not been possible to trace that they ever used it, no doubt because their own soap-rock body was perfectly satisfactory, and the difficulties involved in changing over to a body which was basically different would have involved considerable risk without corresponding advantages.

In 1757 we remark the employment of Robert Hancock, who

had previously worked at the Battersea Enamel Works in London. It was here that transfer-printing was either invented or perfected, and Hancock was its most important practitioner.

Incidentally, his employment may have been the reason for Richard Holdship's defection, since there appears to have been a bitter dispute between the two men. Holdship was probably manager of the printing department, but Hancock resented the position because the former claimed credit which rightly belonged to his subordinate. We find many of the earlier pieces signed by Hancock in full, or with the initials 'RH', to which is often added an anchor – a rebus on the name 'Holdship'.

An amusing exchange is provided by two oft-quoted couplets. This occurred soon after Hancock's arrival. The first appeared in Cave's *Gentleman's Magazine* for December 1757, in reference to a portrait of Frederick the Great, King of Prussia, which was engraved by Hancock. It ran:

> What praise is thine, ingenious Holdship, who
> On the fair porcelain the portrait drew.[1]

These two lines were repeated in the *Worcester Journal* in January 1758, with the addition:

> Hancock, my friend, don't grieve tho' Holdship has the praise,
> 'Tis yours to execute, 'tis his to wear the bays.

Hancock sometimes gave his work a hidden signature concealed among the hatchings of the engraving.

In 1772 there was a readjustment of the proprietorship. The original shareholders retired, and Wall and Davis emerged as the moving spirits of the factory, with Robert Hancock included among the new proprietors. Hancock, however, seems to have been discontented with this arrangement, since he left Worcester in 1774, and joined the newly-formed Caughley factory in 1775. He does not appear to have done any new work at Caughley, and eventually turned to book illustration.

Wall died in 1776, and in 1783 the proprietors decided to dispose of their interest. A purchaser was found in Thomas Flight of London who bought the factory for his sons, Joseph

1. This is a shortened version.

and John. A new body and glaze was introduced, but the alterations caused many difficulties. In 1788 the King and Queen visited the factory, and, upon the King's recommendation, a retail shop was opened in London.

In 1793 Martin Barr joined the firm, which was styled Flight and Barr until 1807. From this year until 1813 the style was Barr, Flight, and Barr, and from 1813 to 1840, Flight, Barr, and Barr. Porcelain of this period is well-marked, and the marks give either the name in full or the initial letters. The approximate date can be deduced therefrom.

In 1783, Robert Chamberlain, one of the factory's decorators, commenced business in partnership with his brother, Humphrey. At first this was merely a decorating establishment, the white porcelain being supplied by Caughley. They soon turned to the manufacture of porcelain, however, with such success that, in 1840, they absorbed the earlier Company. In 1811 the 'Regent' body was introduced, and was first used for a service for the Prince Regent.

Thomas Grainger, a relative of the Chamberlains, founded a factory about 1812 for the manufacture of porcelain, having been an outside decorator since 1800. This was styled Grainger, Lee & Co., and it made an undistinguished porcelain of no very great merit. It was eventually absorbed by the present Company.

In 1850, Messrs Lilly and Kerr entered into partnership, R. W. Binns joining the firm in 1852. The style was then Kerr & Binns, which was changed to the Worcester Royal Porcelain Company in 1862, with R. W. Binns as Managing Director.

James Hadley, principal modeller to the factory, founded a factory of his own in 1896 which was absorbed by the larger Company in 1905.

The factory remains one of the largest and most important manufacturers of fine porcelain in England.

The source of inspiration for the earliest Worcester porcelain is fairly evenly divided between contemporary silver and Chinese porcelain. This was no doubt due to the desire to divide work in reasonable proportion between the moulding shop and the throwers, the former being made in moulds, and the latter, for the most part, on the wheel. Incidentally, motive power for the potter's wheel in this and other factories was provided by small boys.

Many of the early wares were decorated in underglaze blue with a wide variety of patterns mostly based on late Ming and K'ang Hsi prototypes. Among the marks to be observed occasionally we find 玉 which is obviously a mistaken copy of 玉 – the Chinese word, *yü*, meaning *jade*. On Chinese blue-and-white this mark usually signifies a piece of more than ordinarily fine quality. Another mark of the same kind can colourably be related to the late Ming reign marks.

Japanese shapes – fluted and octagonal – are not so often seen at Worcester, and Japanese patterns are not very much in evidence, particularly in the earliest period. Of the Kakiemons, the 'Quail' pattern is infinitely the commonest, but some of these can undoubtedly be attributed to the outside decorator, James Giles, and in such cases the gilding is sometimes replaced with an unusual brownish pigment.

The spirit of the Kakiemon patterns is very imperfectly rendered at Worcester. Despite this, the Imari patterns, which were somewhat more popular, are of finer quality than those of most other factories.

Chinese patterns in a Worcester version of the *verte* palette are relatively common in the early period, as well as the use of *rose* in rendering some floral designs. Towards 1760 and later we notice the use of outline transfer-prints filled in with colour. This expedient was probably adopted to overcome the shortage of skilled china painters, the actual task of filling-in an outline being less difficult than the drawing of an outline in the first place.

By 1760 there is considerable widening in the scope of the themes of decoration, as well as in the manner of their execution. Landscapes, sometimes surrounded by slight *rococo* scroll-work, are both rare and interesting. Some are painted on jugs moulded in the form of overlapping leaves. These jugs were frequently copied elsewhere – at Lowestoft and Caughley particularly – and were popular for many years. The later examples have the addition of a mask lip, a curious development seen at Berlin as early as 1760, and at Vienna in the du Paquier period.

The styles of Meissen began to influence decoration about 1755, somewhat later than in London, and *deutsche Blumen* – natural flower sprays of the German type – were well in evidence by 1760. Dishes of leaf-shape, which had been fashionable at Meissen a few years before, began to be popular about this time.

The earlier Meissen *indianische Blumen* – stylized Oriental flowers – were quite frequently used, as well as such amusing concepts as the *lange Lyzen*, the Long Elizas, which are usually to be seen on blue-and-white porcelain in the Chinese style.

Less often found is the powder-blue ground in conjunction with reserved panels, which was extremely popular at Bow, and can also be seen from Lowestoft and Caughley.

A rare and interesting type of decoration is carried out in black pencilling. At first sight this resembles transfer-printing, but it is actually drawn with a very fine, pointed brush in a technique closely resembling that of the engraver. It would seem to be an example of back-copying from Chinese porcelain of the 'Jesuit' type, although the subjects are Oriental in origin. I have had the opportunity of examining one Worcester cup decorated in this way which appeared to have been painted *in China*, and this was of the typically European subject quite common on transfer-printed Worcester entitled *L'Amour*.

Transfer-printing was extensively employed from 1757 onwards, most of the finest and best-known subjects being engraved by Robert Hancock. A well-known series of mugs bear the portrait of Frederick the Great, King of Prussia, and these are often dated and signed. Other mugs in the same style have portraits of the Marquis of Granby and George III. Apart from Hancock, the work of his pupil, J. Ross, appears occasionally, and differences in style are fairly well-marked. 'Bat' printing was introduced about 1774, although most examples in this *genre* are somewhat later.

When the Chelsea factory partially closed down in 1763, it seems likely that Worcester engaged some of the artists. Shortly after this date, decoration becomes more elaborate, grounds in several colours being undertaken. James Giles flourished between 1763 and 1770, and much of his work was done on Worcester porcelain. The factory at one time supplied him with 'blanks' for this purpose, and occasional specimens with a scale-blue ground, but otherwise undecorated, can be found.

The commonest ground from Worcester is the scale-blue, a pattern in underglaze blue in which overlapping scales are more or less distinctly outlined with a darker blue. As a general rule, the earlier specimens have the more clearly defined scales. Very rarely the scale grounds are found in other colours, yellow, brick-red, pink, and light blue, but these are overglaze, and Giles was certainly responsible for a proportion of them.

A misapprehension, to which I have contributed in the past, is to be found in the assignment of a peculiar light enamel blue of a 'dry' appearance to the factory alone. I have recently had the opportunity of examining an undoubted piece of Giles decoration which had some slight passages of this pigment, and it cannot therefore be regarded as a definitive test of factory decoration.

Transfer-prints which have been coloured over with enamels are almost certainly the work of Giles, or some other outside decorator, and a sale catalogue is in existence which records his purchase of this kind of ware. The section devoted to English outside decorators should be consulted for information on Jeffryes Hamet O'Neale and John Donaldson, who painted some of the finest and most valued of this factory's porcelain.

Porcelain with armorial bearings was frequently made to order, and many services especially painted for the nobility and gentry have been identified in one way or another.

A painter of exotic birds in landscapes, tentatively identified with a Mons. Soqui or Saqui (said to have worked at Plymouth), was more than ordinarily competent, and his style resembles that of some Sèvres painters of similar subjects. He may have worked at that factory before coming to England.

Figure subjects are distinctly rare, although they are com-monest in conjunction with a scale-blue ground, and the 'Fables' of O'Neale and others are particularly desirable.

The influence of Sèvres is strong between 1770 and 1784, and can be seen in the variety of ground colours, the often elaborate but restrained gilding, and the well-rendered floral subjects which abound at this time.

Worcester figures are very few in number, and have mostly come to light only within recent years. The best known are a *Turk and Companion* and a *Gardener and Companion*. These are not unlike some earlier Bow models, and I have tentatively suggested that they may have been modelled by Mr Tebo. Some tureens in the form of a partridge on a nest and a cauliflower are known, but are extremely rare. It is likely that more were made, and is to be expected that they will be discovered in the future.

Worcester porcelain of this period is very precisely potted – much more so than that of other English factories. Some examples, in fact, approach the Chinese 'bodiless' porcelain in the extreme thinness of the body.

The glaze of the earliest examples is apt to be somewhat thicker and richer than on the later which often have an unglazed area immediately inside the foot-ring. This may be due to a retraction of the glaze, and can well be seen if a lead pencil is run round the inside. The 'lead' will mark the *biscuit* unmistakeably, but will slide over the glaze.

The Worcester glaze is never crazed. If crazing is present then the factory of origin must be sought elsewhere. Foot-rings are rarely ground to remove surplus glaze, but this can be noticed occasionally, on some of the later examples in particular. The translucency is usually greenish in hue, but transfer-printed wares will often show an orange tinge.

The first production of the Flight period exhibits some changes. The body assumes a greyish hue, and it is known that difficulties were experienced at this time. Fluted shapes are common, with slight gilding or scattered flowers. There was some repetition of earlier styles and patterns, particularly the Japan patterns, but the colouring is brighter, and the gilding is of the mercuric variety which is thinner and more brassy in appearance than the earlier honey gold. At a slightly later date, a much whiter body was introduced which somewhat resembles that then in use at Derby.

The neo-classical style came to the fore, and can be well seen in vases and wine-coolers which often follow contemporary silver-patterns. Some painting in tones of grey (*en grisaille*), adopted from the Continent, was done by James Pennington. Baxter was principally responsible for the popular feathers and shells, and topographical landscapes, both with and without frames, were frequently used. Flower painting was somewhat in the manner of Derby.

Chamberlain was responsible for illustrative painting, *Paradise Lost* being the inspiration for some of his more distinguished work. His earlier work is to be seen on porcelain bought in white from Caughley and New Hall. Armorial porcelain continued to be popular, and many large services were made of which single specimens can sometimes be acquired.

Some remarks on nineteenth-century Worcester porcelain are contained elsewhere in this chapter, and it is hardly necessary to add to them here. Decoration from this factory is usually restrained in style, and of much better quality than its contemporaries. Much of it, too, was more purely English in flavour than can be seen elsewhere, more particularly on the humbler and useful wares.

(v) LONGTON HALL (STAFFORDSHIRE), ?1750–?60

The Longton Hall factory has already been given passing mention in discussing the porcelain of Derby. For many years the existence of this Staffordshire factory was forgotten, and it was not until 1881 that J. E. Nightingale drew attention to some newspaper advertisements inserted by the proprietors. In 1898 a monograph on the subject was published by W. Bemrose which was, in many ways, a masterpiece of reconstruction from very slight evidence, and his attributions, mostly made by process of elimination, have stood the test of time in a great many instances, although, naturally enough, some were inaccurate.

This was the position until a few years ago when Dr Bernard Watney discovered both the site of the factory and many valuable documents relating to its origin and subsequent history. Ownership was formerly assigned to William Littler, a saltglaze potter of Brownhills, in Staffordshire. Many of the wares were derived from those already existing in saltglazed ware, and its advertisements were signed by William Littler and Company.

Between the publication of Bemrose's monograph and the researches of Dr Watney had come one or two minor and tantalizing additions to its history in the form of advertisements. The most significant were discovered by A. J. B. Kiddell in 1933, and referred to an existing partnership between William Littler, Robert Charlesworth, and Samuel Firmin. Working on these, Dr Watney finally discovered information and documents relating to the factory's history on the premises of a descendant of Samuel Firmin, where they had lain forgotten since the eighteenth century. From these – one of the most remarkable discoveries in the history of the ceramic art – it is now evident that the factory was started in 1750, not 1752 as formerly thought, by William Littler, William Jenkinson, and William Nicklin. It became obvious, too, that William Jenkinson was the leading member of the firm and that he it was who contributed the secret of porcelain-making. It is not certain where he obtained his knowledge, but the Limehouse factory mentioned on page 214 seems the most likely source.

In 1755 Jenkinson sold his interest in the factory to Nathaniel Firmin, a gilder, and the Reverend Robert Charlesworth who provided some essential new capital. Firmin died, and left his share to his son, Samuel Firmin. Littler seems to have been responsible for running the factory, and Nicklin henceforth played a minor part.

In 1760 the three advertisements already mentioned mark the end. These were in *Aris's Birmingham Gazette*, and the first, on 23 May 1760, states that the partnership between William Littler and Robert Charlesworth is dissolved, and that no credit is to be given to the firm on account of Robert Charlesworth.

Littler's reply on 30 June is worth quoting at length:

... William Littler & Company think proper to acquaint the Publick that it's not in Robert Charlesworth's Power to dissolve the Partnership therein mentioned, without consent of the rest of the Partners; that the said William Littler & Co. are far from the Expectation of any Credit on the said Charlesworth's account, and are all very desirous to execute any proper instrument for the Dissolution of the said

Partnership, on having fair Accounts settled, and Damages paid by the said Charlesworth for his many Breaches of Covenant, and his late unjustifiable and illegal, tho' impotent and ineffectual, Attempt to put a Stop to the said Manufactory.

On 8 September the last advertisement signed by Samuel Firmin marks the end. In this he states that he esteems the partnership disolved on 23 May, the date of Charlesworth's advertisement.

From this it seems that Charlesworth had come to the conclusion, by May 1760, that there was no longer any possibility either of running the factory profitably or of securing the return of his capital. Littler, however, attempted to keep the factory in operation until the last possible moment. The stock at the factory was seized by agents acting on behalf of Charlesworth, who took it to Salisbury for sale. It is possible that moulds and equipment were included, although this is uncertain.

Dr Watney's discovery of these early documents did little, by itself, to confirm the attributions already made, and others which were speculative. He carried his researches a step further, however, by digging on the site of the factory, unearthing fragments which not only confirmed many previous attributions but also resolved some earlier difficulties. The main 'waster' heap, and part of the factory, still appears to be covered by some stables subsequently built on the site, and the fragments recovered have been small but adequate for the purpose.

My earlier supposition that the 'Snowman' figures would prove to come from Longton Hall was confirmed by the fragments. They are an interesting group of models, some of which have saltglaze prototypes, and are so-called because they are smothered with a thick glaze. These are the type at one time conjecturally attributed to the earliest Derby manufacture by Frank Hurlbutt.

Perhaps the most characteristic porcelain to come from Longton is in the form of leaves. The veins of the leaves are usually outlined in pink. Strawberry and leaf moulding, especially on the ledges of plates, in conjunction with some good flower or bird painting, can also reasonably be placed to Longton manufacture.

There are a number of pieces which obviously follow saltglaze models, and these, when the porcelain paste and glaze is seen to be in agreement, can safely be regarded as Longton Hall.

Littler is reputed to have been the first potter in Staffordshire to introduce the use of cobalt blue, and a brilliant blue which is found alike on saltglazed stoneware and porcelain has been termed 'Littler's blue'. Occasional specimens decorated with white over the blue ground were made by Littler. On the other hand, some vases made around 1758 with a streaky blue ground were at one time attributed to Longton, and are now more creditably placed to Derby.

The body of Longton wares is usually heavy, with a surface somewhat inclined to be lumpy and uneven. The service-ware generally exhibits 'moons', and the glaze – which contained a percentage of tin oxide – has been well described by W. B. Honey as having the appearance of paraffin wax. Usually specimens are heavier than comparable Derby wares, and figures are inclined to show firecracks, and to be clumsily finished under the base. A fairly large proportion of service ware was made with a flat unglazed base, and no foot-ring.

Of the figures, the *Duke of Brunswick* (Plate 58) here illustrated is characteristic of the most important group ordinarily attributed to this factory. The modelling is exceptionally fine – much finer, in fact, than the greater part of Derby and Bow figures. *Hercules and the Lion* appears in two versions, of which one is more sophisticated than the other. The earlier and more primitive example I have illustrated elsewhere. Both appear to have been taken from seventeenth-century sculpture, the later example being derived without much alteration from a carving by Stefano Maderno called *Hercules and the Lion of Mount Cithaeron*. I record this because the model will be found illustrated elsewhere under the title of *David and the Lion* or *Samson and the Lion*. In the latter case, the story may be a Semitic version of the Greek legend of Hercules.

Some rare examples of topographical painting are known, and these were, apparently, derived from French prints of this nature – at least, the landscapes do not appear to be English in origin. They all seem to be by the same hand, and the artist (unknown) has been termed, for convenience, the 'Castle Painter'. He may have been John Hayfield, whose employment as a painter is recorded.

The Longton palette is soft and very pleasing. It is comparatively easily recognized on the most typical examples. Other things, especially figures, in which the painting closely approaches that of early Derby wares, may have been enamelled at that factory, but differences in the body seem to preclude the possibility of manufacture there.

The finest Longton figures often approach the work of Chelsea in quality, and they represent a very desirable class of English porcelain.

(vi) LOWESTOFT (SUFFOLK), ?1756–?1800

This factory has become internationally famous because of the ludicrous error made by William Chaffers, the author of *Marks and Monograms on Pottery and Porcelain*, which was, unfortunately, believed at the time, and survives even to this day in some less knowledgeable quarters. The error, needless to say, has long since been corrected in the book referred to, and will be found only in the earliest editions.

Chaffers suggested that the enormous quantity of Chinese porcelain with armorial bearings and European subjects, which was painted in Canton to special order, was made and decorated at Lowestoft. Driven from his first position, he endeavoured to maintain that the porcelain was imported from China in white and *decorated* at Lowestoft. Needless to say, it is nothing more than Chinese export porcelain made and decorated in its country of origin. Nevertheless, the trade name for it, 'Oriental Lowestoft', has become hallowed by time, and is still used today, especially in America.

In fact, the porcelain made at Lowestoft is very similar to Bow porcelain. It contains bone-ash in much the same proportions, and pieces decorated in underglaze blue are often virtually impossible to separate from those of the London factory. There can be no possible doubt that only this kind of porcelain was made, because the site of the factory was excavated in 1902, and 'wasters' and fragments submitted to chemical analysis.

The factory had its beginning when Hewlin Luson discovered clay on his estate in 1756. He tried to found a factory, but tradition has it that his workmen were bribed to spoil the mixing. In 1757, a company consisting of Philip Walker, Robert Browne, Obed Aldred, and John Kickman, founded another factory which used the bone-ash paste. It is said that Browne, who was a chemist, somehow managed to get into the Bow factory, and observed the mixing of the body from a hiding-place in a barrel. This romantic story may be true, but it is more likely that they were able to hire a disgruntled Bow workman.

Robert Allen joined the factory in 1757, and subsequently became manager. When the factory closed, he kept a muffle-kiln, and occasionally decorated small items of china. A teapot signed by him is in the Schreiber Collection at the Victoria and Albert Museum, but this was made in China, and was at one time used as evidence in support of Chaffers' theory. Since he did not become an outside decorator until after the Lowestoft factory had closed, obviously he bought porcelain for decorating where he could.

There were a number of artists of the Redgrave family working at Lowestoft, and they have given their names to the 'Redgrave' pattern – a pleasing derivation from the Chinese of rocks and peonies in blue and red.

By far the greater part of existing Lowestoft porcelain is decorated in underglaze blue. Printing in this colour is not uncommon, and some of the pieces thought to be examples of Bow underglaze blue printing may actually be referable to Lowestoft.

Worcester marks were copied very freely, but anyone acquainted with early Worcester porcelain is hardly likely to be deceived. Lowestoft wares are thick, and often clumsily potted, with a thick, greenish or bluish glaze, full of minute bubbles. The body is a creamy colour, and the appearance is in direct contrast to the precisely-potted wares of Worcester.

Inscribed wares form an interesting and important group. These often bear a date in addition to the name of the owner, and we remark at this factory the curious fashion for birth-tablets, which record the name and date of birth of the child.

Less personal are those pieces inscribed 'A Trifle from Lowestoft'.

About 1770 the use of enamel colours became common. A mauve-pink is peculiar to the factory, and was often used with patterns derived from the Chinese 'Mandarin' decoration, specimens of which began to arrive in this country about 1775.

A few small figures were made at Lowestoft, and some portions of moulds for figures and animals were found on the site. Except in a mere handful of instances, however, examples have not been certainly identified.

Writing generally, it may be said that the greater part of Lowestoft production was derived from Chinese porcelain of the simpler kinds, and the more elaborate decorations current at other European factories were not used.

(vii) PLYMOUTH, BRISTOL, AND NEW HALL

Hard-paste porcelain in England was made only at these three factories. The discoverer was William Cookworthy, a Quaker, who was born at Kingsbridge, in Devon, in 1705. He was first apprenticed to a London apothecary, and later returned to Devon to become a member of a firm of Plymouth apothecaries carried on under the name of Bevans & Cookworthy. By 1745 he was interested in the discovery of the secret of the manufacture of Chinese porcelain, and I have already quoted from a letter to a friend on the subject which he wrote in this year.

In 1754 he discovered *kaolin* on the estate of Lord Camelford, and, at a slightly later date, *petuntse*. Camelford himself became interested in the manufacture of porcelain, and assisted Cookworthy financially. In 1765 there is evidence that he was firing experimental bodies in a kiln at Bristol, and it seems that slightly before this date he first met Richard Champion, who was later to take over the manufacture from him.

In 1768 Cookworthy was sufficiently far advanced to apply for a patent, and opened a factory at Coxside, in Plymouth, in the same year. By 1770, despite large sums of money spent both by Cookworthy and Lord Camelford, the Plymouth venture was not paying its way, and the factory was removed to Bristol. Two years later Cookworthy decided to retire from active participation, and Champion continued the manufacture under licence. In 1774 the whole of the patent rights were assigned to Champion.

Richard Champion was born in 1743. His marriage, in 1764, brought him a brother-in-law who was a settler in South Carolina, and there is record of a box of Virginian *unaker* being sent to Bristol. Some of this earth went to Josiah Holdship at Worcester, and a part was used by Champion for experimental purposes.

In 1774, shortly after Cookworthy had assigned his patent, Champion petitioned the House of Commons for an extension of the rights. He was opposed by Josiah Wedgwood on behalf of other Staffordshire potters, but the extension was eventually granted for a total period of twenty-two years.

It would seem, however, that the expenses of meeting this opposition crippled Champion financially, and, by 1778, he was in difficulties. From this year onwards very little work appears to have been done, but the factory by no means went out of existence. An advertisement in the *Bristol Journal* in April 1782 refers to the remaining stock of 'enamels, blue and white, and white Bristol China'.

Champion sold the patent to a company of potters who subsequently opened a factory at New Hall, in Staffordshire. Champion himself went to Staffordshire to oversee the preliminaries of establishing the new manufacture.

This company was in the hands of Samuel Hollins, Jacob Warburton, William Clowes, Charles Bagnal, and Anthony Keeling, and it continued to manufacture true porcelain for some years, until approximately 1810. It then changed to a bone-porcelain of somewhat uneven quality.

Bone-porcelain from New Hall was often marked with the name of the factory, whereas the earlier true porcelain usually bears little but the pattern number.

Plymouth true porcelain falls into two fairly well-marked categories which we can separate by the appearance of the glaze. Some specimens have a thick glaze, full of small bubbles, inclined to pool in hollows and crevices, and, generally, somewhat resembling a soft porcelain glaze. Other examples will show a thin hard glaze, with a surface somewhat akin to the 'orange skin' effect already noted as occurring with some Chinese glazes.

A feature of Plymouth porcelain figures is the very close resemblance which some of them bear to Bow and Longton Hall models. Mr Tebo certainly worked at Plymouth, since his sign-manual has been noticed on Plymouth porcelain, so the origin of the Bow types seems to be fairly obvious. Apart from figures, salts in the form of shells and other marine life are quite common from Plymouth, and we notice these, too, at Bow, with the mark of Tebo.

The Longton Hall types are not, perhaps, so easily accounted for, but it has been assumed that Cookworthy bought some discarded moulds at the Longton Hall sale at Salisbury already mentioned under that heading. There is, quite frequently, slight divergence from the Longton models, particularly in the attributes. Thus cooks become musicians by the simple expedient of replacing pots and pans with musical instruments.

Worcester, too, was copied quite frequently, and we notice this particularly in the shape of some of the tea and coffee pots, as well as in decoration which gives reason to think that Worcester painters were employed.

Some exotic birds have been attributed to a certain Monsieur Soqui, said to have come from Sèvres, whose hand can also be traced on Worcester porcelain. In this case, however, it would seem that he went to Worcester from Plymouth. A few specimens of Plymouth porcelain painted with birds at the studio of James Giles in London are in existence.

Plates are extremely rare. Cups and saucers are not often seen, but sauceboats are not uncommon. Mostly these resemble contemporary silver. Leaf-shaped pickle-trays, made at most of the English factories, are not particularly scarce, although they are mostly decorated in underglaze blue.

A feature of some Plymouth porcelain, also to be seen in porcelain from Bristol, is a peculiar 'wreathing' in the paste. Spiral markings, which start from the bottom, can frequently be felt with the finger-tips, as well as being obvious to the eye. Handles to cups and such things are often slightly askew.

The underglaze blue has a greyish tone usually, although it can assume a blackish tinge, probably the result of firing at too high a temperature.

Of the artists who worked at the factory, the name of Henry Bone, miniaturist and Royal Academician, is best known. He was apprenticed to Cookworthy, and may have done some work for Champion at Bristol.

There are considerable differences between the porcelain of Cookworthy and Champion. The paste and glaze of the latter is more accomplished technically, and styles are obviously derived from Meissen, Sèvres, and Derby.

Floral subjects are by far the more usual in decoration, and green festoons are commonly to be seen. Exotic birds appear occasionally, but are scarce. Gilding is usually over a vermilion base. Underglaze blue was not often used. Most of the existing specimens are painted, but, in a very few instances, transfer-printing was used.

Tebo was at Bristol, and we notice here a type of vase originally derived from Meissen, which has masks on either side, a 'frill' towards the bottom, applied flowers, and, usually, a pierced neck, indicating that it was intended for *pot-pourri*. We notice this type from Bow, Worcester, and Bristol, at all of which factories Tebo worked. It is true that the same vase was made by Derby, but there is no record that Tebo worked here, and this was probably a case of direct copying from Meissen.

Champion made some *plaques* in *biscuit*, with a central coat of arms surrounded by highly modelled flowers. These have been attributed to Thomas Briand, probably the 'French Chemist' discussed in the section referring to Chelsea.

Plates are scarce, and some (especially the larger) have a double foot-ring, used to prevent the centre from sagging during firing.

Bristol figures are of high quality, although a resemblance to work at Derby is to be noticed. It is suggested, with some evidence, that John Bacon modelled for Bristol, and since he also modelled for Duesbury, the resemblance may have more foundation than casual copying.

Coloured grounds were very rarely employed, and then only

to a slight degree, but a bluish-green enamel characterizes much of Champion's decoration.

Many services were made to special order, and some have been identified. Armorial porcelain, sometimes produced at Plymouth, was continued at Bristol.

A certain amount of poorly decorated ware of cheaper quality was made and is referred to as 'cottage Bristol'. Care should be exercised to distinguish between this and some later Staffordshire wares.

The earliest porcelain from New Hall was decorated with such things as the Cantonese 'Mandarin' patterns – over-elaborate and debased Chinese figures with landscapes and buildings especially intended for export to Europe. Very occasionally one sees specimens which are more than usually well-decorated, and these may have been done by the 'outside decorator' Fidèle Duvivier.

A letter from Duvivier to Duesbury in 1791 asks for work, and says that New Hall is giving up elaborate patterns. From then onwards, decoration is mostly of flower-sprigs in a *famille rose* palette, and the forms used were based, principally, on contemporary silver.

Unmarked New Hall porcelain of the nineteenth century is rarely distinguishable from the humbler kinds of contemporary Staffordshire porcelain. The factory was operating until recently, but has now closed.

(viii) CAUGHLEY, COALPORT, AND RIDGWAY, 1772 ONWARDS

The Caughley (Shropshire) manufactory was established shortly after 1750 for the production of earthenware. In 1772 it passed into the hands of Thomas Turner who had been apprenticed at Worcester. Turner married the daughter of the proprietor of the earthenware factory, Ambrose Gallimore, and the manufacture of porcelain was begun in 1772. In 1775 Robert Hancock left Worcester for Caughley, and brought with him some of the engraved plates he had used for transfer-printing at the former factory.

At this period, much blue-and-white china was produced

which, in form and decoration, is not easily distinguished from that of Worcester. The appearance of like designs on the wares of both factories, together with the fact that both were making a soap-rock porcelain almost identical in its essentials, has led to speculation that Worcester sent china to Caughley for decoration, but there is no evidence to support this.

The 'Willow' pattern and the Broseley 'Blue Dragon' were first used here about 1780, and Thomas Minton, who was apprenticed as an engraver to Turner, has been credited with the invention of these famous patterns, both of which, with little alteration, are sometimes used today. The Willow pattern is a true *chinoiserie*, having no Chinese prototype either in decoration or in legend. The story of the Willow pattern is purely a Western invention.

Humphrey Chamberlain, who later founded an independent factory at Worcester, is said to have started by painting Caughley porcelain as an independent decorator.

Most Caughley porcelain is decorated in underglaze blue, either painted or printed. The blue is somewhat variable in shade, but always differs noticeably from that of Worcester, this often being the only method whereby the production of the two factories can be distinguished. A slight pattern of flower-sprigs, somewhat similar to that in use at Chantilly, was frequently employed, together with a certain amount of gilding. More elaborate patterns are not often seen, but were restrained and of excellent quality. Elaborate paintings in enamels can usually more correctly be attributed to Chamberlain, or to some other outside decorator, and are often in a Worcesterish style.

The commonest mark – a capital 'C' – is frequently drawn so as to be virtually indistinguishable from the Worcester crescent, and there is little doubt that the latter mark was copied on some specimens. The porcelain itself is occasionally referred to as 'Salopian', which sometimes appears as an impressed mark.

John Rose was one of Turner's apprentices, and, in 1780, he started a pottery on his own account at Jackfield. In 1799 he purchased Caughley, and continued to operate it in conjunction with a factory at Coalport until 1814. The enterprise was then transferred entirely to Coalport. Incidentally, the latter factory is sometimes referred to as Colebrookdale.

Of Caughley production after the advent of John Rose, it may be said that much, if not all, was sent in white to Coalport for decoration. In 1801 the well-known 'Indian Tree' pattern, a variant of a Chinese *famille rose* style, was introduced at Coalport, and later extensively copied elsewhere on porcelain, ironstone-china, and earthenware.

When John Rose died in 1841, a large manufactory had been developed at Coalport. The undertaking of Billingsley at Nantgarw was taken over in 1819, together with moulds and recipes. Whether or not the Nantgarw impressed mark was added to porcelain made at Coalport in this style is a matter of some controversy, but it is possible.

In 1820 the factory had been awarded the Gold Medal of the Royal Society of Arts for a leadless feldspathic glaze, the lead glaze being a cause of serious illness among operatives. The invention was commemorated by a mark first used about this time.

Apart from services with coloured grounds and flower and fruit painting of fine quality, vases in the style of Chelsea of the gold anchor period, as well as of Meissen and Sèvres, were extensively made, and were sometimes given the marks of those factories. Generally speaking, however, in these days of more specialized knowledge of the early wares, Coalport imitations are not often very deceptive. Some of the flower painting has transfer-printed outlines, which enabled a certain amount of work to be done by less-skilled operatives, a matter of some moment since the demand for Coalport porcelain was both large and growing.

Vases, and other decorative objects, covered with highly-modelled flowers are well known, and these can be regarded as a Coalport speciality, although the same things were produced at Derby during the period of Robert Bloor's proprietorship. Much Coalport porcelain was lavishly gilded, and the quality of the decoration, generally, is often considerably higher than that of contemporary work elsewhere. Services are comparatively common, but are much sought after.

After 1845 the work of Sèvres was increasingly copied under William Frederick Rose. In 1862, William Pugh took over from Rose, who thereupon retired from the business. During Pugh's tenure, the factory suffered a temporary eclipse, and much second-grade porcelain which had been in stock since early in the century was sold off at this time.

Coalport was rescued in 1885 by Peter Bruff. His son, Charles Bruff, who became managing director about 1890, initiated a new period of prosperity. The factory was reorganizing as the Coalport China Company (John Rose & Co.), and at this time started to develop its export business with Canada and the United States which has been continued with increasing success until the present day.

In 1925 Coalport was acquired by the Cauldon Potteries of Shelton, in Staffordshire. Cauldon Place Works were built in 1802 by Job Ridgway, and manufactured pottery, porcelain, and 'stone china' – an opaque semi-porcelain. From 1814 to 1830 the firm was in the hands of the two sons of Job Ridgway, John and William. This partnership was dissolved in 1830, however, and John remained at Cauldon Place, William taking charge of a factory at Bell Bank.

The 'stone china', of which large quantities were made during the nineteenth century, owed its origin to C. J. Mason and is mentioned elsewhere, but Ridgways made it in large quantities. Their porcelain was of extremely good quality, well painted, with coloured grounds and gilding. Services of all kinds were continuously produced, and some important table-services were especially designed for members of the Royal Family. Wedgwood's basaltes and jaspers were occasionally imitated, and the factory patented a number of technical innovations of its own.

Designs mainly followed the Victorian taste, inasmuch as they were derivative, sentimental, and elaborate, but, technically, the workmanship and materials employed left nothing to be desired, and conformed fully to the high standard of quality demanded at the time.

Ridgway's were taken over in 1855 by Messrs T. C. Brown-Westhead, Moore, & Co., under whose guidance the factory continued to expand its business.

In 1932 the Cauldon Potteries went into liquidation, and were, in turn, taken over by the Coalport China Company, the group being acquired in 1936 by Geo. Jones & Son, Ltd, and moved to the present position at Stoke-on-Trent, the Crescent Works.

The factory nowadays manufactures much fine china for export, and is noted for the quality of its coloured grounds and decorative painting.

(ix) DAVENPORT, LONGPORT, NR BURSLEM, STAFFS., 1793–1882

Although this pottery was established in 1793, the exact date at which the manufacture of porcelain was commenced is uncertain.

Much nineteenth-century Davenport porcelain survives, and a good deal of it was excellent in quality. Derby was freely copied, and W. B. Honey records that Thomas Steele, the Derby fruit painter, also worked here. To this may be added the name of the Derby painter, James Rouse, whose hand I have recently observed on two Davenport *plaques* painted in the manner of Birkett Foster.

Tea and dessert services were made in quantity, Japanese and so-called 'Indian' patterns being freely employed.

A celadon glaze and a *rose Pompadour* ground were both in use, and 'stone china' – an opaque semi-porcelain – was manufactured for the cheaper market.

The mark of an anchor, with, usually, the addition of the word 'Davenport', was commonly employed.

(x) PINXTON, NR MANSFIELD, DERBYSHIRE, 1796–1812

This small factory, which worked mainly in the Derby tradition, was started by William Billingsley in 1796. It was situated on the estate of John Coke, who probably provided the necessary capital. Production was very small, and specimens are scarce and often valuable.

Decoration was chiefly flowers in the Derby manner, and

landscapes, which were painted by John Cutts. The hand of Billingsley has not, I believe, yet been identified on wares from this factory.

Many of the forms closely resemble those of early Derby porcelain, the straight-sided coffee-can being made in some quantity. Table-services and small vases formed the greater part of the production, no figures being made.

Billingsley left in 1801, and the factory continued with Cutts as manager until 1812. After 1801 the quality of the porcelain deteriorates greatly. The body was almost opaque, and generally inferior.

(xi) MINTONS, STOKE-ON-TRENT, STAFFS.,
1796 ONWARDS

Thomas Minton was born in 1765, and later apprenticed to an engraver (probably Hancock) at Caughley. He did some patterns for Josiah Spode, for whom he is reputed to have engraved the 'Broseley Blue Dragon' and the 'Willow' patterns, both of which are used today.

The factory, founded in 1796, first made earthenware, porcelain being added about 1798. This early porcelain was a soft-paste, and was abandoned about 1811. In 1821 porcelain was again manufactured, the body then more nearly approaching that in general use in Staffordshire at the time.

The earlier work includes Japan patterns, and some wares with 'bat' printing.

In 1817 the style was Thomas Minton & Sons. In 1836, at the death of Thomas Minton, his son took John Boyle into partnership, the style then being Minton & Boyle. Boyle withdrew in 1842, to be replaced in 1845 by Michael Hollins. The firm was then Minton & Co. In 1849 they were joined by Colin Minton Campbell, and, when Herbert Minton died in 1858, the factory was continued as Hollins & Campbell. The present company was founded in 1883.

In 1825 some of the Derby artists were employed, the flower and fruit painters, Steele, Bancroft, and Hancock, being recorded by Jewitt.

Carrier-Belleuse, the French sculptor, was for some years after 1854 the factory's chief modeller, and Marc-Louis Solon, formerly of Sèvres, introduced the *pâte-sur-pâte* process, specimens of his work signed with the monogram 'MS' being seen occasionally.

Bronzed porcelain, 'Persian' ware – often based on seventeenth-century Near Eastern metal-work – perforated porcelain reminiscent of the *ling lung* work of the Chinese, as well as much Parian statuary, was produced. The work of Sèvres was extensively copied.

The factory is still in existence, and noted for fine-quality porcelain.

(xii) SPODE, STOKE-ON-TRENT, STAFFS.,
c. 1800 ONWARDS

The first Josiah Spode was apprenticed to Thomas Whieldon, the Staffordshire potter, in 1749. He later founded a factory for the manufacture of earthenware which attained a considerable measure of success. The manufacture of porcelain was begun about 1800, and the bone-china body, which is true hard-paste modified by the addition of bone-ash, was probably introduced almost immediately.

William Copeland was taken into partnership about 1813. The style was then Spode & Copeland. The Spodes retired in 1833, and the firm became Copeland & Garrett, Thomas Garrett being taken into partnership. About 1847 the firm first became Copeland late Spode, then W. T. Copeland & Son.

In addition to the manufactory, a London show-room made immense profits for the firm in the early years of the nineteenth century, and extremely large quantities of porcelain were produced.

Little is known of the artists of this factory, but Henry Daniel was principal enameller in the early years of the nineteenth century.

Productions include a number of large and ornate vases in the Empire style, as well as tea, dinner, and dessert services in great variety. A number of new ground colours were introduced, among them being a turquoise, vermilion, and what the factory called 'Sardinian green'. Japan patterns were also employed, especially in the early period.

Many of the wares, particularly towards mid-century, reach depths of vulgarity unplumbed elsewhere, and were replete with excessive gilding, jewelling, and relief work.

'Stone china' was made in some quantity, much of it being decorated with Chinese designs painted over outline transfer-prints in the manner introduced at Worcester in the late 1750s. The elaborate 'Mandarin' styles were employed on vases based on Chinese forms, and often decorated with applied flowers in addition.

About 1846 the Parian body was introduced. This was an imitation of the early Derby and Sèvres *biscuit*, and many figures were modelled in the medium which soon passed beyond the confines of the Spode factory into Staffordshire generally.

The factory is still in existence, and manufactures much porcelain of fine quality.

(xiii) MASONS, FENTON (FORMERLY LANE DELPH), STAFFS., 1802 ONWARDS

This factory was established in the eighteenth century by Miles Mason.

In 1814 Charles James Mason patented an opaque semi-porcelain which he called 'Ironstone China'. This was used for much ware decorated with pseudo-Chinese designs in gaudy colours, as well as enormous vases in the Oriental style. Familiar, too, are moulded jugs made in sizes and decorated with floral patterns in colours. Porcelain of excellent quality, technically, was produced.

The business was purchased in 1851 by Francis Morley, related to the Ridgway family by marriage, and it was later taken over by two brothers named Ashworth.

Most of Mason's pieces were fully marked. Artistically they are negligible.

(xiv) NANTGARW AND SWANSEA, S. WALES, 1814–23

Perhaps the most interesting figure in the history of English porcelain is that of William Billingsley. Born in Derby in 1760 of William and Mary Billingsley, he was apprenticed to the Derby factory in 1774. His father was in business as a japanner and may at one time have been employed at Chelsea as a flower painter.

Young Billingsley was taken in hand by Zachariah Boreman, the Chelsea artist, and his later experiments in the manufacture of porcelain, which were to reach their zenith at Nantgarw, were probably inspired by Boreman who had been at Chelsea during the gold anchor period. If this was indeed the case, then the porcelain of Nantgarw is a lineal descendant of the last, bone-ash, body used at Chelsea, and its superb quality was a short and solitary resurgence of one of the finest of the early-eighteenth-century soft-pastes.

Nevertheless, Billingsley first gained notice as a flower-painter, and, about 1784, he started to paint in a naturalistic manner in which the flower petals were first washed in with full colour, the highlights being wiped out with a dry brush. This mannerism was later extensively copied by other painters, but it is quite distinct from the earlier method, exemplified by the work of Edward Withers at Derby, in which the highlights were left completely unpainted.

The style became so popular that, in 1796, when Billingsley was about to leave Derby, the London agent, Lygo, wrote:

I hope you will be able to make a bargain with Mr Billingsley for him to continue with you, for it will be a great loss to lose such a hand, and not only that, but his going to another factory will put them in the way of doing flowers in the same way, which at present they are entirely ignorant of.

Billingsley, however, was allowed to leave Derby. He went on to Pinxton (see p. 264) and here, for the first time, he was able to experiment with porcelain manufacture. His recipes, which varied somewhat in detail, but were the same in essentials, were all calculated to produce porcelain of superb quality, but they were extremely difficult to fire successfully, and this eventually proved his undoing.

In 1801 he left Pinxton for Mansfield, and here supported himself by working as an 'outside decorator'. He later went to Torksey in Lincolnshire. It has been suggested that he made porcelain here, but this remains unproven. In 1808, now accompanied by his son-in-law, Samuel Walker, he arrived at Worcester, where he worked as a decorator and arcanist. The quality of the Worcester porcelain body at this time probably owes something to Billingsley. He left Worcester, breaking his agreement, and we next hear of him in 1813 at Nantgarw where he had established a small factory. Billingsley and Walker were here joined by William Weston Young.

Billingsley now started to manufacture porcelain in earnest, but although the quality was of the finest, the kiln-wastage was colossal. It is said to have been in the region of nine-tenths, which means, in effect, that out of ten plates put into the kiln, one emerged in a fit condition for decorating. Of course, no factory could continue for long under such conditions, and no doubt improvements were made which reduced this figure to some extent.

In 1814 the partners petitioned the Board of Trade for assistance, and Sir Joseph Banks, a member of the Board and President of the Royal Society, referred the matter to Lewis Dillwyn, proprietor of the Cambrian Pottery at Swansea, for a report on their claims. Dillwyn, who had hitherto manufactured earthenware, was convinced that Billingsley's porcelain could be made a commercial success, and arrangements were made for the removal of the Nantgarw enterprise to Swansea, which probably took place in the same year.

The expected improvements did not materialize, and quarrels became frequent. Dillwyn insisted on the addition of soap-rock to overcome the kiln-wastage factor, and Billingsley left in a huff and returned to Nantgarw with Walker. In 1819 the two men were offered employment by John Rose. This was accepted, and they went to Coalport together. Rose thereupon became possessed of Billingsley's formulas, and it is a matter of common observation that some Coalport porcelain made at this time closely resembles that of Nantgarw.

William Weston Young continued at Nantgarw until 1822, and was principally occupied in decorating stocks of white porcelain in company with Thomas Pardoe.

Dillwyn had already sold his interest in the Swansea undertaking in 1817 to Timothy and John Bevington, who continued to use a soap-rock body until 1823.

Thomas Pardoe, mentioned above, was born in 1770, and apprenticed at Derby in 1785. He was at Worcester for a short time, and in 1795 went to Swansea as a painter of earthenware. In 1809 he was in Bristol, decorating Staffordshire china. He died at Nantgarw in 1823, having been there since 1820. His only son, also Thomas, continued the Bristol decorating establishment for some years after his father's death.

The work of Pardoe *père* took in a considerable range of subjects, of which fruit, birds, landscapes, and flowers in the Billingsley manner have been noted.

Much Nantgarw porcelain was decorated in London by such people as Robins & Randall (see page 282). W. D. John has pointed out that the colours used by these London studios caused an iridescent halo to develop in the glaze immediately surrounding the enamels. This is not always immediately apparent and its occurrence depends on the angle at which light is allowed to fall on the surface.

Most of the London decoration is in the manner of Sèvres, or of such Paris factories as Nast, and the Nantgarw body often resembles that of Sèvres. Because of the shortage of French porcelain to decorate, that of Nantgarw was much in demand.

At Swansea the first body used was similar to that of Nantgarw, but a slightly more stable body with a green translucency was introduced shortly afterwards. This is known as the 'duck egg' paste, and contained a small amount of soap-rock. The bone-ash, contained in the Nantgarw body, was omitted.

A change was made shortly afterwards to a porcelain containing far more soap-rock, and this can be distinguished by the glaze which has been likened to the appearance of pigskin from the small pits in its surface. As specimens often bear an impressed trident as a mark, it is also sometimes called the 'trident body'.

Most Nantgarw porcelain bears the mark 'Nantgarw C.W.', impressed. Although this may be missing from small tureens and such things, it is invariably present on plates. The 'duck egg' paste has the word 'Swansea' impressed or written over-glaze, usually in red, more rarely in blue or gold.

It is possible that a limited amount of porcelain was made at Coalport to the Nantgarw formula.

(xv) ROCKINGHAM, SWINTON, NR ROTHERHAM, YORKS., 1820–42

There appears to have been a pottery on this site from about 1745 onwards. Porcelain was made between 1820 and 1842, the proprietors then being Thomas Brameld and his two brothers. They were granted a subsidy by Earl Fitzwilliam in 1826, and the griffin from the Earl's crest was adopted as a mark.

Porcelain made here was principally in a revived *rococo* style in imitation of Derby and Coalport. 'Named views' were fre-quently used as decoration, and gilding is usually elaborate and of good quality. Coloured grounds were commonly employed for services of all kinds; deep blue, green, and a peculiar grey being the most often seen. Dessert and tea services have not unusually survived, although they are rare in anything like a complete state.

A few figures were made, and amusing cottages and castles in porcelain are to be seen occasionally. Some small vases modelled as tulips are decorative and sought after.

The work of this factory is not particularly important artistic-ally, but quality is somewhat better than at many of its larger contemporaries.

(xvi) H. & R. DANIEL, STOKE-ON-TRENT, STAFFS. 1826–?45

Henry Daniel, chief enameller to Spode, began the manufacture of porcelain in 1826. The quality is comparable with that of most contemporary manufacture.

(xvii) BERNARD MOORE, STOKE-ON-TRENT

At the beginning of this century a potter named Bernard Moore specialized in reproduction of the Chinese *flambé* and *sang de bœuf* glazes. There are usually marked 'BM' in the form of a monogram.

*

During the nineteenth century a large number of factories for the manufacture of porcelain sprang up in Staffordshire. There is no space to mention them in detail here, but their history and productions are described in copious detail by Llewellyn Jewitt. His book, first published in 1877, should be in the library of all students of English porcelain, not only because it is a veritable storehouse of information, even if at times inaccurate, but because it acts as an ever-present example of the fallibility of human judgement in artistic matters.

Describing some of the gaudier excesses of Spode, Jewitt says: '... the massive jewelling, gilding, and enamelling, is of the most costly and elegant character.'[1]

The cuts which illustrate the book form, in themselves, an exhibition of bad taste almost without parallel elsewhere. It has, in fact, long been one of my cherished ambitions to see an exhibition of such porcelain, and if anyone is sufficiently public-spirited to organize one, I commend him to Jewitt for inspiration.

(xviii) LIVERPOOL, LANCS.

There were a number of small factories making porcelain in this city during the eighteenth century.

Very little is known of any of them, but that of Richard Chaffers was the largest, and its wares can be identified with a fair measure of certainty. It was situated at Shaw's Brow, and Podmore, one of the workmen responsible for the transfer of

1. *The Ceramic Art of Great Britain*, 1877 and 1883. (Incidentally this book has not been reprinted, and inquiries should be directed to the second-hand bookseller. Copies are not infrequent.)

the early Bristol factory to Worcester, assisted in its foundation in 1756.

A porcelain made from soap-rock was employed, and the productions much resemble those of Worcester during the early period of that factory. Usually the body is greyish in colour, and somewhat inferior to that of Worcester, but the quality approaches that of Worcester on occasion. Decoration is mostly derived from the Chinese, and was both in underglaze blue and in colour. Specimens can usually be differentiated from those of Worcester by the colouring, by somewhat cruder drawing, and by such details as the shape of foot-rings, and similar small points. A mere handful of pieces decorated by means of transfer-prints in colour are known, and were undoubtedly made here.

There has, in the past, been confusion between some Liverpool wares and those of Longton Hall. I have recently observed a dish of this class marked with the 'LL' of Longton Hall, impressed underglaze. This makes the attribution of such doubtful specimens to Longton Hall the more certain, and it is possible that this factory experimented with a soap-rock body.

Both Podmore and Chaffers died in 1765, and little is known of the factory thereafter.

A manufacturer of *delft*, Seth Pennington, made porcelain at Shaw's Brow. The production may be referable to a type of porcelain, having a glaze with a little tin oxide added, to be seen occasionally. W. B. Honey ascribed to Pennington a group of porcelain painted with a blue which he aptly described as having a 'sticky' appearance.

Another factory belonging to Zachariah Barnes has been regarded as the source of a mug in the British Museum inscribed, 'Frederick Heinzelman Liverpool 1779'.

Sadler & Green of Liverpool were probably independent discoverers of the art of transfer-printing, and some porcelain decorated in this way, and signed 'Sadler Liverpool', has been recorded. They were not manufacturers.

(xix) WEDGWOOD, ETRURIA, STAFFS., 1759 ONWARDS

Josiah Wedgwood was born in Burslem in 1730, son of Thomas Wedgwood, and member of a family well known in the Potteries since the seventeenth century. In 1754 he entered into partnership with Thomas Whieldon of Fenton who was the manufacturer of an earthenware which enjoys a considerable reputation among collectors of English pottery. In 1759 Wedgwood returned to Burslem and established his own factory. About 1762 he first manufactured cream-ware which enjoyed an almost immediate popularity. It could be made cheaply enough to appeal to a wide market, and it was more attractive than the earthenware which had hitherto been available to the poorer buyer. Cream-ware eventually attracted the attention of Queen Charlotte, and it was then retitled 'Queen's Ware'. Much of the early production was transfer-printed by Sadler & Green of Liverpool, independent discoverers of the art. At a later date Wedgwood opened a decorating establishment at Chelsea.

The popularity of cream-ware was such that Wedgwood had to expand his factory, and he reorganized it to produce large quantities. The process of industrialization was eventually to have a disastrous effect on the artistic value of English pottery and porcelain, and led ultimately to the degeneration of the nineteenth century.

At this time the neo-classical style was becoming popular, helped by the publication of Sir William Hamilton's catalogue of his collection of Greek, Roman, and Etruscan antiquities in 1766. The new fashion was particularly adapted to speedy manufacture, and Wedgwood immediately adopted and popularized it, like William Duesbury at Derby.

In 1769 Wedgwood entered into partnership with Thomas Bentley which lasted until the latter's death in 1780. Bentley was responsible for many of the London interests of the partnership, including the decorating establishment at Chelsea already mentioned. 1768 saw the introduction of the black basaltes body, which was described by Wedgwood as black porcelain, and was sometimes termed 'black Egyptian ware'. This body was used for a number of things, including some imitations of Greek vases on which decoration was carried out in a type of red enamel called (by Wedgwood) 'encaustic painting'. Some large portrait busts were modelled in this medium, and, less often, figures, of which a portrait statuette of Voltaire is probably the finest. Basaltes continued to be popular in the nineteenth century, and occasionally one sees it painted in opaque *famille rose* enamels. *Rosso antico* was a hard red stoneware, and a cane-coloured stoneware enjoyed a certain popularity from about 1779.

The well-known jasper ware was introduced in 1776. This somewhat resembles a *biscuit* porcelain, and was unusual inasmuch as it contained barium sulphate as a constituent of the body. The body was coloured in various shades, of which blue is the commonest, but sage-green, lilac, a kind of lavender, and yellow, were also in use. Decoration was carried out in white in relief over the coloured ground. The earliest jasper was stained throughout. The later varieties are coloured on the surface only. These were known, at the time, as 'solid' and 'dip' for obvious reasons.

Jasper ware was employed for a number of unusual purposes, as well as for the well-known vases, plaques, and such things. It was used for ornamenting furniture, for interior decoration, for personal ornaments, and for such things as chessmen. Portrait medallions are much sought after, particularly those bearing the mark of the Wedgwood and Bentley period. The most notable artists were John Flaxman and William Hackwood.

Jasper ware was much copied in Staffordshire, principally by William Adams, John Turner, and Neale & Palmer. Continental copies are not uncommon as it was exported during the eighteenth century in large quantities. Sèvres made some reproductions, as did a number of German factories, but these are not usually difficult to distinguish. Certain forgeries have been noticed marked 'WEDGEWOOD' impressed. The intrusive 'E' is sufficient indication of the spurious nature of the specimen.

The position of Wedgwood in a volume devoted to porcelain is a little ambiguous. The Company have not at any time manufactured porcelain on a scale comparable with their other products, and this note on their history is included largely because of their influence on the style of porcelain manufactured at English and Continental factories, rather than for their own work.

Wedgwood, however, did make a number of experiments with porcelain. There is record that an English resident of Canton gave him some Chinese materials in 1776, and that he made some experimental pieces of hard porcelain with them. The death of the person in question brought the experiments to an end. At a later date, between 1812 and 1822, bone porcelain was manufactured. This was of excellent quality, and competently decorated in the fashions of the period. Naturally, it is somewhat scarce today. Manufacture of bone porcelain was recommenced towards the end of the nineteenth century, but has until recently occupied a subordinate position in relation to their other products.

Wedgwood productions of the twentieth century have been notable for the enlightened attitude of the Company towards considerations of style, and they have been responsible for some of the most acceptable things to be produced in Staffordshire during the last few decades.

(XX) THE OUTSIDE DECORATORS

The first English outside decorator was William Duesbury, who had a studio in London from about 1750 to 1753. From his surviving account book we know that he painted porcelain from all the factories then in existence, as well as saltglazed stoneware from Staffordshire. His work has not been certainly identified although many conjectures have been put forward. A small class of figures from Chelsea marked with a raised anchor have had the anchor touched with red. It is possible that these were decorated at the Duesbury studio, and, if we accept this premise, we can attribute porcelain from other factories to him on a basis of similarity.

Thomas Hughes is a decorator of whose work we know nothing, although his name has survived.

The first to be certainly identified is James Giles of Clerkenwell who decorated a considerable amount of surviving porcelain between 1760 and 1776. He employed a number of artists, but it is not known whether he also functioned as a painter.

The hand of this studio was for long suspected, but no certain identification was made until four plates were presented to the Victoria and Albert Museum by a descendant, Mrs Dora Grubbe, which confirmed some of the ascriptions previously made.

W. B. Honey attributed to him some colourful 'dishevelled birds' to be seen alike on Chelsea and Worcester porcelain. A decoration of sliced fruit, which appears on porcelain from both these factories, seems to have been certainly by a Giles artist, and some landscapes pencilled in black and washed with green have also been attributed to Giles. This kind of decoration is mentioned in the Chelsea sale catalogue for 1756, however, and in this case he was no more than following a fashion already existing. Some of these landscapes from Chelsea can creditably be given to O'Neale.

Many of the coloured ground decorations to be seen on Worcester porcelain emanated from Giles, particularly an opaque apple green and a claret. The claret is usually to be seen in conjunction with flowers, but I have noticed a single instance of its use in conjunction with figures of musicians in the style of Watteau. This decoration is much better known on Chelsea porcelain, and all such painting from either factory can be attributed to Giles.

Somewhat overdecorated Bow figures bearing the anchor and dagger mark are most probably the handiwork of Giles, and black transfer-prints coloured over were undoubtedly done by him. These date from the time of his dispute with the Worcester factory, when the consequent curtailment of his supplies of white and blank porcelain caused him to search elsewhere for supplies. There is record of the purchase by him of transfer-printed tea services at auction, which could only have been for the purpose of adding further decoration.

Worcester bearing a gold crescent mark is almost always by Giles, and Worcester with a gold anchor mark can certainly be attributed to him. Marks in overglaze red usually appear on porcelain which can reasonably be credited to this studio.

Some of the more usual patterns, such as that of the 'Quail' on porcelain from Worcester and Bow, were undoubtedly painted here.

His gilding is inclined to be thick, and rather crudely chased.

The explanation, formerly accepted, that the appearance of an identical hand on porcelain from different factories necessarily meant that an artist had migrated from one to the other, can only be regarded as partially true, and the existence of Chinese porcelain decorated in England in the manner of the Giles studio helps to put the matter in its proper perspective.

Although Jeffryes Hamet O'Neale, the Irish miniaturist, began by working for the Chelsea factory as a painter, he falls into the category of an outside decorator after about 1758. His work on Worcester porcelain, some of which is signed, may have been done at the instigation of the factory, but there is no reason to suppose that he actually functioned as a factory artist, although he certainly visited this city. It is possible that he was in close touch with Giles, and may have done some work for him. It is probable, too, that he used Giles's kiln. He was not alone in this, since we have a reference by Thomas Craft of Bow (in 1760) to a bowl which he had burned 'in Mr Gyles' Kiln' at a cost of three shillings. O'Neale later worked for Josiah Wedgwood.

His work includes some amusing animals, and figures among ruins, during his Chelsea period. One example signed in full is known at this time. Much valued are some magnificent 'Fable' paintings on Worcester porcelain with a *gros bleu* ground. A series of signed vases for Worcester with hunting scenes and landscapes are of exceptional importance.

John Donaldson was born in Edinburgh in 1737, and came to London in 1759. He, too, was a miniaturist. His work on Worcester vases, mostly figure subjects, is highly valued. His hand may be assumed on some Chelsea vases. The attribution to him of some Derby vases of the early 1760s painted with figure subjects is extremely doubtful. Occasionally his work was signed with the monogram 'JD'.

Fidèle Duvivier, cousin of Henri-Joseph Duvivier who worked both at Chelsea and Tournai, decorated for several factories, including Chelsea, Worcester, Derby, and New Hall.

His most important work was on Worcester porcelain, but one or two interesting examples on that from New Hall have been noted. He was fond of figures of children playing, with potworks as a background.

Wedgwood had a decorating establishment in Chelsea. James Banford was employed here before he went to Derby. Identification of the work done is not always certain.

Zachariah Boreman worked in London for one of the outside decorating studios at the end of the century after he left Derby. W. B. Honey says that none of his work for Derby was signed, but there is in existence a large straight-sided Derby mug *initialled* by him.

Baldock, Robins & Randall, and Thomas Pardoe, have been mentioned elsewhere in this chapter. Donovan of Dublin decorated porcelain, mostly from Minton, in the early part of the nineteenth century.

Independent modellers are few. John Bacon perhaps modelled for Bow, although his work cannot be certainly identified. He started as an apprentice to Crispe of Bow Churchyard, who taught him the art of modelling for porcelain. He later supplied models to Wedgwood and Derby, and probably to Champion at Bristol.

Pierre Stephan may have worked in the first place for Sprimont. He was at Derby between 1770 and 1774, and later went to Wedgwood. Still later, he worked as a free-lance, supplying models to Duesbury. He was responsible for the well-known *Two Virgins awakening Cupid*, *Two Bacchantes adorning Pan*, and *Three Graces distressing Cupid*, all after Angelica Kauffmann.

Louis-François Roubiliac perhaps falls into this category, since it is at least possible that he supplied a few models to his friend, Sprimont, in the early days of Chelsea's history, although there is no reason to suppose that he was at any time employed by the factory.

(xxi) FAKES, FORGERIES, AND REPRODUCTIONS

Generally, there are few really dangerous forgeries of early English porcelain, but fakes are rather more numerous.

Samson's reproductions are in hard-paste porcelain, and the distinction, therefore, is not difficult. Gold anchor marked Chelsea, and Derby of the 1760s, are Samson's favourite sources of inspiration. His colouring is usually inaccurate, and most of the specimens one sees are replete with a large gold anchor in a prominent position. The factory anchor is small and placed in an inconspicuous position, usually at the back near the base. I have observed a tea service probably made by this firm, which bore a red anchor mark, and was complete even to the small bread-and-butter plates which did not form part of the tea service until about 1840. The offer of a more or less complete tea service in Chelsea of the red anchor period, when even a cup and saucer is a scarce and desirable item, demands more than usually careful consideration.

Samson's have done some quite good reproductions of Worcester scale-blue, but, strange as it may seem, pottery reproductions are superficially the more deceptive.

Highly dangerous are a few forgeries of Bow and Chelsea porcelain which appear to have made recently. These have been offered from time to time on the art market, at first with some success. Bow birds are a favourite subject with this particular man. These are deceptive, but have been recognized by the principal dealers, auctioneers, and museums. The material used is a kind of bone-china.

It is, of course, possible to take a mould from a genuine figure, cast it in a porcelain body, and fire it. But it is important to remember that all porcelain bodies shrink in firing between one-fifth and one-eighth, so that remoulds will always be distinctly smaller than the original figure. Figures were issued by Derby in several sizes, and these remarks do not apply. Derby figures, however, are rarely valuable enough to be worth forging in this way, except, perhaps, those of the early period, when the idiosyncrasies of manufacture make the forger's task too difficult to be worth attempting.

Ultra-violet radiation and chemical tests are particularly useful in cases of this kind and no forgeries have yet been produced which will stand up to rigorous examination with scientific techniques.

Fakes in English porcelain are legion, the greater number being on a Worcester porcelain base, although Chelsea has by no means escaped attention.

These are, mainly, of two kinds: those in which a simple decoration has been cleaned off with hydrofluoric acid to leave room for subsequent repainting in more expensive and sumptuous styles, and those in which elaborate decoration is superimposed on sparse painting of, perhaps, a few flower sprays.

Fortunately, however, when soft-paste porcelain which has been made for some years is refired, even in the low-temperature enamelling kiln, changes frequently take place which make the interference obvious. The glaze bubbles, and leaves a 'burst bubble' effect behind when it cools. This can usually be seen quite easily. Black specks in the glaze are likely to be extensive, although this is a fault to be seen in some of the earlier and more primitive porcelains, and, in this case, is due to the use of wood as fuel.

When the new painting has been carried out over an original sparse decoration, the faker usually employs a ground colour opaque enough to cover the original work, but if the piece is examined carefully traces of the original painting may be noted under the ground. Caution needs to be exercised, however, in examining such specimens before they are irrevocably stigmatized as fakes. It is likely that James Giles, towards the end of his career, had great difficulty in obtaining adequate supplies of white porcelain, and he may have redecorated sparsely painted things to help to fill the gap. The ability to recognize instances in which this has occurred comes principally from an acquaintance with characteristic work of the Giles studio.

It is difficult to say how long has to elapse between manufacture and redecoration before the adverse effects described above become sufficiently obvious to help in the detection of a fake, but it is probably of the order of twenty years, varying somewhat with the type of glaze employed, and the uses to which the specimen has been put. If, for example, the suspected piece has been used for cooking, fumes and food juices may have penetrated the glaze, and will carbonize under the heat of the kiln, leaving extensive areas of black specking.

These remarks apply equally to the redecoration of French soft-paste porcelains, but, generally, hard-paste specimens do not react in the same way, and the colouring and the style of the painting is usually the only guide.

A number of nineteenth-century English factories extensively manufactured reproductions of Continental and English porcelain of the eighteenth century. Sèvres and Meissen were the prime targets, but Coalport also imitated Chelsea vases of the gold anchor period. Some 'Goat and Bee' jugs are reputed to have come from this factory, but I feel that there is room for doubt on this point, although there seems little doubt that one of the nineteenth-century English factories was responsible.

Tournai made some fairly close copies of early Chelsea during the nineteenth century. These are apt to be dangerous since they are in a true soft-paste body. At worst, chemical analysis will reveal the fraud. Some soft-paste copies are said to have been made in Staffordshire, but I have not been able to identify a specimen.

A Bond Street china-dealer, Baldock, was responsible for much redecoration of Sèvres china, the best being done for him by T. M. Randall. The porcelain of Nantgarw was intended to imitate soft-paste Sèvres, and much of it was decorated in London.

Randall was in partnership with Richard Robins, who was at one time a painter at Pinxton. Boreman may have worked for Robins & Randall when he left Derby about 1795. Randall later opened a small factory at Madeley, in Shropshire, according to Llewellyn Jewitt, at which he imitated Sèvres porcelain in a body similar to that made by Billingsley at Nantgarw.

Several Continental factories copied Wedgwood's jasper ware during the eighteenth century, and the early part of the nineteenth. Generally, these are not particularly deceptive.

I have noticed one example of a forgery of Longton Hall which was complete with the mark. I have not, so far, seen another, and since the first was not conspicuously successful, the attempt may have been abandoned.

The work of other English factories has not been copied, except in some isolated instances. The most dangerous are forgeries of Bristol porcelain made on the Continent, since these are in the same hard-paste as the originals.

It must be remembered that early porcelain factories were prepared to make replacements for broken items of a service to special order. This, to some extent, accounts for occasional interlopers in the form of more than ordinarily exact copies of one factory's patterns on the porcelain of another. A service needs to be examined carefully, piece by piece.

CHAPTER NINE

Some Miscellaneous European Factories

THERE remain a few factories of some importance which have not been discussed in the preceding chapters. These, for various reasons, fall a little outside the main current of the development of porcelain manufacture in Europe.

The first, and undoubtedly the largest, is that of *Copenhagen* in Denmark, and nineteenth- and twentieth-century productions are much the commonest in England and the United States, the earlier examples being rarely seen.

In 1737, C. K. Hunger offered his services to the Danish Government to help in the establishment of a porcelain factory. His reputation as an arcanist was not particularly good, and his approach was rejected. In 1755, deposits of *kaolin* were discovered on the island of Bornholm, and, in 1759, Louis Fournier was invited to Copenhagen by the Government. Fournier had been a modeller at Vincennes and Chantilly, and he made a soft porcelain of excellent quality at the Danish capital between 1759 and 1765. Surviving examples are few.

In 1774 the Royal factory was founded as the result of experiments by Franz Heinrich Müller. J. G. von Langen, a mining engineer, who had been associated with Benckgraff in the establishment of the Fürstenberg factory, acted as adviser, and, owing to his influence, the modeller and arcanist, A. C. Luplau of Fürstenberg, was engaged in 1776. The Queen, Juliane Marie, was originally the principal shareholder. A portrait bust by Luplau is in existence.

The credit for producing a successful hard porcelain body must be awarded to Luplau, and he appears to have brought with him a number of German workmen who were skilled in the manufacture of porcelain. Not all of these workmen were satisfactory, however, and things did not run smoothly in many directions. In 1780, notwithstanding a subvention from the royal Treasury, the factory was in severe financial straits. It was thereupon decided to offer it to the King who, probably against his better judgement, accepted it, and it was henceforward styled *den Kongelige Danske Porcelains Fabrik*.

The porcelain made after 1780 is principally in the neo-classical style. Many of the *motifs* of the painted decoration were taken from various German factories, the *Mosaik* from Berlin being an example. This latter factory was a particularly frequent source of inspiration.

In 1789 Copenhagen started work on an immense service intended for the Empress Catherine II of Russia. This numbered 1,602 pieces, each painted with exact botanical specimens taken from a work on the national flora. This service – called the *Flora Danica* – is probably the best known of all Copenhagen porcelain, and is in the Rosenborg Castle in that city. Much of the painting was done by Johann Christoph Bayer.

Figures were well modelled, and formed a considerable part of the factory's production. Once again, the sources of inspiration were frequently derived from elsewhere, but some figures of Norwegian peasants are both original and interesting. The work of Luplau at Copenhagen can only be uncertainly attributed. The factory is, of course, still in existence, and produces decorative porcelain of the highest quality. Latterly it has been strongly influenced by Chinese porcelain of the Sung period.

In Sweden, a factory at *Marieberg*, near Stockholm, made both *faïence* and porcelain. The manufacture of the latter began about 1766, and many of the early things show very strongly the influence of Mennecy. This is somewhat to be expected, since Marieberg was managed at this time by Pierre Berthevin who had previously been at the French factory. The enterprise closed finally in 1788.

Porcelain was made in Russia, principally at St Petersburg and Moscow. *St Petersburg* was the Russian Imperial factory, and, here again, Hunger was responsible for the earliest experiments. He was in the city in 1745, but, apart from one or two imperfect specimens, he made no serviceable porcelain. Some experimental pieces were made in the immediately succeeding years by Dmitri Vinogradoff, but, these apart, nothing exists which was made prior to 1762. The factory was then in the hands of Johann Gottfried Müller, a Saxon (?Meissen) arcanist. After 1762 production was on a fairly large scale. Perhaps most often seen are snuff-boxes, many in the form of letters, the lid being painted to represent an envelope. A certain amount of work was done in the style of Sèvres, and some well-executed statuettes of Russian peasants were made towards the end of the century. The neo-classical style predominates.

A factory in *Moscow* was founded by an Englishman named Gardner in 1758, and made, among other things, some excellent figures of Russian peasants. Somewhat later, from about 1806 to 1872, the factory of Popoff was in existence. Gardner occasionally used a mark which was a close copy of the Meissen mark of the Marcolini period.

There were a few other factories elsewhere in Russia, but specimens are so rarely seen that they are hardly worth mentioning. A factory at *Baranovka* made imitation Easter eggs.

In Switzerland a factory was founded at *Zürich* in 1763 under the direction of Adam Spängler (or Spengler) whose son was a modeller at the English Derby factory at a later date. For a short time a soft-paste was made, but specimens are extremely rare, and the transition to hard-paste seems to have taken place by 1765.

Zürich porcelain is scarce, and some is of the highest quality. The earlier work, particularly, is much sought after. The best figures were probably modelled by Johann Valentin Sonnenschein who came from Ludwigsburg, and the influence of this factory is often apparent. Later work is less distinguished.

A factory was founded at *Nyon* (near Geneva) in 1780. The moving spirit was Ferdinand Müller, who came from Frankenthal. Associated with him was Jean-Jacques Dortu who had been at Berlin and Marieberg. The manufacture of porcelain ceased in 1813. Most of the wares made here are based on styles current at the Paris factories, and are not particularly important. One or two figures have been identified, but obviously few were made.

A factory at *Weesp*, in Holland, was established about 1764 where some excellent porcelain was produced. The works were transferred to *Oude Loosdrecht* in 1771, and removed again to

Oude Amstel in 1784. The work of these factories is mostly derivative, both France and Germany providing inspiration.

A factory at *The Hague* commenced operations about 1776. It both manufactured porcelain and decorated that from other factories, more particularly porcelain from Tournai. Soft-paste pieces bearing the mark of The Hague were only decorated at that factory.

This chapter is not by any means exhaustive. It does not mention the large number of small factories which were, for the most part, started in the late eighteenth and nineteenth centuries in Germany, Czechoslovakia, Austria, Bulgaria, Hungary, Rumania, and other European countries. To do so would mean that this volume could be little more than a dreary catalogue of names and dates. The literature dealing with these later factories is very small, but the bibliography gives some further information on the point. In any case, their production is not particularly important. It is mostly of poor quality and largely derivative.

Epilogue

*

CHAPTER TEN

The Art of Porcelain

AT this point I would ask the reader to turn back to the four quotations which preface this book. Each is appropriate to a different aspect of our subject, and it is now time to consider them in a little more detail.

The first, by a noted art critic, may surprise some of my readers who have not previously considered ceramics as belonging to the realm of the fine arts, and quite obviously Sir Herbert Read does not intend to refer to many of the factory products we have been discussing. Nevertheless, the first sentence remains largely true, even of these. The final comment needs to be considered in relation to such things as Chinese porcelain of the Sung period, when pottery can be regarded, not only as one of the fine arts, but as one of the principal manifestations of art at its time and place.

The second quotation is a salutary warning to the collector. I have used it before, and shall undoubtedly do so again, because, in a few apposite words, it provides sound advice which is often neglected.

The *raison d'être* of the third quotation is obvious. It sums up the ultimate purpose of much of the information contained in this book, and, in the realm of *expertise*, the mental processes involved in elucidating a crime, piecing together a diplodocus, or deciding upon the date and provenance of a specimen of porcelain, are all much the same. The laws of evidence apply equally in each case.

The last I do not propose to justify. The philosophical attitude implicit in it is one which I find congenial, even though it be a little unfashionable. As a subject for meditation it is not without value.

Porcelain, like other works of art, is an extension of the artist's imagination given concrete and lasting form. It is not the fault of the material if the imagination is lacking in quality. It is a reflection of the mind of the creator, and can equally well be seen in Chinese and European porcelain. The cliché is not a Western prerogative.

My own preference for figures as best typifying the art of porcelain in Europe is probably fairly obvious, and the reason for it is that, for the most part, European service ware – made to be at once useful and decorative – was also largely derivative. Much of it was strongly influenced by Chinese and Japanese originals, even in cases where the decoration was European in both style and subject matter. Figures, on the other hand, are almost completely European in derivation and feeling, and, for the most part, continue the tradition of such small sculptures as Renaissance bronzes and German ivory-carvings. Those with Oriental affiliations are but few in number, and usually limited to the early period.

Obviously, appreciation of the porcelain of all countries and of all periods demands a taste which is both omnivorous and eclectic. Despite the fact that preceding chapters have ranged over a wide field, my own preferences are for Chinese porcelain of the Sung period, and for Meissen, Chelsea, and some early French figures. I dislike the later *rococo* period, much of the work of Sèvres, and almost anything in the neo-classical style, which I consider unsuited to porcelain. I have deliberately set down my preferences and prejudices, not because I consider them to be in any way of outstanding value, but because I think the reader is entitled to be able to evaluate a chapter of this nature in the light of the author's tastes.

In the formation of porcelain, the wheel is the primary tool. It is personal to the workman responsible for the piece. It is under his direct control, and an artist can play upon it in a way that provides many subtleties and refinements of form which can be appreciated only if the trouble is taken to watch a good thrower at work. Moulding, on the contrary, is primarily the transference into porcelain of something done in another medium, and it is, therefore, rarely 'art freed from any imitative intention'. This applies with much more force to service ware than to figures, where moulding, generally, is not objectionable. The Sung potter used the wheel freely, and most Sung porcelain is made in this way. The use of other methods was, in fact, distinctly rare. Yet subtleties of form are infinite in their variety.

Decoration, usually painted in European and the later Chinese wares, was more in keeping with the nature of the material in the Sung period. Much of it was carved or incised into the raw clay with a skill which has yet to be approached. The floral decoration of white Ting ware, delineated with a magnificent economy and freedom of line, should be compared with the same ware decorated with a moulded design. True, the moulding is often of an extremely high standard, but the two things do not belong on the same plane. Basil Gray (Plates 42 and 43 of his *Early Chinese Pottery and Porcelain*) shows an example of each on opposing pages. Both are the best of their kind, but the superiority of the freehand work is obvious at a glance.

The later wares are by no means inconsiderable, but the spirit had changed. The potter was no longer content with a fine pot decorated by methods appropriate to the clay of its origin. He became a painter in addition. Porcelain has to be considered from two aspects – for the form, and for the painting to be seen thereon. Bad form is sometimes redeemed, to some extent, by fine painting, and bad painting can spoil a good pot.

It has often seemed strange to me that we are content to dismiss a good deal of European porcelain as over-decorated and, at the same time, we accept it from the potters of the Ch'ing period without comment, and even with approbation. We too rarely pass judgement using the same criteria as we should in condemning this fault in European wares.

Porcelain is a beautiful substance in its own right, and does not need to be hidden by enamel colours. It is for this reason that, in an earlier chapter, I referred to certain Japanese porcelain as finer than some Chinese Ch'ing wares. The Kakiemon painters understood the value of white porcelain far better than many of the decorators of Ch'ing-te Chên. The classic examples of bad ceramic decoration appear on some Italian *maiolica* of the middle and late periods – the so-called *istoriato* style – when elaborate architectural paintings metaphorically 'knocked a hole' in a dish or a vase. To a much smaller extent this is to be seen with some later European landscapes on porcelain, but, generally, the eighteenth-century decorators had the good sense to avoid this fault.

It is a matter of common observation that, in the appreciation of the plastic and visual arts, most people fall into two distinct categories – those who receive the greatest pleasure from the sense of sight, and those in whom the sense of touch predominates. Of course this is very much a simplification, since the other senses modify the one which is predominant. In Europe, the visual sense is undoubtedly the more highly cultivated, although whether this is inherent, or whether it has been acquired from training and tradition, is a matter upon which it is difficult to express an opinion. The Chinese, particularly those of the Sung period, understood the aesthetics of touch very well, and there is in existence a Sung bowl on which is inscribed, *For the Imperial Fondling of Ch'ien Lung*.

Porcelain can fruitfully be classed as either sculptural or visual, The difference can be seen comparatively easily by comparing a typical Sung piece with the later painted wares. Its application may not always be so obvious when European figures are considered, but, nevertheless, the distinction exists. Many of the earlier figures in particular have remarkable sculptural qualities. They are truly three-dimensional. An excellent example can be found in the figures of Bustelli. The urge to pick them up and examine them is strong. Many of the later figures, however, are little more than flat patterns, analogous to a painting. Like the bas relief, they bridge the gap between sculpture and painting, and there is, usually, small desire to pick them up. The two-dimensional impression is reinforced by a glance at the back, which is often sketchily finished.

Most *baroque* figures are three-dimensional, with well-marked plastic and sculptural qualities. Many *rococo* figures, on the other hand, are essentially picturesque. Some are no more than elaborate pieces of book-illustration, and some are straightforward adaptations from paintings and engravings.

The eighteenth-century appreciation of white marble as a suitable material for sculpture was something new. The coloured porcelain figure is much more in the tradition of European and Oriental sculpture. No doubt eighteenth-century taste was misled by the fact that, owing to the effect of burial, antique sculpture was always recovered in an uncoloured state. But the Greeks and Romans invariably coloured their statuary, and the practice was common in Europe at least until the Renaissance. These colours, however, were of the kind which have necessarily yielded to the vicissitudes of time, and porcelain offered, for the first time, a material in which it was possible to fix colours permanently. It is valuable, therefore, inasmuch as it shows us what colours were in use at the time of manufacture (and the manner of their use) in all the original freshness, whereas paintings in other media have become faded and dirty. The quality of porcelain painting was often extremely high, and although there is nothing, perhaps, which can be regarded as great art, at least it is often decorative art at its best.

Quality in porcelain is a difficult subject to discuss, because it is, to some extent, bound up with questions of taste. Nevertheless, the question ought to be examined. The factors to be considered are innumerable, and the canons of criticism vary with the porcelain under discussion.

In Sung porcelain, for example, one looks for subtleties of form and a glaze of fine colour. Obviously to pass judgement on such a specimen necessarily means an acquaintance with a large number of representative specimens, since criticism in any branch of the arts must be a process of comparison. The London museums are especially rich in fine porcelain, the provincial museums, except in a few notable instances, being less happily situated. There is much to be said, in fact, for travelling exhibitions which could very profitably spend a week or two in each of the larger towns. The assistance such exhibitions could give to the more enlightened manufacturers in their efforts to raise popular taste in pottery and porcelain would be enormous.

The later Chinese porcelains have to be considered from the viewpoint of form and colour, but, in many cases, form is somewhat secondary to the quality of the painting. When one examines a Sung bowl, attention is first turned to its shape, whereas, in the case of a Ming or Ch'ing bowl, more often than not the painting is examined first.

The finest European porcelain painting undoubtedly belongs

to such things as the Meissen landscapes, river scenes, harbour scenes, and *chinoiseries*, to the 'Fable' decorations of England, and to works of all kinds which show the quality of imagination rather than a slavish dependence upon the Orient. Derivations from book illustration are somewhat uneven in importance, and, whilst they are sought after, often acquire their desirability from the scarcity of specimens rather than from their status as works of art. Such things as imitations of grained wood covering the porcelain surface can obviously be dismissed as artistically negligible.

When we consider the question of figures, we must give due weight to the fact that the 'repairer' intervenes between the modeller and the finished specimen. No matter how fine the original model, it must be sliced up, moulded, cast, and put together again, and nothing is more revealing than to examine several examples of the same model side by side. It is surprising how great the differences in pose and quality can be between one and the other as the result of the 'repairer's' activities. Of course, some things are so few in number that the possibility of finding a better example can be regarded as remote, but with the commoner things, it is more satisfying to wait and acquire as good a specimen as can be found.

Discrimination can only result from study, and from seeing as much porcelain as possible. The student should beware of 'snap' judgements based on insufficient knowledge. The collector, in particular, is likely to be badly misled in the early years of his career if he is the kind of person prone to say that he doesn't understand art, but he knows what he likes. I have seen collections made in this way put to the test of sale by auction, and the prices realized have reflected the manner in which the collection had been put together.

Beware of the gaudy and the meretricious. It is far too often seen in porcelain, more particularly in the later varieties. It looks 'showy', but the spirit wearies of the merely showy in course of time, and there can be no intrinsic value, spiritual or monetary, in porcelain coloured in every conceivable part merely because a brush, a palette, and a porcelain surface, all came together in the hands of a man who did not know when and where to stop.

This brief chapter suffers, perhaps, from the fact that there is no common denominator under which to bring the vast number of objects mentioned in this volume. The reader must form his own judgements with the knowledge he has, but at least it may be said that all works of art have one thing in common – simplicity. The other attributes are more appropriate to country of origin and to period, and cannot be so widely applied.

Appendices

*

Notes on the Pronunciation of Chinese Words

FOR practical purposes the vowel sounds can be taken as similar to those of the Italian language, an unmodified 'a' being given the same sound as in *father*, for instance.

Some of the consonantal sounds are given below:

Ch	J as in *joke*.
Ch'	Ch as in *cheap*.
H	is aspirated as in English.
Hs	approximately -sh as in *ship*.
J	R as in *run*. *Ju-yao* = Roo-yow.
K	G as in *guard*.
K'	K as in *keramic*.
P	B as in *bat*.
P'	P as in *part*.
S	as in *sand*.
Sh	as in *ship*.
Ss	a hissing 'S', somewhat as in *snake*.
T	D as in *distant*. Ting-yao = *Ding-yow*.
T'	T as in *time*.
Ts	Dz.
Ts'	Ts – as in *pots*.
Tz	the nearest approach to this sound is the terminal – ds in *goods*.
Tz'	the terminal -tz in *blitz*.

Other consonants are pronounced in the same way as their English equivalents.

Of the special vowels, *ü* is approximately equivalent to the French *u*. *Ê* and *erh* have much the same sound as the *er* in *earnest*. *Ih* is similar to the *-ir* as in *giraffe*.

These notes are sufficient for the reader to arrive at an approximate equivalent to the Chinese pronunciation of the proper names and terms used in Chapter 1.

Glossary of Oriental Words and Phrases
used in Chapter 1

The definitions are not literal translations, but give the accepted usage. Proper names are included in the Index. The words are Chinese unless otherwise indicated.

An hua. 'Secret' decoration. (See page 76.)

Arhat. See *Lohan*.

Cha-no-yu (Jap.) Tea Ceremony. A traditional ceremony conducted according to fixed rules in which certain kinds of pottery and porcelain are used. See *Temmoku*.

Chi hung. Underglaze copper-red. The so-called 'sacrificial red'.

Ch'ih lung. A kind of dragon. One of the Four Supernatural Creatures.

Ch'i-lin. Kylin. One of the Four Supernatural Creatures.

Ch'ing lung. A blue dragon.

Ch'ui ch'ing. Powder-blue (a ground colour).

Fan hung. Iron-red. An enamel colour.

Fêng huang. The phoenix.

Fên-ting. 'Flour' Ting. A variety of Ting ware.

Fu. The bat. Happiness.

Ho-ho (Jap.). See *Fêng huang*.

Hua shih. The 'slippery stone' of Père d'Entrecolles. Perhaps soap-rock or pegmatite.

Hu. Tiger. Also the name of a particular type of vase.

Hui ch'ing. Mohammedan blue.

Ju'i. A frequent decorative *motif*. (See page 94.)

Kinuta seiji (Jap.). 'Mallet' celadon. A greenish-blue celadon glaze.

Kirin (Jap.). The equivalent of the Chinese *ch'i-lin*.

Ko. 'Elder brother'. In reference to an early type of celadon glaze.

Komori (Jap.). Bat.

Kuei. A kind of dragon.

Kylin. See *Ch'i-lin*.

Lei wên. A border decoration or diaper somewhat resembling the 'key' fret.

Ling chih. Fungus symbolizing longevity.

Ling lung. 'Devil's work'. Porcelain with pierced walls.

Lohan. One of the Sixteen Buddhist Disciples. Equivalent to the Japanese Rakan.

Lung. The Dragon.

Ma chün. A type of ware somewhat resembling Chün. (See page 71.)

Mei jên. Figures of tall girls used as decoration. 'Long Elizas' or 'Lange Lyzen'.

Mei ping. A vase shape. A bulbous body having a short narrow neck with a small aperture. Often used for a single spray of prunus blossom.

Mishima (Jap.). A decoration involving inlaying in differently coloured clays.

Mon (Jap.). An emblem somewhat analogous to the European armorial bearing. That of the Japanese Emperor is a formalized chrysanthemum.

Nien hao. Reign mark.

Pa chi-hsiang. The Eight Buddhist Emblems. (See page 95.)

Pa hsien. The Eight Immortals.

Pa kua. The Eight Trigrams, symbolic of natural forces. (See page 92.)

Pa pao. The Eight Precious Things. (See page 99.)

Pai ma. The white horse of Hsüan Chang used as decoration.

Pai-ting. White Ting ware. The finest variety.

Pai-tun-tzŭ. Petuntse – feldspathic rock used in the manufacture of porcelain.

Pai-tzŭ. White stoneware or porcelain.

Pien yao. Porcelain with *flambé* glaze.

Po ku. The Hundred Antiques. (See page 98.)

Rakan (Jap.). See *Lohan.*

San ts'ai. Three-colour decoration. Used of ware decorated with lead-silicate glazes suitably coloured and kept apart by clay threads or engraving. The colours vary, and may, in fact, occasionally be more than three.

Shou. Long life. Longevity.

Shu t'ai. 'Soft' Chün. A late variety of Chün ware.

Ssŭ ling. The Four Supernatural Creatures.

T'ao t'ieh. A grotesque mask used from the earliest times as decoration.

Temmoku (Jap.). A type of ware used in the Tea Ceremony.

T'o t'ai. 'Bodiless' ware. An extremely thin porcelain.

Tobi seiji (Jap.). 'Buckwheat' celadon. A green celadon glaze splashed with brown spots.

Ts'ui. (Probably) a colour resembling kingfisher's feathers. Perhaps blue.

T'u ting. 'Earthen' Ting. A coarse variety of Ting ware.

Tz'ŭ. A resonant stoneware. The term is open to interpretation.

Wu chin. Mirror black.

Wu ts'ai. Five-colour decoration. Enamel colours painted over the glaze. Used of Ming porcelain.

Yang ts'ai. 'Foreign colour'. The *rose* enamel.

Yang-yin. A symbol representing the male-female principle. (See page 92.)

Yao. Ware.

Ying ch'ing. 'Shadowy blue'.

Chronology of Chinese Porcelain

The name given is that in ordinary use

c. 3500–2000 B.C. Neolithic Culture. Decorated pottery recovered from graves.

c. 1766–1122 B.C. Shang-Yin dynasty. Period of the finest bronze ritual vessels.

1122–249 B.C. Chou dynasty. Ritual bronzes and jades.

c. 722–481 B.C. Period of the Spring and Autumn Annals.

c. 481–205 B.C. Period of the Warring States.

221–206 B.C. Empire of Shih Huang Ti (Ch'in dynasty).

206 B.C.–A.D. 220. Han dynasty. (Proto-porcelain.)

220–589   The Six Dynasties.

       386–535. Period of the Northern Wei.

       502–556. Period of the Liang.

581–618   Sui dynasty.

618–906   T'ang dynasty. (Founding of Sāmarrā.)

907–960   The Five Dynasties.

960–1279 Sung dynasty. (Coloured glazes.)

1280–1368 Yüan dynasty. (First blue-and-white porcelain.)

1368–1644 Ming dynasty.

       1368–1398 Hung Wu. (Decoration in enamel colours.)

       1399–1402 Chien Wên.

       1403–1424 Yung Lo.

       1425   Hung Hsi.

       1426–1435 Hsüan Tê.

       1436–1449 Chêng T'ung.

       1450–1457 Ching T'ai.

       1457–1464 T'ien Shun.

       1465–1487 Ch'êng Hua.

       1488–1505 Hung Chih.

       1506–1521 Chêng Tê.

       1522–1566 Chia Ching.

       1567–1572 Lung Ch'ing.

       1573–1619 Wan Li.

       1620   T'ai Ch'ang.

1621–1627 T'ien Ch'i.
1628–1643 Ch'ung Chêng.
1644–1912 Ch'ing dynasty.
      1644–1661 Shun Chih.
      1662–1722 K'ang Hsi.
      1723–1735 Yung Chêng.
      1736–1795 Ch'ien Lung.
      1796–1820 Chia Ch'ing.
      1821–1850 Tao Kuang.
      1851–1861 Hsien Fêng.
      1862–1873 T'ung Chih.
      1874–1908 Kuang Hsü.
      1909–1911 Hsüan T'ung.
      1912 onwards The Chinese Republic.

MARKS OF IDENTIFICATION
TO BE FOUND ON PORCELAIN

Marks of Identification to be found on Porcelain

THIS list includes the marks most usually seen. For the sake of brevity it omits those which give the name of the factory or the place of manufacture. These can be found by reference to the Index. There are a large number of marks less often seen – workmen's marks are legion – which are for the most part recorded in such standard works as Chaffers's *Marks and Monograms* and Honey's *Dictionary of European Ceramic Art*. The reader is reminded that a mark is not a guarantee of authenticity, and that forged marks are common. This is fully discussed in the text.

CHINESE MARKS

There is a distinct and noticeable difference between English handwriting of the eighteenth century and that of today. Much the same applies to written Chinese. The characters listed below are in standard form, but there are variations between (for example) Ming calligraphy and that of the Ch'ing period.

MING REIGN-MARKS

年製 洪武 Hung Wu 1368–98

大明弘治年製 Hung Chih 1488–1505

年製 永樂 Yung Lo 1403–24

德年製 大明宣 Hsüan Tê 1426–35

德年製 大明正 Chêng Tê 1506–21

化年製 大明成 Ch'êng Hua 1465–87

靖年製 大明嘉 Chia Ching 1522–66

慶年製　大明隆　Lung Ch'ing 1567–72

曆年製　大明萬　Wan Li 1573–1619

啟年製　大明天　T'ien Ch'i 1621–7

崇禎　年製　Ch'ung Chêng 1628–43

CH'ING REIGN-MARKS

治年製　大清順　Shun Chih 1644–61

熙年製　大清康　K'ang Hsi 1662–1722

正年製　大清雍　Yung Chêng 1723–35

隆年製　大清乾　Ch'ien Lung 1736–95

年製　嘉慶　Chia Ch'ing 1796–1820

光年製　大清道　Tao Kuang 1821–50

豐年製　大清咸　Hsien Fêng 1851–61

治年製　大清同　T'ung Chih 1862–73

緒年製　大清光　Kuang Hsü 1874–1909

玉　yü (jade)

MEISSEN: This mark was used, with minor variations, from 1724 onwards. It is found on early pieces in enamel colours, subsequently in underglaze blue.

 The monogram of Augustus the Strong, and of Augustus III. At first used for porcelain for royal palaces or gifts, later used more widely. See also page 174.

The caduceus. Particularly used on coffee cups intended for export to Turkey.

The Academic, Transitional, or 'Dot' period, 1763–74.

The period of Marcolini. 1774–1814.

N = 346
W

Inventory mark of the Johanneum Collection. Incised into the glaze with a diamond.

On defective specimens sold to decorators in white. The cancellation is incised into the glaze.

VIENNA: In overglaze enamel, in underglaze blue, incised, or impressed. First used 1744.

HÖCHST: In red and purple overglaze, in underglaze blue, and impressed.

BERLIN: Wegely's factory. In blue and impressed. Paste and model numbers incised into the base of a figure. Marks are found separately.

G

Gotzkowsky's factory, 1761–3, in underglaze blue.

Royal factory. Introduced about 1765.

KPM

Königliche Porzellan-Manufaktur. A later mark sometimes used in conjunction with an orb or the Prussian eagle.

NYMPHENBURG: First used about 1754. Several variations observed.

F

FÜRSTENBERG: An early mark, usually in blue.

FRANKENTHAL: Monogram of Carl Theodor. First used about 1762.

LUDWIGSBURG: Monogram of Charles Eugene, Duke of Württemburg. In use from 1758 onwards.

 GOTHA: In underglaze blue or impressed. 1783 onwards.

 ANSBACH: 1758 onwards. An early mark probably discontinued after a few years.

 KLOSTER VEILSDORF: 1760–97.

 VOLKSTEDT: 1760–99.

 FULDA: In use at least from 1780, and perhaps earlier.

LIMBACH: From about 1772.

ILMENAU: From about 1792.

 RAUENSTEIN: From about 1783.

ITALY AND SPAIN

FLORENCE (MEDICI PORCELAIN): Several minor variations.

CAPO-DI-MONTE: Quoted as appearing on an early figure, but perhaps Buen Retiro.

NAPLES: 1771 onwards.

DOCCIA: In blue, red, gold, and impressed. Late eighteenth century.

NOVE (VENICE): In red and gold.

VENICE: The Cozzi factory.

VINOVO (NEAR TURIN): Several variations observed.

BUEN RETIRO: In blue and gold. 1760–1804.

Incised. Perhaps a late mark.

S.̤C
                   T

SAINT-CLOUD: In blue. Used separately, but known in conjunction. The letters represent: Saint-Cloud, Trou.

CHANTILLY: In red or blue. The commonest mark, found in several variations.

D.V.

MENNECY: In blue, red, black, and incised. For *de Villeroy*.

SÈVRES: Mark for the year 1753. Nearly always in blue enamel.

Mark for the year 1778.

R.F
Sevres.

Period of the first Republic. About 1800–2.

Period of Charles X. Used between 1824 and 1828. The last two figures of the year are usually added.

In chrome green. Louis Philippe, 1845–8.

SÈVRES (*contd*): Period of Napoleon III, usually on specimens in revived soft-paste.

H

STRASBOURG: Paul Hannong, 1752-5.

NIDERVILLER: Monogram of Custine, 1770-93.

SCEAUX: A rare mark.

ORLEANS: A doubtful mark.

PARIS (DE LA COURTILLE): In underglaze blue and incised.

PARIS (RUE POPINCOURT): For Nast of Paris. 'Nast' is sometimes written in full.

PARIS (CLIGNANCOURT): In underglaze blue.

PARIS (RUE THIROUX): In underglaze blue. For Antoinette.

315

J P.

FONTAINEBLEAU: Factory of Jacob Petit 1795 onwards.

TOURNAI: In various colours.

ENGLAND AND WALES

CHELSEA: Incised, and (rarely) in underglaze blue. 1745–50. The alchemical sign for fire.

In underglaze blue. About 1750. Very rare.

Raised on a medallion, 1750–2. Red, 1752–6; gold, 1756 onwards. Underglaze blue, about 1753. Chocolate, probably decorated by James Giles.

CHELSEA-DERBY: 1770–84.

BOW: Incised on early wares. Perhaps a workman's mark.

In red enamel: perhaps indicative of decoration by James Giles.

In underglaze blue. Worcester mark seen on Bow figures.

DERBY: Incised, and in blue, red, and purple, of which red is commonest. Introduced about 1784.

 About 1795. For Duesbury and Kean.

 The Bloor period. 1811–48.

 Stevenson and Hancock: between 1850 and 1870.

 WORCESTER: A common factory mark. In underglaze blue. Overglaze enamel usually indicates decoration by Giles.

 A factory mark; less common. In underglaze blue.

 In underglaze blue, usually on patterns derived from oriental sources.

 Pseudo-Meissen mark. Most specimens thus marked are referable to James Giles.

Pseudo-Chinese mark. The resemblance to a Ming reign-mark is plain.

317

WORCESTER (*contd.*): On transfer printed wares; usually included in the decoration. The initials of Robert Hancock, and the rebus of Richard Holdship.

LONGTON HALL: ? for Littler-Longton. In blue and impressed. The latter is very rare.

[Lowestoft]

LOWESTOFT: No factory mark. The crescent mark of Worcester and the Meissen crossed swords were both used occasionally.

$2\!\!\!\downarrow$

PLYMOUTH: In underglaze or overglaze blue, red, or gold. This is the alchemical sign for tin.

BRISTOL: In blue enamel.

x

In blue enamel.

ℂ   c

CAUGHLEY: The Worcester crescent, or the initial C, usually in blue.

SALOPIAN.

In blue and impressed.

CDale.

COLEBROOKDALE (COALPORT): In blue and gold, an early mark.

𝒳ₘ

MINTON: In blue enamel. A side-glance at the mark of Sèvres.

318

COPENHAGEN, Denmark: From 1775 onwards.

MB MARIEBERG, Sweden: Known in several forms which include this monogram. From about 1766. Incised, in blue, and in red.

ᴲ ST PETERSBURG, Russia: In blue. Ekaterina (Catherine II). 1762–96.

П The Emperor Paul. 1796–1801.

ГАРДНЕРZ MOSCOW, Russia: Impressed. Gardner's factory. Early nineteenth century.

ΛП Popoff's factory (Monogram AP). Early nineteenth century.

Z ZURICH, Switzerland: In blue.

  NYON, Switzerland: In underglaze blue. Variations common.

✗̇ WEESP, Holland: In underglaze blue, 1759 onwards.

M₀ L OUDE LOOSDRECHT, Holland: Incised, underglaze blue, and enamel colours.

Amstel. OUDE AMSTEL, Holland: In blue and black. Successors to the factory above.

  THE HAGUE, Holland: In blue, under or overglaze. The latter frequently on Tournai porcelain decorated in Holland.

These marks were frequently drawn carelessly and may only approximate to the version given above.

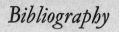

Bibliography

*

Bibliography

THIS Bibliography, which will fill the needs of the student for some time to come, must inevitably contain a large number of scarce and expensive works. Many of them are out of print and can only be purchased through antiquarian book-sellers. Public libraries can procure perhaps three-quarters of those listed through the Regional Library system.

For the reader who does not wish to pursue the subject in so much detail, most of the works listed under the heading of 'General' are fairly easily obtained. Earlier editions of some of the older works are also available, but most contain inaccuracies of fact or attribution. In many cases, in view of the scarcity of documentary evidence and other research material, attributions in some of the later works should not be regarded as fixed and immutable.

It is to be regretted that so many of the works listed are in languages other than English. Books in English dealing with Continental porcelain are distinctly rare, and few of them – a notable exception being J. F. Hayward's Monograph on *Vienna Porcelain of the du Paquier Period* – treat the subject in very much detail. The Faber Monographs on Pottery and Porcelain are useful introductions, and contain a generous selection of illustrations. W. B. Honey's massive two-volume *Dictionary of European Ceramic Art* and Emil Hannover's *Pottery and Porcelain* will supply much information in a concentrated form which will supplement the outline provided by the present volume. Of these two works, the former is to be preferred for up-to-date factual accuracy.

For the rest, it will be necessary to learn the language until such times as detailed monographs or translations are available in English. Nearly all the works cited are copiously illustrated, and a slight knowledge of the language, reinforced by a good dictionary, will assist the reader to acquire much additional information of considerable value.

Volumes marked * are the most useful to the student. The others provide background information, are source books, or are principally concerned with less fundamental aspects of the subject. Titles marked † are intended to provide an extended book-list of easily available works which will supplement the present volume for the general reader.

GENERAL

Behse, A., *Deutsche Fayencenmarken Brevier*. Klinkhardt & Biermann, Braunschweig, 1955.

Burton, W., *Porcelain: its Nature, Art, and Manufacture*. Cassell, London, 1906.

Burton, W., and Hobson, R. L., *Handbook of Marks on Pottery and Porcelain*. London, 1928.

Carolsfeld-Köllman, *Porzellan der europäischen Fabriken*. Revised edition, Klinkhardt & Biermann, Braunschweig, 1956.

*Chaffers, W., *Marks and Monograms on Pottery and Porcelain*. Various English and American editions from 1876 onwards.

Cox, Warren E., *Pottery and Porcelain*. Crown Publishers, New York, 1944.

*Cushion, J. P., *Pocket Book of English Ceramic Marks*. Faber, London, 1959.

*Cushion, J. P., *Pocket Book of German Ceramic Marks*. Faber, London, 1961.

*Cushion J. P., and Honey, W. B., *Handbook of Pottery and Porcelain Marks*. Faber, London, 1956 and 1958.

*Danckert, Ludwig, *Handbuch des Europäischen Porzellans*. Prestel-Verlag, Munich, 1954.

*Hannover, Emil, *Pottery and Porcelain*. Benn, London, 1925.

*Honey, W. B., *A Dictionary of European Ceramic Art*. Faber, London, 1952.

†Honey, W. B., *The Art of the Potter*. Faber, London, 1940.

Leach, Bernard, *A Potter's Book*. London, 1940.

*†Schmidt, Robert, *Das Porzellan als Kunstwerk und Kulturspiegel*. Munich, 1925.

Translated by W. A. Thorpe as: *Porcelain as an Art and Mirror of Fashion*. Harrap, London, 1932.

FAR EASTERN PORCELAIN

Beurdeley, Michel, *Porcelain of the East India Companies*. Barrie & Rockliff, London, 1962.

Goldschmidt, Mme D. Lion, and Moreau Gobard, J.-C., *Chinese Art*. Studio Books, London, 1961.

*†Gray, Basil, *Early Chinese Pottery and Porcelain*. Faber, London, 1953.

Hetherington, A. L., *Early Ceramic Wares of China*. Benn, London, 1922.

*Hetherington, A. L., *Chinese Ceramic Glazes*. P. D. and Ione Perkins, South Pasadena, 1947.

*Hobson, R. L., *Chinese Pottery and Porcelain*. Cassell, London, 1915.

*Hobson, R. L., *The Wares of the Ming Dynasty*. Benn, London, 1922.

Hobson, R. L., and Hetherington, A. L., *The Art of the Chinese Potter*. London, 1923.

Hobson, R. L., *The Later Ceramic Wares of China*. London, 1925.

Hobson, R. L., *The Catalogue of the George Eumofopolous Collection*. London, 1925.

Hobson, R. L., Rackham, Bernard, and King, William, *Chinese Ceramics in Private Collections*. London, 1931.

Hobson, R. L., *A Catalogue of Chinese Pottery and Porcelain in the Collection of Sir Percival David, F.S.A.* London, 1934.

*†Hobson, R. L., *British Museum Handbook of Pottery and Porcelain of the Far East*. London, 1937.

*†Honey, W. B., *The Ceramic Art of China and other Countries of the Far East*. Faber, London, 1945.

*Honey, W. B., *Corean Pottery*. Faber, London, 1947.

*Honey, W. B., *Chinese Porcelain: K'ang Hsi, Yung Chêng, and Ch'ien Lung*. Victoria and Albert Museum, London, 1927.

*†Jenyns, Soame, *Later Chinese Porcelain*. Faber, London, 1952.

Koyama, Fujio, *Céramique ancienne de l'Asie*. Office du Livre, Fribourg, 1960.

†Tsui Chi, *A Short History of Chinese Civilization*. Gollancz, London, 1942.

Zimmermann, Ernst, *Chinesisches Porzellan*. Leipzig, 1923.

The Royal Academy of Arts. Exhibition of Chinese Art. Illustrated Catalogue. London, 1935.

The Transactions of the Oriental Ceramic Society. Annually.

The following catalogues of Sotheby & Company, the London fine art auctioneers:

    The Stephen D. Winkworth Collection. April 1933.

    **The George Eumofopolous Collection*. May 1940.

    The Robert C. Bruce Collection. May 1953.

GERMAN AND AUSTRIAN PORCELAIN

Bayer, A., *Ansbacher Porzellan*. Ansbach, 1933.

Berling, K., *Meissner Porzellan und seine Geschichte*. Leipzig, 1900.

Berling, K., *Festschrift der königlichen sächsischen Porzellanmanufaktur Meissen, 1710–1910*. Leipzig, 1910. Also an English translation entitled: *Publication to Commemorate the 200th Jubilee of the oldest European porcelain factory*. (Very rare.)

*Braun, E. W., and Folnesics, J., *Geschichte der k.k. Wiener Porzellanmanufaktur*. Vienna, 1907.

*Christ, Hans, *Ludwigsburger Porzellanfiguren*. Berlin, 1921.

*Ducret, Siegfried, *German Porcelain and Faïence*. Oldbourne Press, London, 1962.

*Graul, R., and Kurzwelly, A., *Alt-Thüringer Porzellan*. Leipzig, 1909.

*Hannover, Emil, *Pottery and Porcelain*. London, 1925.

*Hayward, J. F., *Vienna Porcelain of the du Paquier period*. Rockliff, London, 1952.

*Hofmann, Friedrich H., *Frankenthaler Porzellan*. F. Bruckmann A.G., Munich, 1911.

*Hofmann, Friedrich H., *Geschichte der bayerischen Porzellan-Manufaktur Nymphenburg*. Karl Hiersemann, Leipzig, 1921–3.

*Hofmann, Friedrich H., *Das Porzellan der europäischen Manufakturen im 18. Jahrhundert*. Propyläenverlag, Berlin, 1932.

*†Honey, W. B., *Dresden China*. Faber, London, 1947.

†Honey, W. B., *German Porcelain*. Faber, London, 1947.

*Lenz, G. *Berliner Porzellan: Die Manufaktur Friedrichs des Grossen, 1763–86*. Berlin, 1913.

Meyer, H., *Böhmisches Porzellan und Steingut*. Leipzig, 1927.

*Pazaurek, Gustav E., *Deutsche Fayence- und Porzellan-Hausmaler*. Hiersemann, Leipzig, 1928.

*Pazaurek, Gustav E., *Meissner Porzellanmalerei des 18. Jahrhunderts*. Stuttgart, 1929 .

*Röder, K., and Oppenheim, M., *Das Höchster Porzellan*. Mainz, 1930.

Sauerlandt, M., *Deutsche Porzellanfiguren des 18. Jahrhunderts*. Cologne, 1923.

*†Savage, George, *Eighteenth Century German Porcelain*. Rockliff, London, 1958.

*Scherer, C., *Das Fürstenberger Porzellan*. Berlin, 1909

*Schnorr von Carolsfeld, L., *Porzellan der europäischen Fabriken des 18. Jahrhunderts*. Berlin, 1912.

Zimmermann, Ernest, *Die Erfindung und Frühzeit des Meissner Porzellans*. Berlin, 1908.

*Zimmermann, Ernst, *Meissner Porzellan*. Leipzig, 1926.

ITALIAN AND SPANISH PORCELAIN

Eisner Eisenhof, Baron A. de, *Le Porcellana di Capo-di-Monte*. Milan, 1925.

Lane, Arthur, *Italian Porcelain*. Faber, London, 1954.

Morazzoni, G., *Le Porcellane italiane*. Milan, 1935.

FRENCH AND BELGIAN PORCELAIN

Auscher, E. S., *A History and Description of French Porcelain*. London, 1905.

Bourgeois, E., *Le biscuit de Sèvres au XVIIIe Siècle*. Paris, 1909.

*Chavagnac, Comte X. de, and Grollier, Marquis A. de, *Histoire des manufactures françaises de porcelaine*. Paris, 1906.

Haug, H., *Les faïences et porcelaines de Strasbourg*. Strasbourg, 1922.

*†Honey, W. B., *French Porcelain of the 18th Century*. Faber, London, 1950.

*Lane, Arthur, *French Faïence*. Faber, London, 1948.

*†Savage, George, *Seventeenth and Eighteenth Century French Porcelain*. Barrie & Rockliff, London, 1960.

*Soil de Moriame, E. J., and Delplace de Formanoir, L., *Les Porcelaines de Tournay*. Tournai, 1937.

ENGLISH PORCELAIN

General

Bemrose, Geoffrey, *Nineteenth-Century English Pottery and Porcelain*. Faber, London, 1952.

Church, Sir Arthur H., *English Porcelain*. Chapman and Hall, London, 1911.

†Dixon, J. L., *English Porcelain of the Eighteenth Century*. Faber, London, 1952.

*English Ceramic Circle, The, *Transactions*. Published irregularly.

*English Ceramic Circle, The, *Commemorative Catalogue of an Exhibition of English Pottery and Porcelain held at the Victoria and Albert Museum*. Routledge, London, 1949.

*Eccles, Herbert, and Rackham, Bernard, *Analysed Specimens of English Porcelain*. Victoria and Albert Museum, 1922.

Fisher, Stanley W., *English Blue and White Porcelain of the Eighteenth Century*. Batsford, London, 1950.

Hobson, R. L., *Catalogue of English Porcelain in the British Museum*. London, 1905.

*†Honey, W. B., *Old English Porcelain*. London, 1945.

*†King, William, *English Porcelain Figures of the Eighteenth Century*. Medici Society, London, 1925.

Nightingale, J. E., *Contributions towards the History of Early English Porcelain*. Bennett Bros, Salisbury, 1881.

*Rackham, Bernard, *Catalogue of the Herbert Allen Collection*. Victoria and Albert Museum, London, 1923.

*Rackham, Bernard, *Catalogue of the Schreiber Collection of English Porcelain, Enamels, and Glass*. Victoria and Albert Museum, London, 1930.

*†Savage, George, *18th-Century English Porcelain*. Rockliff, London: Macmillan, New York, 1952.

*Savage, George, *English Pottery and Porcelain*. Oldbourne Press, London, 1961.

Schreiber, Lady Charlotte, *Journals*. London, 1911.

Bibliographical

*Cook, Cyril, *The Life and Work of Robert Hancock*. London, 1948.

*MacAlister, Mrs D. (ed.), *William Duesbury's London Account Book*. London, 1931.

*Tapp, Major W. H., *Jeffryes Hamett O'Neale*. University of London Press, London, 1938.

Chelsea

Bemrose, William, *Bow, Chelsea, and Derby Porcelain*. Bemrose, London, 1898.

Blunt, R. (ed.), *Cheyne Book of Chelsea Porcelain*. London, 1924.

Bryant, G. F., *Chelsea Porcelain Toys*. Medici Society, London, 1925.

Hurlbutt, F., *Chelsea China*. London, 1937.

*†King, William, *Chelsea Porcelain*. Benn, London, 1922.

*MacKenna, F. Severne, *Chelsea Porcelain: The Triangle and Raised Anchor Wares*. Lewis, Leigh-on-Sea, 1948.

*MacKenna, F. Severne, *Chelsea Porcelain: The Red Anchor Wares*. Lewis, Leigh-on-Sea, 1951.

*MacKenna, F. Severne, *Chelsea Porcelain: The Gold Anchor Wares*. Lewis, Leigh-on-Sea, 1952.

BIBLIOGRAPHY

Bow

Bemrose, W., *Bow, Chelsea, and Derby Porcelain*. Bemrose, London, 1898.

Hurlbutt, Frank, *Bow Porcelain*. Bell, London, 1926.

Tiffin, F. W., *A Chronograph of the Bow, Chelsea, and Derby China Factories*. Salisbury, 1875.

Derby

*Gillespie, F. Brayshaw, *Derby Porcelain*. MacGibbon & Kee, London, 1961.

*Haslem, J., *The Old Derby China Factory*. London, 1875.

Hurlbutt, F., *Old Derby Porcelain and its Artist-Workmen*. T. Werner Laurie, London, 1925.

Worcester

*†Barrett, F. A., *Worcester Porcelain*. Faber, London, 1953.

*Hobson, R. L., *Worcester Porcelain*. Quaritch, London, 1910.

*Hobson, R. L., *Catalogue of the Frank Lloyd Collection of Worcester Porcelain in the British Museum*. London, 1923.

*MacKenna, F. Severne, *Worcester Porcelain*. Lewis, Leigh-on-Sea, 1950.

Longton Hall

*Bemrose, W., *Longton Hall Porcelain*. Bemrose, London, 1898.

Watney, Bernard, *Longton Hall Porcelain*. Faber, London, 1957.

Lowestoft

Murton, A. E., *Lowestoft China*. Lowestoft, 1932.

Spelman, W. W. R., *Lowestoft China*. London and Norwich, 1905. By far the best short account of this factory's productions was given by A. J. B. Kiddell in *The Connoisseur*, September and October 1937.

Liverpool

Boney, Knowles, *Liverpool Porcelain of the Eighteenth Century*. Batsford, London, 1957.

Gatty, C. T., *The Liverpool Potteries*. Liverpool, 1882.

Mayer, Joseph, *History of the Art of Pottery in Liverpool*. Liverpool, 1885.

Plymouth, Bristol, and New Hall

Hurlbutt, F., *Bristol Porcelain*. London, 1928.

*MacKenna, F. Severne, *Cookworthy's Plymouth and Bristol Porcelain*. Lewis, Leigh-on-Sea, 1946.

*MacKenna, F. Severne, *Champion's Bristol Porcelain*. Lewis, Leigh-on-Sea, 1947.

Owen, Hugh, *Two Centuries of Ceramic Art in Bristol*. London, 1873.

Pountney, W. J., *The Old Bristol Potteries*. Arrowsmith, Bristol, 1920.

*Stringer, George Eyre, *New Hall Porcelain*. Rockliff, London, 1949.

Trapnell, Alfred, Esq., *A Catalogue of Plymouth and Bristol Porcelain made by*. Albert Amor, London, 1912.

Wales

*John, W. D., *Nantgarw Porcelain*. London, 1948.

*Nance, Morton, *The Pottery and Porcelain of Swansea and Nantgarw*. London, 1943.

Wedgwood Wares

*Barnard, H., *Chats on Wedgwood Ware*. London, 1924.

*†Honey, W. B., *Wedgwood Ware*. Faber, London, 1948.

MISCELLANEOUS

Ducret, S., *Zürcher Porzellan des 18. Jahrhunderts*. Zürich, 1944.

Hayden, A., *Royal Copenhagen Porcelain*. London, 1911.

Lukomsky, G., *Russisches Porzellan, 1744–1923*. Berlin, 1924.

Molin, A. de, *Histoire documentaire de la manufacture de porcelaine de Nyon, 1781–1813*. Lausanne, 1904.

The best generally available account of the work of the Copenhagen factory is to be found in Volume III of Emil Hannover's *Pottery and Porcelain*. For other minor factories this work may profitably be consulted in conjunction with Honey's *Dictionary of European Ceramic Art*.

Apart from these volumes, *Apollo*, *The Antique Collector*, and *The Connoisseur*, and *The Collector's Guide* frequently publish articles of interest to the student and collector of pottery and porcelain. Much important and original research on the subject may be found in the back-numbers of these periodicals.

Extensive references to these and similar sources may be found in Honey's *Dictionary* cited above.

Index

*

Index

*Two more Pelicans are
described on the
following pages*

WILLIAM MORRIS

SELECTED WRITINGS AND DESIGNS

Edited by Asa Briggs

A521

How are we to regard William Morris? As a brilliant designer who wasted time dabbling in other subjects? As first and foremost a poet? As a political thinker? Or as a successful blend of all these – the last 'universal man' in the Renaissance tradition?

Certainly no one label is adequate for Morris. This selection shows the full range and diversity of his interests – literary, artistic, social, and political. His vitality as a writer emerges throughout, whether he is discussing art or social reform. *News from Nowhere*, the clearest statement of Morris's vision of the Good Life in Utopian terms, takes its place among more ephemeral letters and pamphlets. Morris's poetry is also represented.

Finally, a fully illustrated supplement, prepared by Graeme Shankland, presents Morris the designer, with examples of his tapestries, carpets, wallpaper, and furniture.

ENGLISH FURNITURE STYLES

1500–1830

Ralph Fastnedge

A309

This is a comprehensive, compact, and authoritative historical survey of the evolution of English furniture. In recent years interest in its makers has been growing. Legends have been dispelled, and new facts and material correlated so that our knowledge of the history of furniture design is now very much more exact. Chippendale, Hepplewhite, and Sheraton, for example, are seen no longer as fabulous, isolated figures, but in true perspective; and their famous pattern books (the *Director*, the *Guide*, and the *Drawing Book*), which have been known to collectors for many years, have been studied very closely. Quotations from old memoirs, diaries, and letters, which are often entertaining and very illuminating, help to re-create the social conditions under which the designers and makers were working. The book has several useful appendixes, including glossaries of makers, woods, and specialized terms, and is illustrated by over 100 line drawings and 64 pages of plates.